The
Complete
PRESERVING
Book

Canadian
Living

The
Complete
PRESERVING
Book

By The Canadian Living Test Kitchen

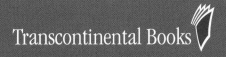

Transcontinental Books

Honey Lavender Jelly
(page 116)

THERE WAS A TIME, not so long ago, when all Canadians were inextricably tied to the growing season. They knew when every locally grown fruit and vegetable was picked so that they could leap on each one, eating their fill right away and preserving the rest for the cold months ahead. Preserving was a necessity: There was no other way to enjoy these foods after the short harvest season.

Nowadays, we live in a world of convenience, in which nearly everything is available year round. But that doesn't mean we don't love local produce. We can taste the stark difference between tiny, sweet, fragrant strawberries from the garden and huge, pale, tasteless ones grown 4,000 kilometres away. We're thrilled when local peaches arrive at the farmer's market. We can taste those first juicy mouthfuls before we even get our hands on them.

Preserving is simply the best way to savour superior, in-season produce. Every time you open a jar of home-canned corn relish, tangy currant jelly or robust tomato-and-pepper salsa, you're deliciously transported back to the warm months when those ingredients were at their peaks. Plus, you're filled with a sense of pride – in our incredible local ingredients, in the people who grow them and in yourself for taking part in a truly Canadian tradition.

Whether you're a beginner and have to regularly turn to our handy how-to instructions and photos (pages 8 to 19) or you're a seasoned canner with lots of experience, I hope you (and the lucky recipients of your efforts) savour these recipes for years to come.

Eat well!

– Annabelle Waugh,
food director

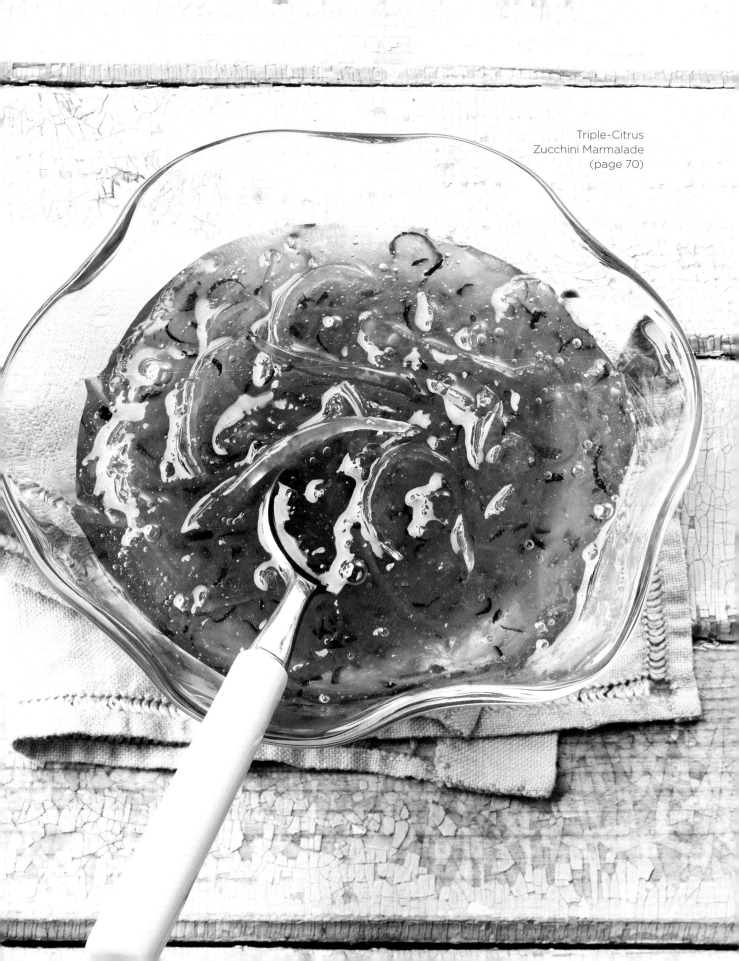

Triple-Citrus
Zucchini Marmalade
(page 70)

Contents

chapter one

Canning Essentials

Canning Basics

This book contains a number of freezer jams and pickles, liqueurs, and refrigerator sauces, but many of the recipes are processed in a boiling water canner. This vacuum-seals jars – keeping air, bacteria and moulds out – so they can be stored safely at room temperature.

Only high-acid foods can be preserved in this way, so follow recipes to ensure that your foods achieve the proper acidity, or pH level. Low-acid preserved foods (not included in this book) must be processed in a pressure canner.

There are a number of steps that go into canning. Below is the basic outline of steps to preserving. Think of this as a cheat sheet.

High-Altitude Canning

Water boils at a lower temperature the higher you go. So if you live in an area where the altitude is more than 1,000 feet (305 metres) above sea level, you'll need to adjust your processing times upward to compensate. Here are the adjustments, according to the canning experts at Bernardin.

- From 1,001 to 3,000 feet (306 to 915 metres): increase by five minutes
- From 3,001 to 6,000 feet (916 to 1,830 metres): increase by 10 minutes
- From 6,001 to 8,000 feet (1,831 to 2,440 metres): increase by 15 minutes
- From 8,001 to 10,000 feet (2,441 to 3,050 metres): increase by 20 minutes

Preparing Equipment

- Use only new discs, and canning jars that are free of nicks and cracks.
- Use only stainless-steel or enamelled pans for cooking preserves. Aluminum and other metals react with acid, giving foods a metallic taste.
- About 30 minutes before filling jars, fill boiling water canner two-thirds full of hot water. Bring to boil.
- Wash, rinse and air-dry jars.
- Ten minutes before filling, place jars in canning rack; heat to hot but not boiling (180°F/82°C).
- Heat discs in saucepan of hot but not boiling water (180°F/82°C) until sealing compound is softened, about five minutes. Bands don't need to be heated.

Filling and Sealing Jars

- Fill hot jars using clean wide-mouth canning funnel and measuring cup, leaving specified headspace.
- Insert nonmetallic utensil and run around inside wall of jar to remove any air bubbles. Readjust headspace if necessary.
- Wipe any spills off rims with damp paper towel to ensure discs will stick.
- Centre hot discs on jars. Screw on bands until resistance is met; increase to fingertip tight.

Processing

- Place filled jars in canning rack. Lower jars into water, ensuring that they are covered by at least 1 inch (2.5 cm) of boiling water. Cover and boil as directed.
- Turn off heat. Uncover and let jars stand in canner for five minutes. Lift up rack. With canning tongs, transfer jars to cooling rack; let cool undisturbed for 24 hours.

Checking for Seal

- Check that lids curve downward. Refrigerate any that do not and use within three weeks.

Headspace

Headspace is the empty space you leave between the top of the preserve and the rim of the jar. It's important to leave the amount called for in the recipe to ensure a solid, safe seal.

Generally, jams and jellies require ¼-inch (5 mm) headspace. Pickles, relishes and chutneys usually require a ½-inch (1 cm). In all cases, check the recipe and make sure you measure accurately. Fill the jar too close to the lid and you risk an overflow in the boiling water bath; fill it too far below the lid and you risk spoilage.

A regular kitchen ruler works fine for checking headspace. But there are also handy clear plastic headspace gauges (see Headspace Gauges, page 15) that make the job even easier.

Pectin

Pectin is a gelling agent that occurs naturally in some fruits, especially citrus. It's one of the essential ingredients in jams and jellies that causes the cooked fruit mixture to firm up to a spreadable consistency.

Old-fashioned jams and jellies relied on the balance between acid and naturally occurring fruit pectin to cause setting. These preserves called for the addition of high-acid, high-pectin ingredients, such as lemon juice, citrus fruits, gooseberries or sour apples. To reach the proper setting point, they needed to be boiled for a relatively long time. (See Testing for Setting Point, page 17.)

Today, there are a number of different types of powdered and liquid pectins available at the grocery store. Adding one to the fruit mixture ensures that it will set, whether or not it contains naturally high-acid, high-pectin fruit. These pectins also shorten the boiling time needed to achieve a proper set. There are pectins specifically designed for the many varieties of jam, including high-sugar, low-sugar and freezer types.

The trick to using store-bought pectin is to stick to the recipe. Different types of pectin aren't interchangeable; each is designed to work with a specific amount of sugar to set a certain amount of fruit mixture. Changing the type of pectin or altering the proportions of the recipe ingredients could leave you with a runny or too-firm result.

What if I Have a Jar That's Not Full?

Don't process jars that aren't filled exactly to the headspace measurement. They won't be safe to keep at room temperature. Refrigerate these less-than-full jars and eat the still-delicious contents within three weeks.

Jar Know-How

• Jars that are labelled 1-cup (250 mL) might not hold the exact amount they say, depending on their shape. Decorative jars often hold less than straight-sided ones.

• When preparing 1-cup (250 mL) jars for canning, you'll usually need one or two fewer than the number of cups of preserve you've made. For example, a jam that yields 8 cups will often fill up only six or seven jars. Keep that in mind, especially when you need a specific number for gifts.

• Always wash and heat a couple more jars than you need, in case your preserve yields more than expected. It's also a good idea to throw in one or two jars that are a size smaller than called for, just in case you have a little extra. Then you can fill the smaller jar up to the recommended headspace and process it like the other larger jars in the batch.

Canning Essentials

Equipment

The right equipment makes preserving easy and safe. All you need to get started is a simple canning kit, available at hardware or kitchenware stores. Later, you can branch out with some convenience gadgets. Here are a number of tools, from basics to luxuries, that make the job go smoothly. Use only stainless-steel or plastic utensils, which can be sterilized.

Boiling Water Canners

A boiling water canner is simply a big pot with a rack in the bottom and a tight-fitting lid. The base should be deep enough to hold jars (without touching the bottom) and allow 1 inch (2.5 cm) of water above jars to maintain a rapid, rolling boil without boiling over. Flat bottoms work on both gas and electric burners. Ridged bottoms are more efficient on gas burners but are not recommended for glass-top stoves. Black porcelain-coated steel pots are popular because they're inexpensive and lightweight.

Preserving Kettles

Jams and jellies (especially those with added pectin) must boil rapidly and will bubble up considerably during cooking. To prevent boiling over, choose a heavy-bottomed stainless-steel Dutch oven or large saucepan. It should hold at least three times the quantity of jam being prepared.

A 36-cup (9 L) stainless-steel preserving kettle or maslin pan [A] is a good investment if you're doing a lot of canning. Its flared side and wide mouth promote maximum evaporation, while its base has an encased layer of aluminum, which holds and distributes heat evenly, preventing hot spots.

Wide-Mouth Canning Funnels

These allow you to ladle preserves into jars without making a hot, sticky mess of the rims (which can keep the lids from sealing). Made especially for the job, these funnels [B] fit standard canning jars perfectly, letting you fill them neatly.

Canning Tongs

These must-have tongs [C] fit jars snugly, preventing slips, splashes and breakage. A rubber coating helps them get a secure grip on jars, while stay-cool handles keep your hands away from hot surfaces and water.

A

B

C

Canning Racks

Canning racks keep jars upright and off the canner bottom to prevent breakage. They also lift jars out of the boiling water all in one go so you don't have to transfer them one-by-one with tongs.

An alternative to investing in a canner with a rack is to purchase a special rack system [D] that fits inside your own pot. These tools come with adjustable-height lifters and either two stainless-steel racks that expand to fit 9½- to 12-inch (24 to 30 cm) diameter pots or one extra-large rack for pots larger than 12 inches (30 cm) in diameter.

Disc-Sterilizing Racks

Instead of fishing around for hot discs with an old pair of tongs, this useful gadget [E] holds 12 standard or wide-mouth discs upright, making them easy to lift out of boiling water.

Magnetic-Tipped Disc Wands

If you don't feel like investing in a disc-sterilizing rack, this inexpensive tool [F] grabs discs, one at a time, in a saucepan of boiling water. It's also great for centring hot discs on jars without direct hand contact.

Headspace Gauges

The stepped end of this tool (photo, page 12) accurately measures headspace. Use the rounded end to swipe though the jar's contents to remove air bubbles.

Jelly Bags and Stands

To make a crystal-clear jelly or syrup, you need to spoon the cooked fruit mixture into a jelly bag or cheesecloth bag and let the juices drip out (don't squeeze – it makes the mixture cloudy). A reusable jelly bag and plastic stand [G] sits neatly on top of most pots, allowing juices to drip, unattended, into the pot.

Kitchen Scales

Whether it's digital or analog, an accurate kitchen scale is excellent for measuring fruits and vegetables exactly. Look for one with a tare button, which zeroes the scale after an empty bowl is added to it.

Canner Cleaning Tip

A buildup of hard water scale often occurs inside canners. To remove: In canner, combine 1 cup white vinegar with 16 cups water; let stand for at least two hours. For heavy scale, increase the vinegar.

Techniques

There are a few steps that are unique to making jams, jellies and marmalades. Here are tried-and-true methods and hints that will help make the process easy, whether you're making your first batch or your hundredth.

Scrubbing Citrus Fruit

When making marmalade or preserves that call for whole citrus fruits, scrub the peels with warm soapy water. This will remove any residues or bacteria that might be hiding. Rinse well to ensure no traces of soap remain on the fruit.

Slicing Citrus Rind Paper-Thin

Make sure the knife you use is very sharp. This will make it easier to cut rind into paper-thin or julienne strips [A], and make it easier on your hands because less pressure will be needed to make each cut. A sharp edge also won't slip and accidentally slice your finger – a good strategy when you're slicing any ingredient.

Creating the Pulp Bag for Marmalade

After you've squeezed the juice, seeds and pulp from your citrus fruit, cut and fold fine cheesecloth to make a double-thickness square.

Pull membranes off peels. Place on cheesecloth square along with pulp and seeds strained out of juice [B]. Bring up corners to form bag; tie tightly.

Look for cheesecloth and kitchen string at grocery, hardware or kitchenware stores. Often called butcher's twine, kitchen string is not treated with inedible chemicals like other types of household string or twine.

Checking Rind Texture

When cooked, the slices of rind should begin to break down. To test that they're fully cooked, pull out a piece of rind; squeeze between your fingers [C]. Rind that's ready will turn to mush when squeezed. If it's still firm, continue cooking, checking every few minutes.

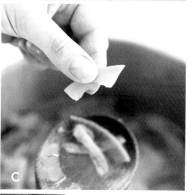

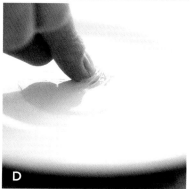

Fixing Floating Fruit

If the rind in a jar of marmalade begins to float after processing, invert jars on cooling rack for 20 minutes, then turn right side up to cool completely.

Testing for Setting Point

Preserves that don't call for added pectin need to be boiled until they reach the proper gelling stage to ensure the mixtures will set.

Chill two small plates in the freezer. Drop ½ tsp hot preserve onto one chilled plate; let cool. Return to freezer for one minute. Tilt plate.

• **Softly set** jams and jellies: Mixture should still flow very slowly.

• **Firmly set** jams, jellies and marmalades: Mixture should be firm and wrinkle when edge is pushed with finger [D].

If mixture remains syrupy, continue to boil, repeating test every few minutes, until proper set is reached, always using coldest clean plate.

Stirring and Skimming Off Foam

This step is often done for jams and jellies that contain chunks of fruit. The set mixture is removed from heat and stirred for five minutes. This allows you to skim off any foam that has formed, and helps distribute the fruit evenly through the mixture so you don't have jars with all the fruit stuck at the top.

Safe Handling and Storage

Home canning has experienced a renaissance in recent years. And with modern canning methods, it's a very safe way to store seasonal food to enjoy year round. Follow these safety and handling tips and you can't go wrong.

• Wash everything well in hot soapy water before you begin. Start with your hands and work your way through all the prep and canning equipment. Don't reuse tools without rewashing first.

• Always follow the recipe. Changing ingredients, proportions or processing times can result in unsafe preserves. Even a small change in acidity can open the door to spoilage. And processing jars for less than the recommended time won't kill dangerous bacteria, such as *Clostridium botulinum*.

• Once processed jars have cooled for 24 hours, check the seals. Lids should be firmly attached to jars and should curve downward. If any don't, the preserves inside will last for up to three weeks in the fridge.

• Clearly label each jar with the name of the preserve and the date it was processed. This way, there's no guessing about the vintage of the contents later.

• Store home-canned goods in a cool, dark, dry place for up to one year, unless otherwise specified. A cool cabinet or shelf in a dry basement is ideal.

• Immediately discard any jars that leak or give off unpleasant odours. Throw out any jars that spurt liquid when opened. (That can be a sign of bacterial contamination.)

• Once opened, store jars in the refrigerator and use within a few weeks.

Avoid Paraffin Seals

Many old recipes call for sealing jars with paraffin wax. Wax seals are no longer recommended because they are not always airtight. As wax cools, it contracts and can pull away from the side of the jar, exposing the preserve to air – an invitation to mould and bacteria.

Measuring Fruits and Vegetables

Here's a handy guide to measuring the main varieties of produce called for in this book, plus their peak harvest times in Canada. These guidelines are based on common supermarket sizes. For chopped or sliced produce, we assume they have been trimmed, pitted, stemmed and peeled where appropriate.

Fruits

Apples: late August to April
- 1 lb (450 g) = 2 to 3 apples
- 1 apple = 1 cup grated or chopped = 1½ cups sliced

Apricots: July to August
- 1 lb (450 g) = 5 to 7 apricots
- 1 apricot = ½ cup sliced

Bananas: year round
- 1 lb (450 g) = 4 bananas
- 1 banana = 1 cup sliced = ¾ cup mashed

Blackberries: July to August (some varieties until November)
- 1 lb (450 g) = 4 cups

Blueberries: July to September
- 1 pint = 12 oz (340 g) = 2 cups

Cherries: late June to early August
- 1 lb (450 g) = 50 cherries = 3 cups
- 1 lb (450 g) = 2 cups pitted

Cranberries: September to late December
- 1 pkg = 12 oz (340 g) = 3 cups

Currants: July and August
- 1 lb (450 g) = 4 cups

Grapefruit: year round; peak in winter
- 1 lb (450 g) = 1 to 3 grapefruit
- 1 grapefruit = 1 cup sections = ¾ cup juice

Grapes: August through early October
- 1 lb (450 g) = 3 cups stemmed

Lemons: year round; peak in winter
- 1 lb (450 g) = 2 to 3 lemons
- 1 lemon = 1 tbsp grated zest and ¼ cup juice

Limes: year round; peak in fall
- 1 lb (450 g) = 4 limes
- 1 lime = 2 tsp grated zest and 3 tbsp juice

Mandarins: November to January
- 1 lb (450 g) = 3 to 4 mandarins
- 1 mandarin = 1 cup sections = 2 tsp grated zest and ⅓ cup juice

Nectarines: August to mid-September
- 1 lb (450 g) = 4 nectarines
- 1 nectarine = 1 cup sliced or chopped

Oranges: year round; peak in winter
- 1 lb (450 g) = 2 to 3 oranges
- 1 orange = 1 cup sections = 1 tbsp grated zest and ⅓ cup juice

Peaches: mid-July to mid-September
- 1 lb (450 g) = 2 to 4 peaches
- 1 peach = 1 cup sliced, chopped or diced

Pears: August to late November
- 1 lb (450 g) = 2 to 3 pears
- 1 pear = 1 cup sliced or chopped

Pineapples: year round; peak in winter
- 2½ lb (1.125 kg) = 1 pineapple = 5 cups chopped

Plums: mid-July to late September
- 1 lb (450 g) = 5 plums
- 1 plum = ½ cup chopped or sliced

Raspberries: July (some varieties until September)
- 1 pint = 12 oz (340 g) = 2 cups = 1 cup puréed = ⅓ cup puréed with seeds strained out

Rhubarb: forced, January to April; outdoor, early May to July
- 1 lb (450 g) = 10 stalks, trimmed
- 1 stalk, trimmed = ½ cup chopped

Strawberries: early June to mid/late July (some varieties until September)
- 1 quart = 1½ lb (675 g) = 30 strawberries = 4 cups hulled, sliced or chopped = 2½ cups puréed

Vegetables
Asparagus: April to late June
- 1 bunch = 1 lb (450 g) = 24 stalks = 3 cups chopped

Beans (green or yellow wax): July to late September
- 1 lb (450 g) = 6 cups whole = 4 cups chopped

Beets: July to mid-October
- 1 bunch = 1 lb (450 g) = 3 to 4 beets = 2 cups quartered = 2⅓ cups chopped or sliced

Cabbage (green): July to November
- 4 lb (1.8 kg) = 1 large cabbage
- 1 lb (450 g) = 6 cups shredded

Carrots: July to September
- 1 lb (450 g) = 4 large carrots
- 1 large carrot = ¾ cup chopped or sliced = ⅔ cup grated
- 1 bunch = 12 oz (340 g) = 9 small carrots, tops removed
- 1 small carrot = ⅓ cup chopped or sliced = ¼ cup grated

Cauliflower: August to late October
- 2¾ lb (1.2 kg) = 1 large cauliflower = 12 cups trimmed florets

Celery: August to September
- 1 bunch = 1½ lb (675 g)
- 1 rib = ½ cup sliced = 6 celery sticks

Corn: late July to late September
- 8 oz (225 g) = 1 cob = 1 cup kernels

Cucumbers: English, year round; field, June to early September
- 1 lb (450 g) = 1 English cucumber (12 inches/ 30 cm) = 4 cups sliced = 2½ cups chopped
- 1 lb (450 g) = 2 to 8 small field cucumbers

Eggplant: August to late September
- 1 lb (450 g) = 1 large Italian eggplant = 7 cups sliced or cubed
- 6 oz (170 g) = 1 small Asian eggplant = 2 cups sliced or cubed

Garlic: August to October
- 2 oz (55 g) = 1 head = 10 cloves
- 1 clove = 1 tsp minced

Green onions: July to September
- 1 bunch = 4 oz (115 g) = 6 green onions = 1½ cups chopped (white and light green parts only)

Onions, cooking: August to May
- 1 lb (450 g) = 3 to 4 cooking onions
- 1 onion = 1½ cups sliced = 1 cup chopped

Onions, red: August to October
- 1 lb (450 g) = 2 red onions = 2½ cups sliced
- 1 onion = 2 cups chopped

Onions, Spanish and other large, sweet varieties: August to October
- 1 lb (450 g) = 1 large Spanish onion = 3 cups sliced
- 1 onion = 2 cups chopped

Rutabaga: October to December
- 2½ lb (1.125 kg) = 1 rutabaga = 5 cups cubed

Sweet peppers: greenhouse, year round; outdoor, August to September
- 1 lb (450 g) = 2 to 4 peppers
- 1 pepper = 1½ cups sliced = 1¼ cups chopped

Tomatoes: late July to late September
- 1 lb (450 g) = 2 to 3 tomatoes
- 1 tomato = 1 cup chopped

Zucchini: July to late September
- 1 lb (450 g) = 4 zucchini
- 1 zucchini = 2 cups sliced halved = 1½ cups chopped

chapter two

Jams
& Marmalades

Blackberry Jam

Fresh blackberries are in season for such a short time that you need to gobble them up as fast as you can. Here's a delightful spread for toast, scones and crumpets that preserves these gorgeous berries for cooler days ahead.

10 cups **fresh blackberries**

2 tbsp freshly squeezed **lemon juice**

1 pkg (57 g) **fruit pectin crystals**

6 cups **granulated sugar**

In food processor, purée half of the blackberries. Press through fine-mesh sieve to remove seeds.

In large bowl and using potato masher, crush remaining blackberries; stir in strained purée. Measure 4½ cups fruit mixture.

In large Dutch oven, stir blackberries with lemon juice; stir in pectin. Bring to boil over high heat, stirring often.

Gradually stir in sugar. Return mixture to full rolling boil, stirring often. Boil hard, stirring constantly, for 1 minute.

Remove from heat. Stir and skim off foam for 5 minutes.

Fill hot 1-cup (250 mL) canning jars, leaving ¼-inch (5 mm) headspace. Cover with prepared discs. Screw on bands until resistance is met; increase to fingertip tight. Boil in boiling water canner for 10 minutes. (See Canning Basics, page 10.)

Turn off heat. Uncover and let jars stand in canner for 5 minutes. Lift up rack. With canning tongs, transfer jars to cooling rack; let cool undisturbed for 24 hours.

MAKES ABOUT 8 CUPS. PER 1 TBSP: about 42 cal, trace pro, 0 g total fat (0 g sat. fat), 11 g carb, trace fibre, 0 mg chol, 0 mg sodium, 16 mg potassium. % RDI: 2% vit C.

tip

Straining the puréed blackberries may seem unnecessary, but the resulting jam has a less-seedy texture that's worth the extra effort.

Jams & Marmalades

Strawberry Gooseberry Jam

High-pectin, high-acid gooseberries are often blended with other fruits to help jams and jellies set. They're quite tart, but the sweet strawberries balance them out.

3 cups **fresh strawberries,** hulled

3 cups **fresh gooseberries,** topped and tailed

5 cups **granulated sugar**

In large Dutch oven and using potato masher, crush half each of the strawberries and gooseberries to just break up but not completely crush. Add remaining strawberries, gooseberries and ⅓ cup water.

Cover and cook over medium-high heat, stirring often, until berries are tender, about 8 minutes. Add sugar; stir to blend.

Bring to full rolling boil over high heat, uncovered and stirring often. Boil hard, stirring constantly, until firmly set, about 9 minutes. (See Testing for Setting Point, page 17.)

Remove from heat. Stir and skim off foam for 5 minutes.

Fill hot 1-cup (250 mL) canning jars, leaving ¼-inch (5 mm) headspace. Cover with prepared discs. Screw on bands until resistance is met; increase to fingertip tight. Boil in boiling water canner for 10 minutes. (See Canning Basics, page 10.)

Turn off heat. Uncover and let jars stand in canner for 5 minutes. Lift up rack. With canning tongs, transfer jars to cooling rack; let cool undisturbed for 24 hours.

MAKES 6 CUPS. PER 1 TBSP: about 44 cal, 0 g pro, 0 g total fat (0 g sat. fat), 11 g carb, trace fibre, 0 mg chol, 0 mg sodium. % RDI: 5% vit C.

Light Strawberry Jam

This strawberry jam – and the other fruity variations below – contains less sugar but has all the fresh flavour of regular jam. It is more softly set than jams that contain added pectin, but the old-fashioned fruit taste is perfect.

8 cups halved hulled **fresh strawberries**

1 cup **granulated sugar**

½ cup **corn syrup**

2 tbsp freshly squeezed **lemon juice**

In large Dutch oven and using potato masher, crush half of the strawberries. Add remaining strawberries and ½ cup water; bring to boil over medium heat. Reduce heat to medium-low; cover and simmer for 10 minutes.

Stir in sugar, corn syrup and lemon juice; bring to full rolling boil, uncovered and stirring often. Boil hard, stirring constantly, just until softly set, 15 to 20 minutes. (See Testing for Setting Point, page 17.) Remove from heat. Skim off foam.

Fill hot 1-cup (250 mL) canning jars, leaving ¼-inch (5 mm) headspace. Cover with prepared discs. Screw on bands until resistance is met; increase to fingertip tight. Boil in boiling water canner for 10 minutes. (See Canning Basics, page 10.)

Turn off heat. Uncover and let jars stand in canner for 5 minutes. Lift up rack.

With canning tongs, transfer jars to cooling rack; let cool undisturbed for 24 hours.

Store in cool, dry, dark place for up to 4 months. Once opened, store in refrigerator for up to 4 weeks.

MAKES ABOUT 4 CUPS. PER 1 TBSP: about 26 cal, trace pro, trace total fat (0 g sat. fat), 7 g carb, 1 g fibre, 0 mg chol, 3 mg sodium, 34 mg potassium. % RDI: 1% iron, 15% vit C, 1% folate.

Variations

Light Raspberry Jam: Substitute fresh raspberries for the strawberries. Omit lemon juice.

Light Peach Apricot Jam: Substitute 4 cups each chopped peeled peaches and apricots for the strawberries. Reduce lemon juice to 1 tbsp.

Light Plum Jam: Substitute chopped peeled plums for the strawberries. Reduce lemon juice to 1 tbsp.

Strawberry Freezer Jam

Kids love strawberry jam, and this no-cook freezer jam is a terrific recipe they can help make. They can have fun mashing the berries and measuring the sugar.

8 cups **fresh strawberries,** hulled

1 pkg (49 g) **light fruit pectin crystals**

3¼ cups **granulated sugar**

In large bowl and using potato masher, crush strawberries, 1 cup at a time. Measure 4 cups fruit.

Mix pectin with ¼ cup of the sugar; stir into strawberries. Let stand for 30 minutes.

Add remaining sugar, stirring until sugar is dissolved, about 3 minutes.

Fill 1-cup (250 mL) airtight containers, leaving ¼-inch (5 mm) headspace. Seal with lids. Let stand undisturbed at room temperature until set, about 24 hours.

Refrigerate for up to 3 weeks or freeze for up to 8 months.

MAKES 6 CUPS. PER 1 TBSP: about 31 cal, 0 g pro, 0 g total fat (0 g sat. fat), 8 g carb, trace fibre, 0 mg chol, 0 mg sodium. % RDI: 1% iron, 12% vit C, 1% folate.

Variation

Low-Sugar Strawberry Freezer Jam: Reduce sugar to 1½ cups. Crush strawberries as directed. Stir in sugar; let stand for 15 minutes. Stirring constantly, gradually add 1 pkg (45 g) freezer jam pectin; stir for 3 minutes. Let stand for 5 minutes. Fill 1-cup (250 mL) airtight containers, leaving ½-inch (1 cm) headspace. Seal with lids. Refrigerate for up to 3 weeks or freeze for up to 1 year.

MAKES 5 CUPS.

Strawberry Mint Freezer Jam

A fragrant mint-infused syrup livens up and adds sophistication to a simple freezer jam.

8 cups **fresh strawberries, hulled**

1 pkg (49 g) **light fruit pectin crystals**

2¾ cups **granulated sugar**

SYRUP:

½ cup **granulated sugar**

½ cup packed **fresh mint leaves** or fresh lemon verbena leaves

SYRUP: In small saucepan, bring sugar, mint leaves and ¼ cup water to boil. Reduce heat to medium and simmer, stirring, until sugar is dissolved, about 2 minutes. Remove from heat; cover and let cool for 20 minutes.

Meanwhile, in large bowl and using potato masher, crush strawberries, 1 cup at a time. Measure 4 cups fruit.

Strain syrup into berries. Mix pectin with ¼ cup of the sugar; stir into strawberry mixture. Let stand for 30 minutes.

Add remaining sugar, stirring until sugar is dissolved, about 3 minutes.

Fill 1-cup (250 mL) airtight containers, leaving ½-inch (1 cm) headspace. Seal with lids. Let stand undisturbed at room temperature until set, about 24 hours.

Refrigerate for up to 3 weeks or freeze for up to 1 year.

MAKES 6 CUPS. PER 1 TBSP: about 31 cal, trace pro, 0 g total fat (0 g sat. fat), 8 g carb, trace fibre, 0 mg chol, 1 mg sodium, 15 mg potassium. % RDI: 10% vit C, 1% folate.

Variation
Strawberry Raspberry Freezer Jam: Make syrup as directed, replacing mint leaves with 2 strips (each 2 inches/5 cm long) orange zest. Continue with recipe, replacing half of the strawberries with 4 cups fresh raspberries.

Jams & Marmalades

Swedish Tea
Rings (page 43)
made with
Strawberry Jam
(opposite)

Strawberry Jam

This classic, straight-up strawberry jam is sensational on sandwiches, toast and baked goods. It's especially lovely in Swedish Tea Rings (page 43).

8 cups **fresh strawberries,** hulled

4 cups **granulated sugar**

¼ cup freshly squeezed **lemon juice**

In large bowl and using potato masher, crush strawberries, 1 cup at a time. Measure 4 cups fruit.

In large Dutch oven, combine strawberries, sugar and lemon juice; stir over low heat until sugar is dissolved.

Bring to full rolling boil over high heat, stirring often. Boil hard, stirring almost constantly, until firmly set, about 10 minutes. (See Testing for Setting Point, page 17.)

Remove from heat. Stir and skim off foam for 5 minutes.

Fill hot 1-cup (250 mL) canning jars, leaving ¼-inch (5 mm) headspace. Cover with prepared discs. Screw on bands until resistance is met; increase to fingertip tight. Boil in boiling water canner for 10 minutes. (See Canning Basics, page 10.)

Turn off heat. Uncover and let jars stand in canner for 5 minutes. Lift up rack. With canning tongs, transfer jars to cooling rack; let cool undisturbed for 24 hours.

MAKES ABOUT 5 CUPS. PER 1 TBSP: about 42 cal, trace pro, trace total fat (0 g sat. fat), 11 g carb, trace fibre, 0 mg chol, 0 mg sodium. % RDI: 1% iron, 12% vit C, 1% folate.

Variation
Strawberry Rhubarb Jam: Substitute 3 cups crushed strawberries and 2 cups thickly sliced rhubarb for the strawberries. Precook strawberries with rhubarb over medium-high heat until rhubarb is softened, about 10 minutes. Reduce sugar to 3 cups. Boil hard for 8 minutes.

Jams & Marmalades

Strawberry Raspberry Jam

Raspberry cocktail concentrate adds intense berry flavour to this ruby-red, softly set preserve.

10 cups hulled **fresh strawberries**

4 cups **granulated sugar**

½ cup **frozen raspberry cocktail concentrate,** thawed

¼ cup freshly squeezed **lemon juice**

In large Dutch oven and using potato masher, crush 4 cups of the strawberries, 1 cup at a time. Add remaining strawberries, sugar, raspberry concentrate and lemon juice; stir over low heat until sugar is dissolved.

Bring to full rolling boil over high heat, stirring often. Boil hard, stirring almost constantly, until softly set, 12 to 15 minutes. (See Testing for Setting Point, page 17.)

Remove from heat. Stir and skim off foam for 5 minutes.

Fill hot 1-cup (250 mL) canning jars, leaving ¼-inch (5 mm) headspace. Cover with prepared discs. Screw on bands until resistance is met; increase to fingertip tight. Boil in boiling water canner for 10 minutes. (See Canning Basics, page 10.)

Turn off heat. Uncover and let jars stand in canner for 5 minutes. Lift up rack. With canning tongs, transfer jars to cooling rack; let cool undisturbed for 24 hours.

MAKES ABOUT 5½ CUPS. PER 1 TBSP: about 42 cal, trace pro, 0 g total fat (0 g sat. fat), 11 g carb, trace fibre, 0 mg chol, 0 mg sodium. % RDI: 1% iron, 10% vit C, 1% folate.

Jams & Marmalades

Strawberry Vanilla Jam

Strawberry jam is even more heavenly when enhanced with the fresh, warm flavour and aroma of vanilla.

12 cups **fresh strawberries,** hulled

1 pkg (49 g) **light fruit pectin crystals**

4½ cups **granulated sugar**

1 **vanilla bean**

In large Dutch oven and using potato masher, crush strawberries, 1 cup at a time. Measure 6 cups fruit.

Mix pectin with ¼ cup of the sugar; stir into strawberries. Slit vanilla bean lengthwise; scrape out seeds. Stir seeds and vanilla pod into strawberry mixture.

Bring to boil over high heat, stirring often. Add remaining sugar; return to full rolling boil. Boil hard, stirring constantly, for 1 minute.

Remove from heat. Skim off foam; discard vanilla pod.

Fill hot 1-cup (250 mL) canning jars, leaving ¼-inch (5 mm) headspace. Cover with prepared discs. Screw on bands until resistance is met; increase to fingertip tight. Boil in boiling water canner for 10 minutes. (See Canning Basics, page 10.)

Turn off heat. Uncover and let jars stand in canner for 5 minutes. Lift up rack. With canning tongs, transfer jars to cooling rack; let cool undisturbed for 24 hours.

MAKES ABOUT 8 CUPS. PER 1 TBSP: about 32 cal, 0 g pro, 0 g total fat (0 g sat. fat), 8 g carb, trace fibre, 0 mg chol, 0 mg sodium. % RDI: 7% vit C.

Strawberry Pineapple Jam

When you want fresh jam but berries aren't in season, this sweet spread is just the thing.

3 pkg (each 300 g) **frozen unsweetened whole strawberries,** thawed

1 can (14 oz/398 mL) **crushed pineapple packed in juice**

1 tbsp freshly squeezed **lemon juice**

2 tsp finely grated **orange zest**

1 pkg (49 g) **light fruit pectin crystals**

4½ cups **granulated sugar**

In large Dutch oven and using potato masher, crush strawberries. Measure 4 cups fruit.

Add pineapple and juice, lemon juice and orange zest.

Stir pectin with ¼ cup of the sugar; stir into fruit mixture. Bring to boil over high heat, stirring often.

Stir in remaining sugar; return mixture to full rolling boil. Boil hard, stirring constantly, for 1 minute.

Remove from heat. Stir and skim off foam for 5 minutes.

Fill hot 1-cup (250 mL) canning jars, leaving ¼-inch (5 mm) headspace. Cover with prepared discs. Screw on bands until resistance is met; increase to fingertip tight. Boil in boiling water canner for 10 minutes. (See Canning Basics, page 10.)

Turn off heat. Uncover and let jars stand in canner for 5 minutes. Lift up rack. With canning tongs, transfer jars to cooling rack; let cool undisturbed for 24 hours.

MAKES ABOUT 7 CUPS. PER 1 TBSP: about 37 cal, 0 g pro, 0 g total fat (0 g sat. fat), 10 g carb, trace fibre, 0 mg chol, 0 mg sodium. % RDI: 1% iron, 5% vit C.

tip

In the summer, find a local U-pick or farmer's market and pick up local berries at the height of ripeness. Freeze them whole on a baking sheet until firm, then transfer to resealable freezer bags.

Strawberry Balsamic Black Pepper Jam

Sweet strawberries, tangy vinegar and a little spicy pepper create a perfect balance to enjoy with cheese and crackers.

12 cups **fresh strawberries,** hulled

1 pkg (49 g) **light fruit pectin crystals**

4½ cups **granulated sugar**

¼ cup **balsamic vinegar**

1 tsp coarsely cracked **black pepper**

In large Dutch oven and using potato masher, crush strawberries, 1 cup at a time. Measure 6 cups fruit.

Mix pectin with ¼ cup of the sugar; stir into strawberries. Bring to boil over high heat, stirring often.

Stir in remaining sugar; return mixture to full rolling boil. Boil hard, stirring constantly, for 1 minute.

Remove from heat. Skim off foam. Stir in balsamic vinegar and pepper.

Fill hot 1-cup (250 mL) canning jars, leaving ¼-inch (5 mm) headspace. Cover with prepared discs. Screw on bands until resistance is met; increase to fingertip tight. Boil in boiling water canner for 10 minutes. (See Canning Basics, page 10.)

Turn off heat. Uncover and let jars stand in canner for 5 minutes. Lift up rack. With canning tongs, transfer jars to cooling rack; let cool undisturbed for 24 hours.

MAKES ABOUT 8 CUPS. PER 1 TBSP: about 32 cal, 0 g pro, 0 g total fat (0 g sat. fat), 8 g carb, trace fibre, 0 mg chol, 0 mg sodium. % RDI: 1% iron, 7% vit C.

tip
A full rolling boil (220°F/ 104°C) is rapid, usually foaming or spurting, and cannot be stirred down.

Strawberry Banana Jam

The touch of tropical sweetness is delightful in this jam. It's terrific smeared on hot-out-of-the-oven Buttermilk Scones (opposite).

8 cups **fresh strawberries,** hulled

1 cup mashed **banana**

2 tbsp freshly squeezed **lemon juice**

1 pkg (49 g) **light fruit pectin crystals**

4½ cups **granulated sugar**

In large Dutch oven and using potato masher, crush strawberries, 1 cup at a time. Measure 4 cups fruit.

Add banana and lemon juice. Mix pectin with ¼ cup of the sugar; stir into fruit mixture.

Bring to boil over medium-high heat, stirring often. Stir in remaining sugar; return to full rolling boil. Boil hard, stirring constantly, for 1 minute.

Remove from heat. Stir and skim off foam for 5 minutes.

Fill hot 1-cup (250 mL) canning jars, leaving ¼-inch (5 mm) headspace. Cover with prepared discs. Screw on bands until resistance is met; increase to fingertip tight. Boil in boiling water canner for 10 minutes. (See Canning Basics, page 10.)

Turn off heat. Uncover and let jars stand in canner for 5 minutes. Lift up rack. With canning tongs, transfer jars to cooling rack; let cool undisturbed for 24 hours.

MAKES ABOUT 7 CUPS. PER 1 TBSP: about 37 cal, trace pro, 0 g total fat (0 g sat. fat), 10 g carb, trace fibre, 0 mg chol, 1 mg sodium, 20 mg potassium. % RDI: 7% vit C.

Jams & Marmalades

Buttermilk Scones

Buttermilk gives these scones a slightly tart edge and tender texture. They're delicious with jam or as the base for homemade strawberry shortcakes.

1⅔ cups **all-purpose flour**

3 tbsp **granulated sugar**

1 tbsp **baking powder**

¼ tsp **salt**

6 tbsp cold **unsalted butter,** cubed

1 **egg**

⅓ cup **buttermilk**

TOPPING:

1 tbsp **buttermilk**

2 tsp **coarse sugar**

In large bowl, whisk together flour, sugar, baking powder and salt. Using pastry blender or 2 knives, cut in butter until in coarse crumbs with a few larger pieces.

Whisk egg with buttermilk; pour over flour mixture and stir with fork just until dough comes together.

Turn out onto lightly floured surface; pat out into 1-inch (2.5 cm) thick round. Transfer to parchment paper–lined baking sheet.

TOPPING: Brush with buttermilk; sprinkle with sugar. Cut into 8 wedges, but do not separate.

Bake in 425°F (220°C) oven until golden and firm to the touch, about 16 minutes.

MAKES 8 SCONES. PER SCONE: about 211 cal, 4 g pro, 10 g total fat (6 g sat. fat), 27 g carb, 1 g fibre, 47 mg chol, 203 mg sodium, 63 mg potassium. % RDI: 7% calcium, 10% iron, 9% vit A, 26% folate.

Jams & Marmalades

Concord Grape Jam

Grape jellies are more common, but a jam like this will make you wonder why. Concord grapes have a rich, full flavour that's ideal for many types of preserves.

12 cups **Concord grapes**

3 cups **granulated sugar**

Wash grapes and pinch off skins; reserve pulp and skins separately. In large Dutch oven, bring pulp to boil; cook over medium heat, stirring to break down fruit, until soft, 10 minutes. Press through fine-mesh sieve into clean Dutch oven; discard seeds.

Add skins to pulp to make about 6 cups. Cook over medium-high heat until skins are tender, about 10 minutes.

Add sugar; bring to full rolling boil over high heat, stirring often. Boil hard, stirring constantly, until firmly set, 4 to 6 minutes. (See Testing for Setting Point, page 17.)

Remove from heat. Stir and skim off foam for 5 minutes.

Fill hot 1-cup (250 mL) canning jars, leaving ¼-inch (5 mm) headspace. Cover with prepared discs. Screw on bands until resistance is met; increase to fingertip tight. Boil in boiling water canner for 10 minutes. (See Canning Basics, page 10.)

Turn off heat. Uncover and let jars stand in canner for 5 minutes. Lift up rack. With canning tongs, transfer jars to cooling rack; let cool undisturbed for 24 hours.

MAKES ABOUT 4 CUPS. PER 1 TBSP: about 48 cal, trace pro, trace total fat (0 g sat. fat), 12 g carb, trace fibre, 0 mg chol, 0 mg sodium, 32 mg potassium. % RDI: 1% iron.

Jams & Marmalades

Blueberry Jam

This intensely flavoured jam is softly set and a bit lower in sugar than some traditional jams, thanks to light pectin crystals. It is excellent in yogurt, on pancakes or as an ice-cream topping.

8 cups **fresh blueberries**

1 pkg (49 g) **light fruit pectin crystals**

2½ cups **granulated sugar**

In large Dutch oven and using potato masher, crush blueberries, 1 cup at a time. Measure 5 cups fruit. Add 1 cup water.

Mix pectin with ¼ cup of the sugar; stir into blueberries.

Bring to boil over high heat, stirring often. Stir in remaining sugar; return to full rolling boil. Boil hard, stirring, for 1 minute.

Remove from heat. Skim off foam.

Fill hot 1-cup (250 mL) canning jars, leaving ¼-inch (5 mm) headspace. Cover with prepared discs. Screw on bands until resistance is met; increase to fingertip tight. Boil in boiling water canner for 10 minutes. (See Canning Basics, page 10.)

Turn off heat. Uncover and let jars stand in canner for 5 minutes. Lift up rack. With canning tongs, transfer jars to cooling rack; let cool undisturbed for 24 hours.

MAKES ABOUT 6 CUPS. PER 1 TBSP: about 28 cal, 0 g pro, 0 g total fat (0 g sat. fat), 7 g carb, trace fibre, 0 mg chol, 1 mg sodium. % RDI: 2% vit C.

Light Blueberry Jam

This jam uses pectin designed to work with a reduced amount of sugar. It requires a shorter cooking time, so the jam has a fresh, intense blueberry flavour. It sets up quite firm – perfect to spread on toasted crumpets.

12 cups **fresh wild blueberries**

¼ cup freshly squeezed **lemon juice**

1 pkg (49 g) **light fruit pectin crystals** or no-sugar-needed fruit pectin crystals

3 cups **granulated sugar**

In Dutch oven and using potato masher, crush blueberries, 1 cup at a time. Measure 6 cups fruit.

Add lemon juice to blueberries. Mix pectin with ¼ cup of the sugar; stir into blueberry mixture. Bring to boil over high heat, stirring often.

Gradually stir in remaining sugar; return to full rolling boil. Boil hard, stirring constantly, for 1 minute.

Remove from heat. Stir and skim off foam for 5 minutes.

Fill hot 1-cup (250 mL) canning jars, leaving ¼-inch (5 mm) headspace. Cover with prepared discs. Screw on bands until resistance is met; increase to fingertip tight. Boil in boiling water canner for 10 minutes. (See Canning Basics, page 10.)

Turn off heat. Uncover and let jars stand in canner for 5 minutes. Lift up rack. With canning tongs, transfer jars to cooling rack; let cool undisturbed for 24 hours.

MAKES ABOUT 8 CUPS. PER 1 TBSP: about 26 cal, trace pro, 0 g total fat (0 g sat. fat), 7 g carb, trace fibre, 0 mg chol, 1 mg sodium, 10 mg potassium. % RDI: 2% vit C.

tips
- If you prefer a smoother jam, purée the blueberries in a food processor instead of crushing them with a potato masher.
- Certo Light Fruit Pectin Crystals and Bernardin No-Sugar-Needed Fruit Pectin Crystals can be used interchangeably in this recipe.

Jams & Marmalades

Wild Blueberry Freezer Jam

No-cook jams are the ultimate in easy preparation. They're fun to make with kids, without the worry of hot stoves and boiling fruit mixtures. And because they aren't cooked, their fruit flavour is vibrant and fresh.

3 cups crushed **fresh wild blueberries**

1 tbsp freshly squeezed **lemon juice**

2 tbsp **granulated sugar**

1 pkg (49 g) **light fruit pectin crystals**

In large bowl, stir crushed blueberries with lemon juice.

Add sugar. Mix in pectin; let stand for 30 minutes, stirring occasionally.

Fill 1-cup (250 mL) airtight containers, leaving ¼-inch (5 mm) headspace. Seal with lids. Let stand undisturbed at room temperature until set, about 24 hours.

Refrigerate for up to 3 weeks or freeze for up to 8 months.

MAKES 3 CUPS. PER 1 TBSP: about 14 cal, trace pro, trace total fat (0 g sat. fat), 4 g carb, 1 g fibre, 0 mg chol, 2 mg sodium, 12 mg potassium. % RDI: 3% vit C.

tip

If you can't find wild blueberries, you can use cultivated ones instead. However, the jam won't have quite as strong a flavour or as deep a colour.

Wild Blueberry and Lemon Preserve

This softly set preserve is scrumptious on scones or rolled up in crêpes. Because there's the option to use frozen berries, you can make this recipe year round.

4 cups **fresh wild blueberries** or frozen wild blueberries

4 cups **granulated sugar**

1 pkg (85 mL) **liquid fruit pectin**

1 tsp grated **lemon zest**

2 tbsp freshly squeezed **lemon juice**

In large Dutch oven and using potato masher, gently crush half of the blueberries to just break up. Stir in sugar and remaining blueberries. Heat over low heat, stirring often, until sugar is dissolved.

Bring to boil over high heat, stirring constantly. Stir in pectin; return to full rolling boil. Boil hard for 1 minute, stirring constantly.

Stir in lemon zest and juice; return to full rolling boil over high heat.

Remove from heat. Stir and skim off foam for 5 minutes.

Fill hot 1-cup (250 mL) canning jars, leaving ¼-inch (5 mm) headspace. Cover with prepared discs. Screw on bands until resistance is met; increase to fingertip tight. Boil in boiling water canner for 10 minutes. (See Canning Basics, page 10.)

Turn off heat. Uncover and let jars stand in canner for 5 minutes. Lift up rack. With canning tongs, transfer jars to cooling rack; let cool undisturbed for 24 hours.

MAKES 4 CUPS. PER 1 TBSP: about 53 cal, 0 g pro, 0 g total fat (0 g sat. fat), 14 g carb, trace fibre, 0 mg chol, 1 mg sodium. % RDI: 2% vit C.

Jams & Marmalades

Blueberry Raspberry Jam

The crown jewels of summer fruit combine in this royal purple jam. In winter, make it with slightly thawed frozen berries.

4 cups **fresh blueberries**

2 cups **fresh raspberries**

1 pkg (49 g) **light fruit pectin crystals**

3½ cups **granulated sugar**

In large Dutch oven and using potato masher, crush blueberries with raspberries.

Mix pectin with ¼ cup of the sugar; stir into berry mixture. Bring to boil over high heat, stirring constantly.

Stir in remaining sugar; return to full rolling boil. Boil hard, stirring constantly, for 1 minute.

Remove from heat. Stir and skim off foam for 5 minutes.

Fill hot 1-cup (250 mL) canning jars, leaving ¼-inch (5 mm) headspace. Cover with prepared discs. Screw on bands until resistance is met; increase to fingertip tight. Boil in boiling water canner for 10 minutes. (See Canning Basics, page 10.)

Turn off heat. Uncover and let jars stand in canner for 5 minutes. Lift up rack. With canning tongs, transfer jars to cooling rack; let cool undisturbed for 24 hours.

MAKES ABOUT 5 CUPS. PER 1 TBSP: about 41 cal, 0 g pro, 0 g total fat (0 g sat. fat), 11 g carb, 0 g fibre, 0 mg chol, 1 mg sodium. % RDI: 2% vit C.

Jams & Marmalades

Swedish Tea Rings

These cookies are delicious with any jam or jelly you like, so feel free to substitute apricot, raspberry, strawberry or any favourite. For the best flavour, use California walnut halves, or substitute pecans, almonds or Brazil nuts.

1 cup **butter,** softened
⅔ cup **granulated sugar**
2 **eggs,** separated
1 tsp **vanilla**
¼ tsp **salt**
2 cups **all-purpose flour**
1½ cups finely chopped **walnuts**
¼ cup **red currant jelly** (approx)

Line rimless baking sheets with parchment paper or grease; set aside.

Beat butter with sugar until fluffy. Beat in egg yolks, vanilla and salt. Stir in flour, blending with hands if necessary.

Using 1 tbsp for each, shape into 32 balls. In shallow bowl, beat egg whites lightly. Place walnuts in separate bowl.

Using 2 spoons to hold dough balls, dip into egg whites, letting excess drip off. Roll in walnuts. Place on prepared pans. Press thimble or small bottle cap into each cookie to make indentation. Bake in 350°F (180°C) oven for 5 minutes.

Remove from oven; press hole again and fill with small dab of jelly. Bake until golden, about 12 minutes.

Let cool on pans on racks for 2 minutes. Transfer to racks; let cool completely. *(Make-ahead: Layer between waxed paper in airtight container and freeze for up to 1 month.)*

MAKES ABOUT 32 COOKIES. PER COOKIE: about 144 cal, 2 g pro, 9 g total fat (5 g sat. fat), 14 g carb, 1 g fibre, 29 mg chol, 63 mg sodium. % RDI: 2% iron, 7% vit A, 7% folate.

Jams & Marmalades

Pure and Simple Raspberry Jam

Raspberry jam is easy and quick to make in small quantities. If you don't have time in the summer, freeze fresh berries to make this jam when the weather is cooler.

3 cups **granulated sugar**

2 cups crushed **fresh raspberries**

¼ cup freshly squeezed **lemon juice**

In large Dutch oven, combine sugar, raspberries and lemon juice; let stand until sugar is dissolved, about 1½ hours.

Bring to full rolling boil over high heat, stirring constantly. Boil hard until firmly set. (See Testing for Setting Point, page 17.)

Remove from heat. Skim off foam.

Fill hot 1-cup (250 mL) canning jars, leaving ¼-inch (5 mm) headspace. Cover with prepared discs. Screw on bands until resistance is met; increase to fingertip tight. Boil in boiling water canner for 10 minutes. (See Canning Basics, page 10.)

Turn off heat. Uncover and let jars stand in canner for 5 minutes. Lift up rack. With canning tongs, transfer jars to cooling rack; let cool undisturbed for 24 hours.

MAKES ABOUT 3 CUPS. PER 1 TBSP: about 53 cal, trace pro, trace total fat (0 g sat. fat), 14 g carb, 1 g fibre, 0 mg chol, 0 mg sodium, 14 mg potassium. % RDI: 1% iron, 3% vit C.

Raspberry Red Currant Jam

The natural pectin in red currants makes commercial pectin unnecessary for this softly set jam. This recipe is adapted from one in the *Bernardin Complete Book of Home Preserving* (Robert Rose, 2006).

6 cups stemmed **fresh red currants**

4 cups **fresh raspberries**

3 cups **granulated sugar**

In saucepan and using potato masher, crush red currants with ½ cup water.

Cover and bring to boil over medium-high heat; reduce heat and simmer, mashing often, until softened, about 5 minutes. Press through fine-mesh sieve or food mill to remove seeds.

In large Dutch oven, stir together strained red currants, raspberries and sugar. Bring to full rolling boil over high heat, stirring often. Boil hard, stirring constantly, until clear, foam subsides and jam is softly set, about 10 minutes. (See Testing for Setting Point, page 17.)

Remove from heat. Skim off foam.

Fill hot 1-cup (250 mL) canning jars, leaving ¼-inch (5 mm) headspace. Cover with prepared discs. Screw on bands until resistance is met; increase to fingertip tight. Boil in boiling water canner for 10 minutes. (See Canning Basics, page 10.)

Turn off heat. Uncover and let jars stand in canner for 5 minutes. Lift up rack. With canning tongs, transfer jars to cooling rack; let cool undisturbed for 24 hours.

MAKES ABOUT 5 CUPS. PER 1 TBSP: about 36 cal, trace pro, 0 g total fat (0 g sat. fat), 9 g carb, trace fibre, 0 mg chol, 0 mg sodium. % RDI: 1% iron, 7% vit C.

Jams & Marmalades

Summer-Fresh Raspberry Freezer Jam

With a thinner consistency and intensely fresh raspberry taste that captured our taste buds, this is the Test Kitchen's hands-down favourite freezer jam.

8 cups **fresh raspberries**

1½ cups **granulated sugar**

1 pkg (45 g) **freezer jam pectin**

In large bowl and using potato masher, crush raspberries, 1 cup at a time. Measure 4 cups fruit.

Whisk sugar with pectin; add to raspberries and stir for 3 minutes.

Fill 1-cup (250 mL) airtight containers, leaving ½-inch (1 cm) headspace. Seal with lids. Let stand undisturbed at room temperature until set, about 24 hours.

Refrigerate for up to 3 weeks or freeze for up to 1 year.

MAKES 5 CUPS. PER 1 TBSP: about 23 cal, trace pro, 0 g total fat (0 g sat. fat), 6 g carb, 1 g fibre, 0 mg chol, 0 mg sodium. % RDI: 1% iron, 5% vit C, 1% folate.

Rasp-Pear Jam

With a brilliant red colour and a fruity flavour, this jam is a luxurious taste of summer for winter tables.

3 pkg (each 300 g) **frozen raspberries**

3 cups diced peeled **pears**

1 tbsp freshly squeezed **lemon juice**

1 pkg (49 g) **light fruit pectin crystals**

4½ cups **granulated sugar**

Reserving juice, thaw and drain raspberries. In large Dutch oven and using potato masher, crush raspberries. Measure 2 cups fruit. Add enough of the reserved juice to make 3 cups.

Add pears and lemon juice. Stir pectin with ¼ cup of the sugar; stir into berry mixture. Bring to boil over high heat, stirring constantly.

Stir in remaining sugar. Return to full rolling boil; boil hard, stirring constantly, for 1 minute.

Remove from heat. Stir and skim off foam for 5 minutes.

Fill hot 1-cup (250 mL) canning jars, leaving ¼-inch (5 mm) headspace. Cover with prepared discs. Screw on bands until resistance is met; increase to fingertip tight. Boil in boiling water canner for 10 minutes. (See Canning Basics, page 10.)

Turn off heat. Uncover and let jars stand in canner for 5 minutes. Lift up rack. With canning tongs, transfer jars to cooling rack; let cool undisturbed for 24 hours.

MAKES ABOUT 7 CUPS. PER 1 TBSP: about 39 cal, trace pro, trace total fat (0 g sat. fat), 10 g carb, 1 g fibre, 0 mg chol, 1 mg sodium, 18 mg potassium. % RDI: 1% iron, 3% vit C.

Jams & Marmalades

Cranberry Pear Jam

This versatile jam is terrific on toast and scones, and delectable with hot or cold turkey, duck or chicken.

6 cups **fresh cranberries**

3 cups diced peeled **pears**

1 tsp coarsely grated **lemon zest**

2 tbsp freshly squeezed **lemon juice**

4½ cups **granulated sugar**

In large Dutch oven, combine cranberries, pears, and lemon zest and juice; bring to boil. Cover and cook over medium heat, stirring occasionally, until tender, 12 to 15 minutes.

Stir in sugar; bring to full rolling boil over high heat, stirring often. Boil hard, stirring constantly, until softly set. (See Testing for Setting Point, page 17.)

Remove from heat. Stir and skim off foam for 5 minutes.

Fill hot 1-cup (250 mL) canning jars, leaving ¼-inch (5 mm) headspace. Cover with prepared discs. Screw on bands until resistance is met; increase to fingertip tight. Boil in boiling water canner for 10 minutes. (See Canning Basics, page 10.)

Turn off heat. Uncover and let jars stand in canner for 5 minutes. Lift up rack. With canning tongs, transfer jars to cooling rack; let cool undisturbed for 24 hours.

MAKES 6 CUPS. PER 1 TBSP: about 42 cal, 0 g pro, 0 g total fat (0 g sat. fat), 11 g carb, trace fibre, 0 mg chol, 0 mg sodium, 12 mg potassium. % RDI: 2% vit C.

Summer Berry Jam

This old-fashioned jam, often called jewel jam because of its rich ruby colour, is made with fresh fruit that's not in season for long. Make it while the summer sun shines.

2½ cups crushed stemmed **fresh red currants**

1½ cups chopped pitted **fresh tart cherries**

¾ cup crushed hulled **fresh strawberries**

¾ cup crushed **fresh raspberries**

3½ cups **granulated sugar**

In large Dutch oven, combine red currants, cherries, strawberries and raspberries. Bring to boil, stirring often. Reduce heat to medium-low and simmer, stirring occasionally, for 15 minutes. Remove from heat.

Stir in sugar; bring to full rolling boil over high heat, stirring often. Boil hard, stirring constantly, until firmly set, 12 to 15 minutes. (See Testing for Setting Point, page 17.)

Remove from heat. Skim off foam.

Fill hot 1-cup (250 mL) canning jars, leaving ¼-inch (5 mm) headspace. Cover with prepared discs. Screw on bands until resistance is met; increase to fingertip tight. Boil in boiling water canner for 10 minutes. (See Canning Basics, page 10.)

Turn off heat. Uncover and let jars stand in canner for 5 minutes. Lift up rack. With canning tongs, transfer jars to cooling rack; let cool undisturbed for 24 hours.

MAKES ABOUT 5 CUPS. PER 1 TBSP: about 41 cal, trace pro, trace total fat (0 g sat. fat), 10 g carb, 1 g fibre, 0 mg chol, 0 mg sodium. % RDI: 1% iron, 7% vit C.

tip

As a general rule, you need to double the volume of whole berries, cherries or currants to obtain the specified amount of crushed fruit.

Jams & Marmalades

Winter Berry Jam

When you can't get fresh in-season fruit, this jam comes to the rescue. Its full berry flavour will transport you to lazy summer days with each bite.

2 pkg (each 600 g) **frozen mixed berries,** thawed and juices reserved

2 tsp grated **lemon zest**

1 tbsp freshly squeezed **lemon juice**

1 pkg (49 g) **light fruit pectin crystals**

4½ cups **granulated sugar**

2 tbsp **berry-flavoured vodka** (optional)

In large Dutch oven, crush berries, 1 package at a time. Measure 5 cups fruit.

Stir lemon zest and juice into fruit mixture. Mix pectin with ¼ cup of the sugar; stir into berry mixture. Bring to boil over high heat, stirring constantly.

Stir in remaining sugar; return to full rolling boil. Boil hard, stirring constantly, for 1 minute.

Remove from heat. Stir in vodka (if using). Stir and skim off foam for 5 minutes.

Fill hot 1-cup (250 mL) canning jars, leaving ¼-inch (5 mm) headspace. Cover with prepared discs. Screw on bands until resistance is met; increase to fingertip tight. Boil in boiling water canner for 10 minutes. (See Canning Basics, page 10.)

Turn off heat. Uncover and let jars stand in canner for 5 minutes. Lift up rack. With canning tongs, transfer jars to cooling rack; let cool undisturbed for 24 hours.

MAKES ABOUT 7 CUPS. PER 1 TBSP: about 38 cal, 0 g pro, 0 g total fat (0 g sat. fat), 10 g carb, trace fibre, 0 mg chol, 0 mg sodium. % RDI: 1% iron, 5% vit C, 1% folate.

Jams & Marmalades

Mixed Berry Freezer Jam

Sometimes you want jam quickly, without the fuss of boiling all those jars. This recipe satisfies that urge in no time flat and tastes so good.

1 cup crushed **fresh wild blueberries** or fresh cultivated blueberries

1 cup crushed **fresh raspberries**

1 cup crushed **fresh blackberries**

4 tsp freshly squeezed **lemon juice**

2 tbsp **granulated sugar**

1 pkg (49 g) **light fruit pectin crystals**

In large bowl, stir together blueberries, raspberries, blackberries and lemon juice.

Add sugar; mix in pectin. Let stand for 30 minutes, stirring occasionally.

Fill 1-cup (250 mL) airtight containers, leaving ¼-inch (5 mm) headspace. Seal with lids. Let stand undisturbed at room temperature until set, about 24 hours.

Refrigerate for up to 3 weeks or freeze for up to 8 months.

MAKES 3 CUPS. PER 1 TBSP: about 12 cal, trace pro, trace total fat (0 g sat. fat), 3 g carb, 1 g fibre, 0 mg chol, 1 mg sodium, 18 mg potassium. % RDI: 1% iron, 5% vit C, 1% folate.

Jams & Marmalades

Clockwise from top left: Wild Blueberry Freezer Jam (page 40), Cherry Raspberry Freezer Jam (page 60) and Mixed Berry Freezer Jam (opposite)

Light Berry Currant Jam

This jam uses relatively little sugar but gets a hit of natural sweetness from apple juice concentrate.

4 cups hulled **fresh strawberries**

3 cups **fresh raspberries**

2 cups **fresh blueberries**

1½ cups stemmed **fresh red currants**

1 can (355 mL) **frozen apple juice concentrate,** thawed

¾ cup **granulated sugar**

In large Dutch oven and using potato masher, crush strawberries. Add raspberries, blueberries and red currants; lightly crush.

Stir in apple juice concentrate, making sure pan is no more than half full. Bring to boil over medium heat; reduce heat, cover and simmer for 10 minutes.

Stir in sugar. Return to full rolling boil over high heat, uncovered and stirring often. Boil hard, stirring almost constantly, just until softly set, about 25 minutes. (See Testing for Setting Point, page 17.)

Remove from heat. Skim off foam.

Fill hot 1-cup (250 mL) canning jars, leaving ¼-inch (5 mm) headspace. Cover with prepared discs. Screw on bands until resistance is met; increase to fingertip tight. Boil in boiling water canner for 10 minutes. (See Canning Basics, page 10.)

Turn off heat. Uncover and let jars stand in canner for 5 minutes. Lift up rack. With canning tongs, transfer jars to cooling rack; let cool undisturbed for 24 hours.

MAKES 5 CUPS. PER 1 TBSP: about 24 cal, trace pro, trace total fat (0 g sat. fat), 6 g carb, 1 g fibre, 0 mg chol, 2 mg sodium, 52 mg potassium. % RDI: 1% iron, 17% vit C, 1% folate.

tip
The specified amount of sugar is crucial to getting the right consistency. Do not reduce it or replace it with artificial sweeteners.

Jams & Marmalades

Very Cherry Jam

Lower in sugar than most cherry jams, this softly set spread has a tart-fresh flavour.

7 cups pitted halved **fresh tart cherries**

3¼ cups **granulated sugar**

1 tsp grated **lemon zest**

1 pkg (49 g) **light fruit pectin crystals**

In large bowl, stir cherries with 1 cup of the sugar. Let stand at room temperature until juicy, about 1 hour.

In large Dutch oven, combine cherry mixture with lemon zest. Mix pectin with ¼ cup of the remaining sugar; stir into cherry mixture. Bring to boil over high heat, stirring constantly.

Stir in remaining sugar; return to full rolling boil over high heat. Boil hard, stirring constantly, for 1 minute.

Remove from heat. Stir and skim off foam for 5 minutes.

Fill hot 1-cup (250 mL) canning jars, leaving ¼-inch (5 mm) headspace. Cover with prepared discs. Screw on bands until resistance is met; increase to fingertip tight. Boil in boiling water canner for 10 minutes. (See Canning Basics, page 10.)

Turn off heat. Uncover and let jars stand in canner for 5 minutes. Lift up rack. With canning tongs, transfer jars to cooling rack; let cool undisturbed for 24 hours.

MAKES 6 CUPS. PER 1 TBSP: about 33 cal, trace pro, 0 g total fat (0 g sat. fat), 9 g carb, trace fibre, 0 mg chol, 0 mg sodium. % RDI: 1% vit A, 2% vit C.

Apricot Jam

Fresh ripe apricots are a real luxury, so why not preserve them for year-round enjoyment? This old-fashioned jam is delicious as a glaze over grilled meats.

5 cups chopped **fresh apricots**

3 cups **granulated sugar**

¼ cup freshly squeezed **lemon juice**

In large Dutch oven, combine apricots, sugar and lemon juice. Stir over low heat until sugar is dissolved.

Bring to full rolling boil over high heat, stirring often. Boil hard, stirring constantly, until firmly set, 10 to 14 minutes. (See Testing for Setting Point, page 17.)

Remove from heat. Stir and skim off foam for 5 minutes.

Fill hot 1-cup (250 mL) canning jars, leaving ¼-inch (5 mm) headspace. Cover with prepared discs. Screw on bands until resistance is met; increase to fingertip tight. Boil in boiling water canner for 10 minutes. (See Canning Basics, page 10.)

Turn off heat. Uncover and let jars stand in canner for 5 minutes. Lift up rack. With canning tongs, transfer jars to cooling rack; let cool undisturbed for 24 hours.

MAKES ABOUT 4 CUPS. PER 1 TBSP: about 43 cal, trace pro, trace total fat (0 g sat. fat), 11 g carb, trace fibre, 0 mg chol, 0 mg sodium, 39 mg potassium. % RDI: 1% iron, 3% vit A, 2% vit C.

Jams & Marmalades

Peach Melba Jam

Named for Australian opera singer Nellie Melba, this classic combination of peaches and raspberries is best made with the ripest fresh fruit you can find.

4 cups sliced peeled **fresh peaches**

4 cups **fresh raspberries**

1 tbsp freshly squeezed **lemon juice**

1 pkg (49 g) **light fruit pectin crystals**

3½ cups **granulated sugar**

In large Dutch oven and using potato masher, crush peaches. Measure 3 cups fruit.

In separate bowl, crush raspberries. Measure 2 cups fruit; add to peaches. Stir in lemon juice.

Mix pectin with ¼ cup of the sugar; stir into peach mixture. Bring to boil over high heat, stirring often.

Add remaining sugar; return to full rolling boil over high heat. Boil hard, stirring constantly, for 1 minute.

Remove from heat. Skim off foam.

Fill hot 1-cup (250 mL) canning jars, leaving ¼-inch (5 mm) headspace. Cover with prepared discs. Screw on bands until resistance is met; increase to fingertip tight. Boil in boiling water canner for 10 minutes. (See Canning Basics, page 10.)

Turn off heat. Uncover and let jars stand in canner for 5 minutes. Lift up rack. With canning tongs, transfer jars to cooling rack; let cool undisturbed for 24 hours.

MAKES ABOUT EIGHT 1-CUP (250 mL) JARS. PER 1 TBSP: about 26 cal, 0 g pro, 0 g total fat (0 g sat. fat), 7 g carb, trace fibre, 0 mg chol, 1 mg sodium. % RDI: 2% vit C.

tip

To peel peaches: With sharp knife, score X into bottom of each peach. In saucepan of boiling water, blanch each peach for 30 seconds. With slotted spoon, transfer to cold water. Remove and peel. Place in mixture of 4 cups water and ¼ cup freshly squeezed lemon juice to prevent browning.

Jams & Marmalades

Peach Jam

Freestone peaches are the best for making jam. The flesh doesn't cling to the stone, making them easy to pit. If you can get peaches with a red blush, they add a beautiful, rich colour to the jam.

6 cups sliced peeled **fresh peaches**

2 tbsp freshly squeezed **lemon juice**

1 pkg (49 g) **light fruit pectin crystals**

3½ cups **granulated sugar**

In large Dutch oven and using potato masher, crush peaches. Measure 4 cups fruit.

Add lemon juice. Mix pectin with ¼ cup of the sugar; stir into peaches. Bring to boil over high heat, stirring often.

Add remaining sugar; return to full rolling boil. Boil hard, stirring constantly, for 1 minute.

Remove from heat. Skim off foam.

Fill hot 1-cup (250 mL) canning jars, leaving ¼-inch (5 mm) headspace. Cover with prepared discs. Screw on bands until resistance is met; increase to fingertip tight. Boil in boiling water canner for 10 minutes. (See Canning Basics, page 10.)

Turn off heat. Uncover and let jars stand in canner for 5 minutes. Lift up rack. With canning tongs, transfer jars to cooling rack; let cool undisturbed for 24 hours.

MAKES ABOUT FIVE 1-CUP (250 mL) JARS. PER 1 TBSP: about 41 cal, trace pro, 0 g total fat (0 g sat. fat), 11 g carb, trace fibre, 0 mg chol, 1 mg sodium. % RDI: 2% vit C.

Clockwise from top left: Peach Jam (opposite);
Crab Apple Jelly (page 92) and Blueberry Jam (page 37)

Cherry Raspberry Freezer Jam

This tart-sweet jam is a snap to make, and the light pectin crystals allow you to use a small amount of sugar.

1½ cups finely chopped pitted **fresh tart cherries**

1½ cups crushed **fresh raspberries**

1 tbsp freshly squeezed **lemon juice**

¼ cup **granulated sugar**

1 pkg (49 g) **light fruit pectin crystals**

In large bowl, stir together cherries, raspberries and lemon juice.

Add sugar. Stir in pectin; let stand for 30 minutes, stirring occasionally.

Fill 1-cup (250 mL) airtight containers, leaving ¼-inch (5 mm) headspace. Seal with lids. Let stand undisturbed at room temperature until set, about 24 hours.

Refrigerate for up to 3 weeks or freeze for up to 8 months.

MAKES 3 CUPS. PER 1 TBSP: about 14 cal, trace pro, trace total fat (0 g sat. fat), 4 g carb, 1 g fibre, 0 mg chol, 2 mg sodium, 23 mg potassium. % RDI: 1% iron, 1% vit A, 3% vit C, 1% folate.

Slow-Cook Plum Jam

A thick German-style preserve, this jam has a unique caramelized taste created by long, slow cooking.

8 cups halved **fresh prune plums**

4 cups **granulated sugar**

¼ cup freshly squeezed **lemon juice**

1 **cinnamon stick**

In large Dutch oven, stir together plums, sugar, lemon juice, cinnamon stick and ¼ cup water; cover and bring to boil.

Reduce heat to low; simmer, uncovered and stirring often, until firmly set, about 2 hours. (See Testing for Setting Point, page 17.)

Remove from heat. Stir and skim off foam for 5 minutes.

Fill 1-cup (250 mL) hot canning jars, leaving ¼-inch (5 mm) headspace. Cover with prepared discs. Screw on bands until resistance is met; increase to fingertip tight. Boil in boiling water canner for 10 minutes. (See Canning Basics, page 10.)

Turn off heat. Uncover and let jars stand in canner for 5 minutes. Lift up rack. With canning tongs, transfer jars to cooling rack; let cool undisturbed for 24 hours.

MAKES 6 CUPS. PER 1 TBSP: about 40 cal, trace pro, 0 g total fat (0 g sat. fat), 10 g carb, trace fibre, 0 mg chol, 0 mg sodium. % RDI: 2% vit C.

Jams & Marmalades

Rhubarb Cherry Spread

This tasty combination produces a softly set jam that's ideal for filling a layer cake or for spooning over ice cream, frozen yogurt, a slice of cake or even toast.

3 cups chopped **fresh rhubarb**

2 cups pitted **fresh tart cherries**

1 pkg (49 g) **light fruit pectin crystals**

2¾ cups **granulated sugar**

In large Dutch oven, stir rhubarb with cherries. Mix pectin with ¼ cup of the sugar; stir into rhubarb mixture. Bring to boil over high heat, stirring constantly.

Stir in remaining sugar; return to full rolling boil. Boil hard, stirring constantly, for 1 minute.

Remove from heat. Stir and skim off foam for 5 minutes.

Fill hot 1-cup (250 mL) canning jars, leaving ¼-inch (5 mm) headspace. Cover with prepared discs. Screw on bands until resistance is met; increase to fingertip tight. Boil in boiling water canner for 10 minutes. (See Canning Basics, page 10.)

Turn off heat. Uncover and let jars stand in canner for 5 minutes. Lift up rack. With canning tongs, transfer jars to cooling rack; let cool undisturbed for 24 hours.

MAKES 5 CUPS. PER 1 TBSP: about 31 cal, 0 g pro, 0 g total fat (0 g sat. fat), 8 g carb, trace fibre, 0 mg chol, 0 mg sodium. % RDI: 2% vit C.

Pineapple Rhubarb Jam

Rhubarb, grown from the Atlantic to the Pacific and popular with home gardeners everywhere, makes a fine jam, especially when its tartness is complemented by a sweet fruit such as pineapple.

1 pkg (49 g) **light fruit pectin crystals**

4 cups **granulated sugar**

6 cups chopped **fresh rhubarb**

1 tbsp freshly squeezed **lemon juice**

1 can (19 oz/540 mL) **pineapple tidbits,** drained

Mix pectin with ¼ cup of the sugar; set aside.

In large Dutch oven, combine rhubarb, lemon juice and remaining sugar; cook, stirring, over medium heat until sugar is dissolved. Bring to boil, stirring constantly; reduce heat and simmer until rhubarb is tender, about 5 minutes.

Stir in pineapple and pectin mixture; bring to full rolling boil over high heat, stirring often. Boil hard, stirring constantly, for 1 minute.

Remove from heat. Skim off foam.

Fill hot 1-cup (250 mL) canning jars, leaving ¼-inch (5 mm) headspace. Cover with prepared discs. Screw on bands until resistance is met; increase to fingertip tight. Boil in boiling water canner for 10 minutes. (See Canning Basics, page 10.)

Turn off heat. Uncover and let jars stand in canner for 5 minutes. Lift up rack. With canning tongs, transfer jars to cooling rack; let cool undisturbed for 24 hours.

MAKES ABOUT 7 CUPS. PER 1 TBSP: about 32 cal, trace pro, trace total fat (0 g sat. fat), 8 g carb, trace fibre, 0 mg chol, 0 mg sodium. % RDI: 1% calcium, 2% vit C.

Rum Pot Jam

All the traditional flavours of a rumtopf – a rum-soaked fruit and berry mixture – come together in this irresistible jam. Use raspberries, blackberries, blueberries and strawberries, or another favourite combination.

8 cups **fresh mixed berries**

2 cups **fresh red currants**

1 pkg (49 g) **light fruit pectin crystals**

4 cups **granulated sugar**

¼ cup **amber rum**

In large Dutch oven and using potato masher, crush mixed berries with red currants. Measure 5⅔ cups fruit; add ⅓ cup water.

Mix pectin with ¼ cup of the sugar; stir into berry mixture. Bring to boil over high heat, stirring often.

Stir in remaining sugar; return to full rolling boil. Boil hard, stirring constantly, for 1 minute.

Remove from heat. Stir in rum; skim off foam.

Fill hot 1-cup (250 mL) canning jars, leaving ¼-inch (5 mm) headspace. Cover with prepared discs. Screw on bands until resistance is met; increase to fingertip tight. Boil in boiling water canner for 10 minutes. (See Canning Basics, page 10.)

Turn off heat. Uncover and let jars stand in canner for 5 minutes. Lift up rack. With canning tongs, transfer jars to cooling rack; let cool undisturbed for 24 hours.

MAKES ABOUT 7 CUPS. PER 1 TBSP: about 36 cal, trace pro, 0 g total fat (0 g sat. fat), 9 g carb, 1 g fibre, 0 mg chol, 1 mg sodium. % RDI: 1% iron, 5% vit C.

Jams & Marmalades

Fig and Anise Jam

The floral flavour of fresh figs is beautiful with the subtle licorice flavour of aniseed. This jam is softly set at room temperature but firms up considerably when chilled. Try it on crackers with a sharp cheese for an appetizer.

1 tsp **aniseed**

2½ lb (1.125 kg) **fresh figs** (about 26)

Lemon seeds from 1 lemon

⅓ cup freshly squeezed **lemon juice**

4¼ cups **granulated sugar**

In large Dutch oven, combine aniseed with ¾ cup water. Bring to boil over high heat. Remove from heat; let stand for 15 minutes.

Meanwhile, in large heatproof bowl, cover figs with boiling water. Let stand for 10 minutes.

Drain figs well; cut off and discard stems. Chop figs into ⅓-inch (8 mm) pieces. Measure 6 cups fruit.

Tie lemon seeds in square of cheesecloth to form bag; add to anise mixture along with figs and lemon juice.

Gradually stir in sugar. Bring to boil over medium heat, stirring often. Reduce heat and simmer, stirring often, until thickened and softly set, 30 to 32 minutes. (See Testing for Setting Point, page 17.)

Remove from heat. Discard lemon seed bag. Stir and skim off foam for 5 minutes.

Fill hot 1-cup (250 mL) canning jars, leaving ¼-inch (5 mm) headspace. Cover with prepared discs. Screw on bands until resistance is met; increase to fingertip tight. Boil in boiling water canner for 10 minutes. (See Canning Basics, page 10.)

Turn off heat. Uncover and let jars stand in canner for 5 minutes. Lift up rack. With canning tongs, transfer jars to cooling rack; let cool undisturbed for 24 hours.

MAKES ABOUT 6½ CUPS. PER 1 TBSP: about 40 cal, trace pro, 0 g total fat (0 g sat. fat), 10 g carb, trace fibre, 0 mg chol, 0 mg sodium, 26 mg potassium.

tip

Fresh figs deteriorate quickly, so call your local market to see which day the delivery arrives. Then buy the freshest figs you can and make this jam as soon as possible after purchasing them.

Seville Orange Marmalade

Seville oranges make the finest marmalade, producing a clear jelly around shreds of refreshingly bitter peel. Since Sevilles are available for such a short time, make this large batch to last throughout the year.

8 **Seville oranges** (4 lb/1.8 kg)

2 **lemons**

15 cups **granulated sugar**

Scrub oranges and lemons; cut out stem and blossom ends and any blemishes. Cut in half crosswise; squeeze out juice and seeds. Reserving seeds and pulp, strain juice into large Dutch oven.

Pull membranes off peels; tie pulp, seeds and membranes in 8-inch (20 cm) square of double-thickness cheesecloth to form bag. Add to pan.

Cut orange and lemon halves into thirds. Cut each crosswise into scant ¼-inch (5 mm) thick strips. Add to pan along with any juices.

Add 16 cups water; bring to simmer over medium heat. Simmer, stirring often and pressing bag to release pectin, until peel turns to mush when pressed between fingers, 2½ to 3 hours.

Remove bag; let cool. Squeeze liquid from bag into pan. Measure 15 cups fruit mixture. (See Tip, left.)

Divide fruit mixture into 3 batches. For each batch, in clean Dutch oven, bring fruit mixture and 5 cups of the sugar to full rolling boil over high heat, stirring. Boil hard, stirring constantly, until free of foam, thickened and firmly set, 8 minutes. (See Testing for Setting Point, page 17.)

Fill hot 1-cup (250 mL) canning jars, leaving ¼-inch (5 mm) headspace. Cover with prepared discs. Screw on bands until resistance is met; increase to fingertip tight. Boil in boiling water canner for 10 minutes. (See Canning Basics, page 10.)

Turn off heat. Uncover and let jars stand in canner for 5 minutes. Lift up rack. With canning tongs, transfer jars to cooling rack; let cool undisturbed for 24 hours.

MAKES ABOUT 18 CUPS. PER 1 TBSP: about 43 cal, trace pro, trace total fat (0 g sat. fat), 11 g carb, trace fibre, 0 mg chol, 1 mg sodium. % RDI: 1% iron, 8% vit C.

tip

If your fruit mixture measures less than called for, top it up with water. If it measures more, continue simmering until reduced to correct amount.

Jams & Marmalades

Mandarin Marmalade

For the best marmalade with attractive shreds, look for fruit with thick skins. Members of the sweet mandarin family include clementines, satsumas, honey and royal. You can also use anything else under the tangerine name.

6 **large mandarins** (3 lb/1.35 kg)
4 **lemons**
10 cups **granulated sugar**

Scrub mandarins and lemons; cut out stem and blossom ends and any blemishes. Cut lemons in half; squeeze out juice and seeds. Reserving seeds and pulp, strain juice into large Dutch oven.

Peel mandarins; reserving seeds, chop flesh. Tie mandarin and lemon seeds and pulp in 8-inch (20 cm) square of double-thickness cheesecloth. Add to pan.

Cut lemon and mandarin peels into paper-thin strips. Add lemon peel to pan; set mandarin peel aside. Add 8 cups water; bring to simmer over medium heat. Simmer, stirring, for 1½ hours.

Add mandarin peel; simmer until peel turns to mush when pressed between fingers, about 30 minutes. Remove bag; let cool. Squeeze liquid from bag into pan. Measure 10 cups fruit mixture. (See Tip, opposite.)

Divide fruit mixture into 2 batches. For each batch, in clean Dutch oven, bring fruit mixture and 5 cups of the sugar to full rolling boil over high heat, stirring. Boil hard, stirring constantly, until free of foam, thickened and firmly set, 8 minutes. (See Testing for Setting Point, page 17.)

Fill hot 1-cup (250 mL) canning jars, leaving ¼-inch (5 mm) headspace. Cover with prepared discs. Screw on bands until resistance is met; increase to fingertip tight. Boil in boiling water canner for 10 minutes. (See Canning Basics, page 10.)

Turn off heat. Uncover and let jars stand in canner for 5 minutes. Lift up rack. With canning tongs, transfer jars to cooling rack; let cool undisturbed for 24 hours.

MAKES ABOUT 12 CUPS. PER 1 TBSP: about 44 cal, 0 g pro, 0 g total fat (0 g sat. fat), 12 g carb, trace fibre, 0 mg chol, 1 mg sodium. % RDI: 1% vit A, 10% vit C.

Triple-Citrus Zucchini Marmalade

Zucchini gives this spread a lovely colour and is a nice contrast to the delicate shreds of citrus zest. It's a terrific way to use up the late-summer harvest in your garden.

2 **large oranges**

2 **large lemons**

1 **lime**

3 cups shredded **zucchini** (about 2)

1 pkg (57 g) **fruit pectin crystals**

6½ cups **granulated sugar**

Scrub oranges, lemons and lime; cut out stem and blossom ends and any blemishes. Using vegetable peeler, peel strips of zest off oranges, lemons and lime, avoiding white pith. Cut zest crosswise into thin strips. Measure 1 cup zest.

Cut any remaining zest and pith off oranges, lemons and lime; discard. Coarsely chop fruit, discarding tough centre membrane and seeds, and reserving any accumulated juice. Measure 2 cups total fruit and juice.

In Dutch oven, combine zest, fruit mixture and 1 cup water; bring to boil over medium-high heat. Reduce heat and simmer, stirring often, until zest starts to soften, about 8 minutes.

Stir in zucchini; simmer, stirring often, until zest and zucchini are translucent, about 15 minutes.

Stir in pectin. Bring to boil over high heat, stirring often.

Gradually stir in sugar; return to full rolling boil, stirring often. Boil hard, stirring constantly, for 1 minute.

Remove from heat. Stir and skim off foam for 7 minutes.

Fill hot 1-cup (250 mL) canning jars, leaving ¼-inch (5 mm) headspace. Cover with prepared discs. Screw on bands until resistance is met; increase to fingertip tight. Boil in boiling water canner for 10 minutes. (See Canning Basics, page 10.)

Turn off heat. Uncover and let jars stand in canner for 5 minutes. Lift up rack. With canning tongs, transfer jars to cooling rack; let cool undisturbed for 24 hours.

MAKES ABOUT 6½ CUPS. PER 1 TBSP: about 53 cal, trace pro, 0 g total fat (0 g sat. fat), 14 g carb, trace fibre, 0 mg chol, 1 mg sodium, 16 mg potassium. % RDI: 5% vit C, 1% folate.

tips

• Use the coarse side of a box grater to shred the zucchini, leaving the pretty green skin on.

• When slicing citrus zest, use a very sharp knife. Stack a few strips at a time and cut strips as thinly as possible.

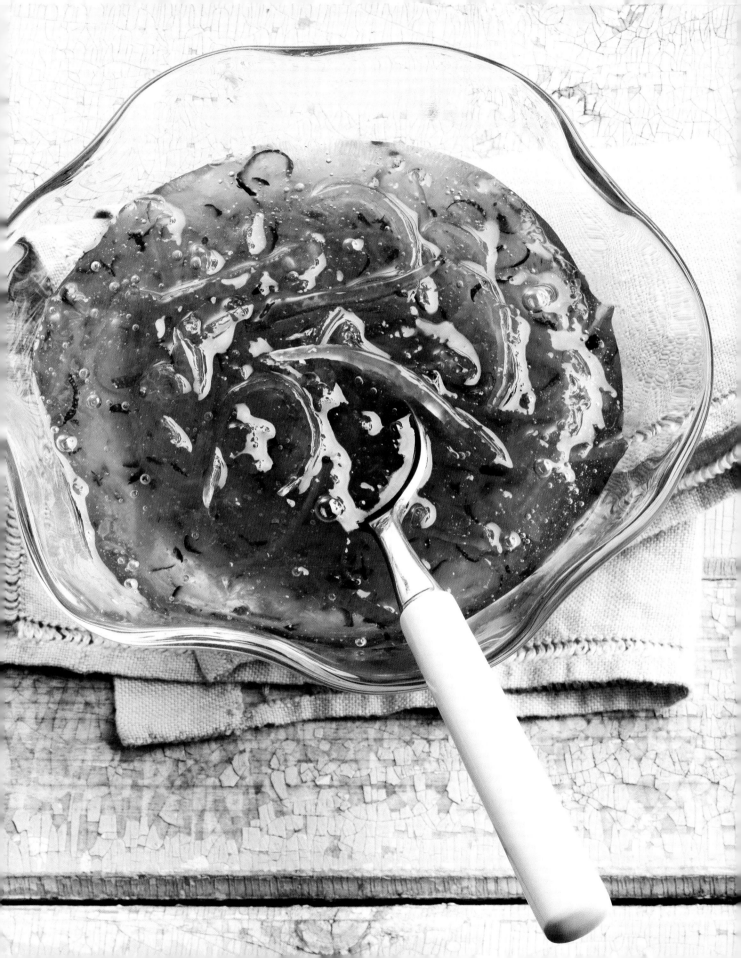

Five-Fruit Marmalade

Orange, clementine, grapefruit, lime and lemon combine to make a wonderfully fresh and citrusy wake-up.

4 **small clementines**
1 **orange**
1 **pink grapefruit**
1 **lemon**
1 **lime**
7 cups **granulated sugar**

Scrub clementines, orange, grapefruit, lemon and lime; cut out stem and blossom ends and any blemishes.

Cut each fruit in half crosswise; squeeze out juice. Reserving seeds and pulp, strain juice into large Dutch oven.

Pull membranes off peels; tie pulp, seeds and membranes in 15-inch (38 cm) square of double-thickness fine cheesecloth to form bag. Add to pan. Cut fruit halves in half; cut each crosswise into paper-thin strips. Add to pan.

Add 6 cups water; bring to simmer over medium heat. Simmer, stirring often and pressing bag to release pectin, until peel turns to mush when pressed between fingers, 1 to 1½ hours.

Remove bag; let cool. Squeeze liquid from bag into pan. Measure 7 cups fruit mixture. (See Tip, page 68.)

In clean Dutch oven, bring sugar and fruit mixture to full rolling boil, stirring often. Boil hard, stirring constantly, until free of foam, thickened and firmly set, 10 to 12 minutes. (See Testing for Setting Point, page 17.)

Fill hot 1-cup (250 mL) canning jars, leaving ¼-inch (5 mm) headspace. Cover with prepared discs. Screw on bands until resistance is met; increase to fingertip tight. Boil in boiling water canner for 10 minutes. (See Canning Basics, page 10.)

Turn off heat. Uncover and let jars stand in canner for 5 minutes. Lift up rack. With canning tongs, transfer jars to cooling rack; let cool undisturbed for 24 hours.

MAKES ABOUT 8 CUPS. PER 1 TBSP: about 45 cal, 0 g pro, 0 g total fat (0 g sat. fat), 12 g carb, 0 g fibre, 0 mg chol, 0 mg sodium. % RDI: 5% vit C.

Jams & Marmalades

Grapefruit Ginger Marmalade

Zingy ginger complements the bitterness of grapefruit in this preserve, which has lots of chunky peel.

3 **red grapefruit** or pink grapefruit

2 **lemons**

7 cups **granulated sugar**

⅓ cup chopped **crystallized ginger**

Scrub grapefruit and lemons; cut out stem and blossom ends and any blemishes. Cut in half crosswise; squeeze out juice and seeds. Reserving seeds and pulp, strain juice into large Dutch oven.

Pull membranes off peels; tie pulp, seeds and membranes in 15-inch (38 cm) square of double-thickness fine cheesecloth to form bag. Add to pan.

Cut grapefruit and lemon halves in half; cut crosswise into paper-thin strips. Add to pan.

Add 6 cups water; bring to simmer over medium heat. Simmer, stirring often and pressing bag to release pectin, until peel turns to mush when pressed between fingers, 1 to 1½ hours.

Remove bag; let cool. Squeeze liquid from bag into pan. Measure 7 cups fruit mixture. (See Tip, page 68.)

In clean Dutch oven, bring sugar, ginger and fruit mixture to full rolling boil over high heat, stirring often. Boil hard, stirring constantly, until free of foam, thickened and firmly set, 12 to 15 minutes. (See Testing for Setting Point, page 17.)

Fill hot 1-cup (250 mL) canning jars, leaving ¼-inch (5 mm) headspace. Cover with prepared discs. Screw on bands until resistance is met; increase to fingertip tight. Boil in boiling water canner for 10 minutes. (See Canning Basics, page 10.)

Turn off heat. Uncover and let jars stand in canner for 5 minutes. Lift up rack. With canning tongs, transfer jars to cooling rack; let cool undisturbed for 24 hours.

MAKES ABOUT 8 CUPS. PER 1 TBSP: about 49 cal, 0 g pro, 0 g total fat (0 g sat. fat), 13 g carb, trace fibre, 0 mg chol, 1 mg sodium. % RDI: 1% iron, 10% vit C.

Rhubarb Grapefruit Marmalade

Rhubarb provides a subtle background flavour in this grapefruit marmalade and gives it a lovely pink hue.

3 **red grapefruit**

1 **lemon**

6 cups **granulated sugar**

4 cups sliced **fresh rhubarb**

Scrub grapefruit and lemon; cut out stem and blossom ends and any blemishes. Cut grapefruit and lemon in half crosswise; squeeze out juice and seeds. Reserving seeds and pulp, strain juice into Dutch oven.

Pull membranes off peels; tie pulp, seeds and membranes in 8-inch (20 cm) square of double-thickness fine cheesecloth to form bag. Add to pan. Discard lemon peel.

Cut grapefruit halves into thirds, trimming off excess white pith. Cut each crosswise into scant ¼-inch (5 mm) thick strips. Add to pan along with any juices.

Add 5 cups water; bring to boil over medium heat. Reduce heat, cover and simmer gently, stirring often, until peel turns to mush when pressed between fingers, about 2½ hours. Remove bag; let cool.

Squeeze liquid from bag into pan. Measure 5 cups fruit mixture. (See Tip, page 68.)

In clean Dutch oven, bring fruit mixture, sugar and rhubarb to full rolling boil, stirring. Boil hard, stirring, until firmly set, 20 minutes. (See Testing for Setting Point, page 17.) Skim off foam.

Fill hot 1-cup (250 mL) canning jars, leaving ¼-inch (5 mm) headspace. Cover with prepared discs. Screw on bands until resistance is met; increase to fingertip tight. Boil in boiling water canner for 10 minutes. (See Canning Basics, page 10.)

Turn off heat. Uncover and let jars stand in canner for 5 minutes. Lift up rack. With canning tongs, transfer jars to cooling rack; let cool undisturbed for 24 hours.

MAKES ABOUT 6 CUPS. PER 1 TBSP: about 55 cal, trace pro, 0 g total fat (0 g sat. fat), 14 g carb, 1 g fibre, 0 mg chol, 1 mg sodium. % RDI: 1% calcium, 1% iron, 13% vit C, 1% folate.

Jams & Marmalades

Red Grapefruit Marmalade

This amber marmalade has a bittersweet flavour that's delicious spread over warm, buttery croissants.

2 **large red grapefruit** or pink grapefruit (4 lb/1.8 kg)

2 **lemons**

7 cups **granulated sugar**

Scrub grapefruit and lemons; cut out stem and blossom ends and any blemishes. Cut in half crosswise; squeeze out juice and seeds. Reserving seeds and pulp, strain juice into large Dutch oven.

Pull membranes off peels; tie pulp, seeds and membranes in 15-inch (38 cm) square of double-thickness cheesecloth to form bag. Add to pan.

Cut grapefruit and lemon halves into paper-thin strips; add to pan.

Add 6 cups water; bring to simmer over medium heat. Simmer, stirring often and pressing bag to release pectin, until peel turns to mush when pressed between fingers, 1 to 1½ hours.

Remove bag; let cool. Squeeze liquid from bag into pan. Measure 7 cups fruit mixture, adding water or boiling further to reduce to correct amount if needed.

In clean Dutch oven, bring sugar and grapefruit mixture to full rolling boil over high heat, stirring often. Boil hard, stirring constantly, until free of foam, thickened and firmly set, about 10 minutes. (See Testing for Setting Point, page 17.)

Fill hot 1-cup (250 mL) canning jars, leaving ¼-inch (5 mm) headspace. Cover with prepared discs. Screw on bands until resistance is met; increase to fingertip tight. Boil in boiling water canner for 10 minutes. (See Canning Basics, page 10.)

Turn off heat. Uncover and let jars stand in canner for 5 minutes. Lift up rack. With canning tongs, transfer jars to cooling rack; let cool undisturbed for 24 hours.

MAKES ABOUT 8 CUPS. PER 1 TBSP: about 46 cal, 0 g pro, 0 g total fat (0 g sat. fat), 12 g carb, trace fibre, 0 mg chol, 1 mg sodium. % RDI: 8% vit C.

From left: Mandarin
Marmalade (page 69),
Red Grapefruit
Marmalade (opposite)
and Lemon Shred
Marmalade (page 84)

Red Onion Marmalade

Vibrantly coloured and deliciously tangy, this savoury marmalade pairs well with meat, such as pork, lamb or beef, or with crackers and a creamy cheese.

1 **orange**

3 cups **granulated sugar**

1½ cups thinly sliced **red onion**

¾ cup **red wine vinegar**

½ tsp **salt**

1 pkg (85 mL) **liquid fruit pectin**

Using vegetable peeler, peel zest from orange in long strips (save flesh for another use). Scrape any white pith off zest; slice zest lengthwise into paper-thin strips.

In large saucepan, bring zest strips, sugar, onion, vinegar and salt to boil; boil for 1 minute. Stir in pectin, mixing well. Remove from heat.

Using tongs, divide onion and orange zest among 3 hot 1-cup (250 mL) canning jars. Pour in liquid, leaving ¼-inch (5 mm) headspace.

Cover with prepared discs. Screw on bands until resistance is met; increase to fingertip tight. Boil in boiling water canner for 10 minutes. (See Canning Basics, page 10.)

Turn off heat. Uncover and let jars stand in canner for 5 minutes. Lift up rack. With canning tongs, transfer jars to cooling rack; let cool undisturbed for 24 hours.

MAKES 3 CUPS. PER 1 TBSP: about 51 cal, 0 g pro, 0 g total fat (0 g sat. fat), 13 g carb, trace fibre, 0 mg chol, 24 mg sodium. % RDI: 2% vit C.

Variation
Pepper and Red Onion Marmalade: Add ½ tsp coarsely ground pepper or hot pepper flakes.

tip
Use a mandoline to get the most delicate, paper-thin slices of onion.

Jams & Marmalades

Choosing and Storing Summer Fruits

In the summer, farm stands and markets overflow with fresh, ripe fruit. Here's how to pick and keep some of the most popular fruits for jams, jellies, pickles and preserves.

RASPBERRIES AND BLACKBERRIES

These are the most fragile of all berries. Look for berries that are deep red, golden or purple, depending on the variety. They should be plump with no green spots. Discard any soft, mouldy or mildewed fruit. Raspberries and blackberries don't last long in the refrigerator, so buy only what you need. Refrigerate unwashed berries, uncovered, in a single layer on a paper towel–lined tray for a day or two.

PLUMS

Buy local fruit that's ripe, smooth and deep purple, red or yellow, depending on the variety. Really ripe plums should smell sweet and fruity. Avoid any that are too hard or too soft, and toss any that are leaky or bruised. Store at room temperature out of direct sunlight.

BLUEBERRIES

Whether you're using wild or cultivated, look for firm, sweet-smelling blueberries that are dark purple-blue with a powdery bloom. Discard any that are wrinkled or mouldy. Refrigerate unwashed berries in a single layer on a paper towel–lined tray and cover lightly for a couple of days.

CHERRIES

Look for plump cherries that are deeply coloured – rich crimson, black-red or pinkish red. The stems should look fresh and green. Discard any cherries with bruises, tears or soft spots. Cherries will last for a few days in the refrigerator. Spread them, unwashed, in a single layer on a paper towel–lined tray and cover lightly.

PEACHES, NECTARINES AND APRICOTS

Choose peaches and nectarines with an orange-pink blush, and apricots that are an even yellow. Choose fruit that's sweet, perfumy and plump, avoiding any that is soft or overly bruised (you can cut out small bruises when preparing preserves). Store slightly underripe fruit at room temperature, out of direct sunlight, for a day or two. Refrigerate ripe fruit and store only a couple of days before using.

STRAWBERRIES

Look for plump, sweet-smelling, fully red berries without any white or green spots. Discard any that are bruised or show signs of mould or spoilage. Buy just what you need – strawberries don't keep well for more than a day or two. Refrigerate whole unwashed berries, hulling them just before use.

Jams & Marmalades

Bacon and Onion Jam

Sweet and savoury, this bacon jam – a cross between a chutney and a potted meat – is wonderful on whole grain toast, hamburgers and even peanut butter sandwiches.

1 pkg (500 g) sliced **bacon,** thinly sliced crosswise

2 lb (900 g) **red onions,** finely chopped

½ tsp **salt**

⅔ cup **maple syrup**

¼ cup **malt vinegar**

½ tsp **dried rubbed savory**

¼ tsp **ground cloves**

Pinch **pepper**

tip

Jars that will be boiled in a boiling water canner for 10 minutes or more don't need to be sterilized. But this low-acid meat-based jam isn't processed, so it's a good idea to sterilize the jars before filling them to be sure they're free of bacteria. Simply submerge the jars in boiling water in a large canning pot; boil for 10 minutes. Leave them in the water and dry them just before you're ready to fill them.

In large skillet over medium heat, fry bacon until crisp. Reserving fat, drain bacon in sieve set over heatproof bowl.

Return ¼ cup of the reserved fat to skillet. Fry onions and salt, stirring often, until onions are deep brown and very soft, about 50 minutes.

Scrape onions into saucepan. Mince bacon; add to pan along with maple syrup, vinegar, ¼ cup water, savory, cloves and pepper. Bring to boil; simmer over medium heat, uncovered and stirring often, until liquid no longer pools and mixture is thick and jam-like, 20 minutes.

Spoon into 3 hot sterilized 1-cup (250 mL) canning jars. Stir mixture to remove any air pockets; tap jars on surface to pack down mixture. Smooth tops.

Cover with prepared discs. Screw on bands until resistance is met; increase to fingertip tight. Let cool completely. Refrigerate for up to 1 month.

Let jar stand at room temperature for 30 minutes before serving.

MAKES 3 CUPS. PER 1 TBSP: about 43 cal, 1 g pro, 2 g total fat (1 g sat. fat), 5 g carb, trace fibre, 4 mg chol, 94 mg sodium, 51 mg potassium. % RDI: 1% calcium, 1% iron, 2% vit C, 1% folate.

Carrot Orange Marmalade

Carrots add a new dimension – not to mention vibrant colour – to familiar marmalade. Now that's orange!

3 **lemons**

2 **oranges**

5 cups **granulated sugar**

3 cups grated **carrots** (about 12 oz/340 g)

Scrub lemons and oranges; cut out stem and blossom ends and any blemishes. Cut in half crosswise; squeeze out juice and set aside.

Cut lemon and orange halves into thirds. Cut each crosswise into thin strips.

In large Dutch oven, bring lemon and orange strips, reserved juice and 3 cups water to simmer over medium heat. Cover and simmer, stirring often, until peel turns to mush when pressed between fingers, about 45 minutes.

Add sugar and carrots. Bring to full rolling boil over high heat, uncovered and stirring often. Boil hard, stirring constantly, until thickened and firmly set, 8 to 12 minutes. (See Testing for Setting Point, page 17.)

Remove from heat. Stir and skim off foam for 5 minutes.

Fill hot 1-cup (250 mL) canning jars, leaving ¼-inch (5 mm) headspace. Cover with prepared discs. Screw on bands until resistance is met; increase to fingertip tight. Boil in boiling water canner for 10 minutes. (See Canning Basics, page 10.)

Turn off heat. Uncover and let jars stand in canner for 5 minutes. Lift up rack. With canning tongs, transfer jars to cooling rack; let cool undisturbed for 24 hours.

MAKES 7 CUPS. PER 1 TBSP: about 37 cal, 0 g pro, 0 g total fat (0 g sat. fat), 10 g carb, 0 g fibre, 0 mg chol, 2 mg sodium. % RDI: 1% iron, 8% vit A, 7% vit C.

Meyer Lemon Marmalade

Tasty Meyer lemons aren't interchangeable with other lemons and are only in season in the winter. If you can't find them, try Lemon Shred Marmalade (page 84).

2 lb (900 g) **Meyer lemons** (about 10)

5 cups **granulated sugar**

Scrub lemons; cut out stem and blossom ends and any blemishes. Cut in half crosswise; squeeze out juice and seeds. Reserving seeds and pulp, strain juice into large Dutch oven.

Pull membranes off peels; tie pulp, seeds and membranes in 15-inch (38 cm) square of double-thickness fine cheesecloth to form bag. Add to pan.

Cut lemon halves in half; cut crosswise into paper-thin strips. Add to pan.

Add 5 cups water; bring to simmer over medium heat. Simmer, stirring often and pressing bag to release pectin, until peel turns to mush when pressed between fingers, about 45 minutes.

Remove bag; let cool. Squeeze liquid from bag into pan. Measure 5 cups fruit mixture. (See Tip, page 68.)

In clean Dutch oven, bring sugar and fruit mixture to full rolling boil over high heat, stirring often. Boil hard, stirring constantly, until free of foam, thickened and firmly set, 7 to 10 minutes. (See Testing for Setting Point, page 17.)

Fill hot 1-cup (250 mL) canning jars, leaving ¼-inch (5 mm) headspace. Cover with prepared discs. Screw on bands until resistance is met; increase to fingertip tight. Boil in boiling water canner for 10 minutes. (See Canning Basics, page 10.)

Turn off heat. Uncover and let jars stand in canner for 5 minutes. Lift up rack. With canning tongs, transfer jars to cooling rack; let cool undisturbed for 24 hours.

MAKES 6 CUPS. PER 1 TBSP: about 43 cal, 0 g pro, 0 g total fat (0 g sat. fat), 11 g carb, trace fibre, 0 mg chol, 0 mg sodium. % RDI: 10% vit C.

Jams & Marmalades

Lemon Shred Marmalade

Straining the juice and using only the zest produces a crystal-clear jelly with elegant fine shreds. This zippy marmalade makes an excellent glaze for grilled chicken.

9 **lemons**

8 cups **granulated sugar**

Scrub lemons; cut out stem and blossom ends and any blemishes. Using vegetable peeler, peel off zest, avoiding white pith; cut zest into paper-thin strips. Set aside.

Cut lemons in half crosswise; squeeze out juice and seeds. Reserving seeds and pulp, strain juice into large Dutch oven. Add zest to pan.

Chop lemon pith and membranes; tie along with pulp and seeds in 15-inch (38 cm) square of double-thickness fine cheesecloth to form bag. Add to pan.

Add 10 cups water; bring to simmer over medium heat. Simmer, stirring often and pressing bag to release pectin, until peel turns to mush when pressed between fingers, about 1 hour.

Remove bag; let cool. Squeeze liquid from bag into pan. Measure 8 cups fruit mixture. (See Tip, page 68.)

Divide fruit mixture into 2 batches. For each batch, in clean Dutch oven, bring fruit mixture and 4 cups of the sugar to full rolling boil, stirring. Boil hard, stirring constantly, until free of foam, thickened and firmly set, 8 minutes. (See Testing for Setting Point, page 17.)

Fill hot 1-cup (250 mL) canning jars, leaving ¼-inch (5 mm) headspace. Cover with prepared discs. Screw on bands until resistance is met; increase to fingertip tight. Boil in boiling water canner for 10 minutes. (See Canning Basics, page 10.)

Turn off heat. Uncover and let jars stand in canner for 5 minutes. Lift up rack. With canning tongs, transfer jars to cooling rack; let cool undisturbed for 24 hours.

MAKES ABOUT 8 CUPS. PER 1 TBSP: about 52 cal, trace pro, 0 g total fat (0 g sat. fat), 14 g carb, 1 g fibre, 0 mg chol, 1 mg sodium. % RDI: 1% calcium, 1% iron, 15% vit C.

Jams & Marmalades

chapter three

Jellies

Grape Jelly

These luscious Canadian grapes produce a delicious, glistening jelly with the classic grape flavour that any kid – or adult – will love on a PB and J sandwich.

3¾ lb (1.7 kg) **Concord grapes** or Coronation grapes

1 pkg (57 g) **fruit pectin crystals**

5 cups **granulated sugar**

Rinse grapes; drain well. Remove enough grapes from stems to make 10 cups, discarding any that are wrinkled or bruised.

In large Dutch oven and using potato masher, crush grapes. Add 1 cup water; bring to boil, stirring often. Reduce heat, cover and simmer for 10 minutes.

Scoop cooked grapes into damp jelly bag suspended over large glass measure or bowl. Let drip, without squeezing bag, until juice measures 4 cups, about 2 hours. (See Tip, page 90.)

In clean Dutch oven, bring juice and pectin to boil. Stir in sugar; bring to full rolling boil over high heat, stirring often. Boil hard, stirring constantly, for 1 minute.

Remove from heat. Skim off any foam.

Fill hot 1-cup (250 mL) canning jars, leaving ¼-inch (5 mm) headspace. Cover with prepared discs. Screw on bands until resistance is met; increase to fingertip tight. Boil in boiling water canner for 10 minutes. (See Canning Basics, page 10.)

Turn off heat. Uncover and let jars stand in canner for 5 minutes. Lift up rack. With canning tongs, transfer jars to cooling rack; let cool undisturbed for 24 hours.

MAKES ABOUT 7 CUPS. PER 1 TBSP: about 42 cal, 0 g pro, 0 g total fat (0 g sat. fat), 11 g carb, 0 g fibre, 0 mg chol, 0 mg sodium.

tip

If you don't have a jelly bag and frame, you can make a simple substitute. Scoop cooked fruit mixture into colander lined with damp square of triple-thickness fine cheesecloth. Bring up sides; tie with kitchen string to form bag. Tie bag to cupboard handle over large glass measure or bowl. Let drip as directed.

Jellies

Grape Plum Jelly

Small prune plums infuse this jelly with a light flavour that tones down the strong grape taste.

2 lb (900 g) **Coronation grapes** or Concord grapes

2 lb (900 g) **fresh prune plums**

1 pkg (49 g) **light fruit pectin crystals**

4½ cups **granulated sugar**

Rinse grapes; drain well. Remove enough grapes from stems to make 10 cups, discarding any that are wrinkled or bruised.

Rinse grapes; drain well. Remove enough grapes from stems to make 10 cups, discarding any that are wrinkled or bruised.

Pit and quarter plums. In large Dutch oven and using potato masher, crush grapes. Add plums and 2 cups water; bring to boil, stirring often. Reduce heat, cover and simmer until fruit is softened, about 25 minutes.

Scoop into damp jelly bag suspended over large glass measure or bowl. Let drip, without squeezing bag, until juice measures 6½ cups, 2 hours. (See Tip, page 90.)

Mix pectin with ¼ cup of the sugar. In clean Dutch oven, stir pectin mixture with juice; bring to full rolling boil over high heat.

Stir in remaining sugar; return to full rolling boil, stirring. Boil hard, stirring constantly, for 1 minute.

Remove from heat. Skim off foam.

Fill hot 1-cup (250 mL) canning jars, leaving ¼-inch (5 mm) headspace. Cover with prepared discs. Screw on bands until resistance is met; increase to fingertip tight. Boil in boiling water canner for 10 minutes. (See Canning Basics, page 10.)

Turn off heat. Uncover and let jars stand in canner for 5 minutes. Lift up rack. With canning tongs, transfer jars to cooling rack; let cool undisturbed for 24 hours.

MAKES ABOUT EIGHT 1-CUP (250 mL) JARS. PER 1 TBSP: about 34 cal, 0 g pro, 0 g total fat (0 g sat. fat), 9 g carb, 0 g fibre, 0 mg chol, 1 mg sodium.

tip
To reduce foaming, add ½ tsp unsalted butter to fruit juice before cooking.

Jellies

Tart Cherry Vanilla Jelly

Spread this sweet-tart vanilla-laced jelly on a peanut butter sandwich and you'll want to lick the plate clean.

3¾ cups pitted **fresh tart cherries**

Half **vanilla bean**

1 pkg (57 g) **fruit pectin crystals**

4 cups **granulated sugar**

In large Dutch oven, combine cherries and ½ cup water. Cut vanilla bean in half lengthwise; scrape seeds into pan. Discard pod.

Using potato masher, crush cherries; bring to boil over medium heat, stirring often. Reduce heat and simmer, crushing and stirring often, until cherries are soft and well mashed, 10 minutes.

Scoop cherry mixture into damp jelly bag suspended over large glass measure or bowl. Let drip, without squeezing bag, until juice measures 3¾ cups, about 4 hours. (See Tip, left.) If juice measures less, pour boiling water slowly over cherry mixture and let drip until correct amount.

In clean Dutch oven, stir juice with pectin. Bring to boil over high heat, stirring often. Gradually stir in sugar; return to full rolling boil, stirring often. Boil hard, stirring constantly, for 1 minute.

Remove from heat. Stir and skim off foam for 5 minutes.

Fill hot 1-cup (250 mL) canning jars, leaving ¼-inch (5 mm) headspace. Cover with prepared discs. Screw on bands until resistance is met; increase to fingertip tight. Boil in boiling water canner for 10 minutes. (See Canning Basics, page 10.)

Turn off heat. Uncover and let jars stand in canner for 5 minutes. Lift up rack. With canning tongs, transfer jars to cooling rack; let cool undisturbed for 24 hours.

MAKES ABOUT 6 CUPS. PER 1 TBSP: about 37 cal, trace pro, 0 g total fat (0 g sat. fat), 10 g carb, 0 g fibre, 0 mg chol, 0 mg sodium, 11 mg potassium. % RDI: 1% iron.

tip
When measuring juice or a herbal infusion for jelly, use a 1-cup measuring cup multiple times rather than a single large cup (such as a 4-cup). Large glass measures tend to be less accurate, and the different amount of liquid can throw off the balance of ingredients.

Jellies

Crab Apple Jelly

This clear, stunning jelly ranges from coral to red, depending on the apples. Serve with roast pork or pâté, or pair with cream cheese for a delicious toast topping.

6 lb (2.7 kg) **crab apples**

4½ cups **granulated sugar**

Cut out stem and blossom ends from crab apples. (Do not peel or core.)

In large Dutch oven, bring crab apples and 6 cups water to boil. Reduce heat, cover and simmer, stirring occasionally, until softened, about 10 minutes. Using potato masher, crush crab apples; cook for 5 minutes.

Scoop crab apples into damp jelly bag suspended over large glass measure or bowl. Let drip, without squeezing bag, until juice measures 6½ cups, about 2 hours. (See Tip, page 90.) Add up to 1½ cups water if not enough juice.

In clean Dutch oven, bring juice and sugar to full rolling boil over medium-high heat, stirring. Boil hard, stirring constantly, until firmly set, 15 to 18 minutes. (See Testing for Setting Point, page 17.)

Remove from heat. Skim off foam.

Fill hot 1-cup (250 mL) canning jars, leaving ¼-inch (5 mm) headspace. Cover with prepared discs. Screw on bands until resistance is met; increase to fingertip tight. Boil in boiling water canner for 10 minutes. (See Canning Basics, page 10.)

Turn off heat. Uncover and let jars stand in canner for 5 minutes. Lift up rack. With canning tongs, transfer jars to cooling rack; let cool undisturbed for 24 hours.

MAKES ABOUT EIGHT 1-CUP (250 mL) JARS. PER 1 TBSP: about 30 cal, 0 g pro, 0 g total fat (0 g sat. fat), 8 g carb, 0 g fibre, 0 mg chol, 0 mg sodium.

Jellies

Spiced Apple Mint Jelly

The sweet-and-sour flavour of early McIntosh apples is excellent for this jelly, but any tasty cooking apple, such as Gravenstein, Winesap or Empire, will work. Serve with roast lamb or a cheese plate (see page 137).

4½ lb (2.025 kg) **apples** (unpeeled and uncored), chopped

3-inch (8 cm) piece **cinnamon stick**

2½-inch (6 cm) piece **fresh ginger,** thinly sliced

2½ tsp **black peppercorns**

4 cups lightly packed **fresh mint leaves**

4 cups **granulated sugar**

¼ cup freshly squeezed **lemon juice**

In large Dutch oven, bring apples, 4 cups water, cinnamon, ginger and peppercorns to boil. Reduce heat; simmer, stirring and breaking up apples, until apples are completely mushy, 30 to 40 minutes. Remove from heat; stir in mint. Cover and let stand for 10 minutes.

Scoop apple mixture into damp jelly bag suspended over large glass measure or bowl. Let drip, without squeezing bag, for 8 hours or overnight.

Bring juice, sugar and lemon juice to boil; boil over medium-high heat until firmly set, 25 to 30 minutes. (See Testing for Setting Point, page 17.)

Remove from heat. Skim off foam.

Fill hot 2-cup (500 mL) canning jars, leaving ¼-inch (5 mm) headspace. Cover with prepared discs. Screw on bands until resistance is met; increase to fingertip tight. Boil in boiling water canner for 10 minutes. (See Canning Basics, page 10.)

Turn off heat. Uncover and let jars stand in canner for 5 minutes. Lift up rack. With canning tongs, transfer jars to cooling rack; let cool undisturbed for 24 hours.

MAKES FOUR 2-CUP (500 ML) JARS.
PER 1 TBSP: about 51 cal, 0 g pro, 0 g total fat (0 g sat. fat), 13 g carb, 0 g fibre, 0 mg chol, 1 mg sodium, 13 mg potassium. % RDI: 1% iron, 1% vit C.

tip

If you don't have a jelly bag and frame, you can make a simple substitute. Scoop cooked fruit mixture into colander lined with damp square of triple-thickness fine cheesecloth. Bring up sides; tie with kitchen string to form bag. Tie bag to cupboard handle over large glass measure or bowl. Let drip as directed.

Jellies

Black Currant Gooseberry Jelly

These two old-fashioned berries often grow in kitchen gardens and might have been the stars of some of your grandmother's favourite preserves. Look for them in farmer's markets during the all-too-brief harvest.

3 cups stemmed **fresh black currants**

3 cups **fresh gooseberries,** topped and tailed

1 pkg (57 g) **fruit pectin crystals**

4 cups **granulated sugar**

In large Dutch oven and using potato masher, crush currants with gooseberries. Add 1½ cups water; bring to boil, stirring occasionally. Reduce heat, cover and simmer until berries are tender, about 10 minutes.

Scoop berry mixture into damp jelly bag suspended over large glass measure or bowl. Let drip, pressing bag lightly, until juice measures 3 cups, about 2 hours. (See Tip, page 90.)

In clean Dutch oven, bring juice and pectin to boil, stirring. Stir in sugar; return to full rolling boil, stirring often. Boil hard, stirring constantly, for 1 minute.

Remove from heat. Skim off any foam.

Fill hot 1-cup (250 mL) canning jars, leaving ¼-inch (5 mm) headspace. Cover with prepared discs. Screw on bands until resistance is met; increase to fingertip tight. Boil in boiling water canner for 10 minutes. (See Canning Basics, page 10.)

Turn off heat. Uncover and let jars stand in canner for 5 minutes. Lift up rack. With canning tongs, transfer jars to cooling rack; let cool undisturbed for 24 hours.

MAKES ABOUT 5 CUPS. PER 1 TBSP: about 28 cal, 0 g pro, 0 g total fat (0 g sat. fat), 7 g carb, 0 g fibre, 0 mg chol, 0 mg sodium. % RDI: 1% iron, 7% vit C.

Jellies

Raspberry Red Currant Jelly

Bright and refreshing, both in colour and flavour, this jelly can do double duty, working in sweet and savoury dishes.

6 cups stemmed **fresh red currants**

6 cups **fresh raspberries**

1 pkg (49 g) **light fruit pectin crystals**

4½ cups **granulated sugar**

In large Dutch oven and using potato masher, crush red currants with raspberries. Add 1½ cups water; bring to boil, stirring occasionally. Reduce heat, cover and simmer for 10 minutes.

Scoop currant mixture into damp jelly bag suspended over large glass measure or bowl. Let drip, without squeezing bag, until juice measures 6½ cups, about 2 hours. (See Tip, page 90.) Add up to 1½ cups water if not enough juice.

Mix pectin with ¼ cup of the sugar. In clean Dutch oven, stir pectin mixture with juice; bring to full rolling boil over high heat. Stir in remaining sugar; return to full rolling boil, stirring often. Boil hard, stirring constantly, for 1 minute.

Remove from heat. Skim off foam.

Fill hot 1-cup (250 mL) canning jars, leaving ¼-inch (5 mm) headspace. Cover with prepared discs. Screw on bands until resistance is met; increase to fingertip tight. Boil in boiling water canner for 10 minutes. (See Canning Basics, page 10.)

Turn off heat. Uncover and let jars stand in canner for 5 minutes. Lift up rack. With canning tongs, transfer jars to cooling rack; let cool undisturbed for 24 hours.

MAKES ABOUT EIGHT 1-CUP (250 mL) JARS. PER 1 TBSP: about 33 cal, trace pro, 0 g total fat (0 g sat. fat), 8 g carb, 0 g fibre, 0 mg chol, 1 mg sodium. % RDI: 1% iron, 3% vit C.

Two-Currant Jelly

Look for cultivated white currants in farmer's markets, or grow your own. Their light sweetness blends nicely with the puckery tang of red currants in this clear light-red jelly. Brush it over a pork roast for a sensational dinner.

6 cups stemmed **fresh red currants**

6 cups stemmed **fresh white currants**

1 pkg (57 g) **fruit pectin crystals**

7 cups **granulated sugar**

In large Dutch oven and using potato masher, crush red and white currants. Add 1½ cups water; bring to boil, stirring occasionally. Reduce heat, cover and simmer until currants are softened and deflated, about 10 minutes.

Scoop cooked currants into damp jelly bag suspended over large glass measure or bowl. Let drip, pressing bag lightly, until juice measures 6½ cups, about 2 hours. (See Tip, page 90.)

In clean Dutch oven, bring juice and pectin to boil, stirring. Stir in sugar; return to full rolling boil, stirring constantly. Boil hard, stirring constantly, for 1 minute.

Remove from heat. Skim off foam.

Fill hot 1-cup (250 mL) canning jars, leaving ¼-inch (5 mm) headspace. Cover with prepared discs. Screw on bands until resistance is met; increase to fingertip tight. Boil in boiling water canner for 10 minutes. (See Canning Basics, page 10.)

Turn off heat. Uncover and let jars stand in canner for 5 minutes. Lift up rack. With canning tongs, transfer jars to cooling rack; let cool undisturbed for 24 hours.

MAKES ABOUT 10 CUPS. PER 1 TBSP: about 39 cal, trace pro, 0 g total fat (0 g sat. fat), 10 g carb, 0 g fibre, 0 mg chol, 0 mg sodium. % RDI: 1% iron, 3% vit C.

Variation

Red Currant Jelly: Replace fresh white currants with fresh red currants.

Jellies

Ginger Peach Jelly

The pep of ginger complements the floral fruitiness of the peaches like magic in this rosy-hued jelly. It is lovely on scones and toast, of course, but it also makes a shiny, flavourful glaze on fruit tarts, pies or even ham.

4½ lb (2.025 kg) **fresh peaches** (about 16)

⅔ cup thinly sliced **fresh ginger** (about 6-inch/15 cm piece)

2 tbsp freshly squeezed **lemon juice**

1 pkg (57 g) **fruit pectin crystals**

6 cups **granulated sugar**

Rub peaches under cool running water to remove excess fuzz. Pit and cut into quarters, or sixths if large.

In large Dutch oven, combine peaches, 1 cup water and ginger. Using potato masher, crush peach mixture. Bring to boil over high heat, stirring often. Reduce heat and simmer, crushing and stirring often, until peaches are very soft and well mashed and ginger is translucent, about 25 minutes.

Scoop peach mixture into damp jelly bag suspended over large glass measure or bowl. Let drip, without squeezing bag, until juice measures 4 cups, 4 hours. (See Tip, page 90.) If juice measures less, pour up to 3 cups boiling water slowly over peach mixture and let drip until correct amount.

In clean Dutch oven, stir together peach juice, lemon juice and pectin.

Bring to boil over high heat, stirring often. Gradually stir in sugar; return to full rolling boil over high heat, stirring often. Boil hard, stirring constantly, for 1 minute.

Remove from heat. Stir and skim off foam for 5 minutes.

Fill hot 1-cup (250 mL) canning jars, leaving ¼-inch (5 mm) headspace. Cover with prepared discs. Screw on bands until resistance is met; increase to fingertip tight. Boil in boiling water canner for 10 minutes. (See Canning Basics, page 10.)

Turn off heat. Uncover and let jars stand in canner for 5 minutes. Lift up rack. With canning tongs, transfer jars to cooling rack; let cool undisturbed for 24 hours.

MAKES ABOUT 6 CUPS. PER 1 TBSP: about 53 cal, trace pro, 0 g total fat (0 g sat. fat), 14 g carb, 0 g fibre, 0 mg chol, 0 mg sodium, 16 mg potassium. % RDI: 2% vit C.

tip

For the best flavour, use the freshest ginger possible. It should have shiny, taut skin and juicy, fragrant flesh. Avoid pieces with shrivelled skin or signs of mould.

Jellies

Crantini Jelly

Adapted from a Certo recipe, this cranberry-scented, martini-inspired jelly is terrific with roasted meat or poultry when you're entertaining.

3½ cups **granulated sugar**

2 cups **cranberry juice**

1 pkg (85 mL) **liquid fruit pectin**

¼ cup **vodka**

¼ cup **white vermouth**

In large saucepan, bring sugar and cranberry juice to full rolling boil over high heat, stirring constantly. Boil hard, stirring constantly, for 1 minute.

Remove from heat. Stir in pectin, vodka and vermouth.

Fill hot 1-cup (250 mL) canning jars, leaving ¼-inch (5 mm) headspace. Cover with prepared discs. Screw on bands until resistance is met; increase to fingertip tight. Boil in boiling water canner for 10 minutes. (See Canning Basics, page 10.)

Turn off heat. Uncover and let jars stand in canner for 5 minutes. Lift up rack. With canning tongs, transfer jars to cooling rack; let cool undisturbed for 24 hours.

MAKES 4 CUPS. PER 1 TBSP: about 49 cal, 0 g pro, 0 g total fat (0 g sat. fat), 12 g carb, 0 g fibre, 0 mg chol, 0 mg sodium. % RDI: 2% vit C.

Jellies

Rachel

Clockwise from top right: Red Grapefruit Marmalade (page 76), Crantini Jelly (opposite) and Apple Chutney (page 211)

Cranberry Red Wine Jelly

Be sure to use 100 per cent cranberry juice and choose a fruity dry red wine, such as a Merlot, for this easy preserve. When canned in small jars, it makes a lovely gift.

1 cup **100% cranberry juice**

1 cup **fruity dry red wine**

2 tbsp freshly squeezed **lemon juice**

1 pkg (57 g) **fruit pectin crystals**

3½ cups **granulated sugar**

In large saucepan over high heat, combine cranberry juice, wine and lemon juice. Stir in pectin; bring to boil, stirring constantly.

Stir in sugar; bring to full rolling boil, stirring often. Boil hard, stirring constantly, for 1 minute.

Remove from heat. Skim off any foam.

Fill hot ½-cup (125 mL) canning jars, leaving ¼-inch (5 mm) headspace. Cover with prepared discs. Screw on bands until resistance is met; increase to fingertip tight. Boil in boiling water canner for 10 minutes. (See Canning Basics, page 10.)

Turn off heat. Uncover and let jars stand in canner for 5 minutes. Lift up rack. With canning tongs, transfer jars to cooling rack; let cool undisturbed for 24 hours.

MAKES 3½ CUPS. PER 1 TBSP: about 57 cal, 0 g pro, 0 g total fat (0 g sat. fat), 14 g carb, 0 g fibre, 0 mg chol, 1 mg sodium. % RDI: 2% vit C.

tip

This jelly is versatile. Serve it with roast turkey, chicken, duck or goose, or add a spoonful to poultry gravy. For an easy glaze, heat and spoon jelly over roast pork or ham two or three times during the last 30 minutes of cooking. It also makes a delicious appetizer: Spread over a block of cream cheese and serve with crackers.

Jellies

Port Jelly

Rich with spices and luscious ruby Port, this jelly is the perfect colour and flavour for the festive season.

6 **whole cloves**

4 **black peppercorns**

2 **cinnamon sticks,** broken

3 cups **granulated sugar**

2 cups **ruby Port**

¼ cup freshly squeezed **orange juice**

1 **orange,** thinly sliced

1 pkg (85 mL) **liquid fruit pectin**

Tie cloves, peppercorns and cinnamon in cheesecloth square to form bag.

In large saucepan, bring sugar, Port, orange juice, orange and spice bag to boil; boil, stirring constantly, for 2 minutes.

Remove from heat. Using tongs, remove orange slices and spice bag. Squeeze liquid from bag into pan. Stir in pectin, mixing well.

Fill hot ½-cup (125 mL) canning jars, leaving ¼-inch (5 mm) headspace. Cover with prepared discs. Screw on bands until resistance is met; increase to fingertip tight. Boil in boiling water canner for 10 minutes. (See Canning Basics, page 10.)

Turn off heat. Uncover and let jars stand in canner for 5 minutes. Lift up rack. With canning tongs, transfer jars to cooling rack; let cool undisturbed for 24 hours.

MAKES 4 CUPS. PER 1 TBSP: about 44 cal, 0 g pro, 0 g total fat (0 g sat. fat), 10 g carb, 0 g fibre, 0 mg chol, 1 mg sodium.

Jellies

Cabernet Franc Wine Jelly

Fresh thyme accentuates the herbaceous notes of Cabernet Franc, making this jelly a wonderful accompaniment to a cheese plate (see page 137). Stir up a batch to give as gifts to friends and family.

1¾ cups **Cabernet Franc wine**
   or Merlot wine

¼ cup **red wine vinegar**

2 large sprigs **fresh thyme**

3½ cups **granulated sugar**

1 pkg (85 mL) **liquid fruit pectin**

In large saucepan, bring wine, vinegar and thyme to boil over high heat. Remove from heat; cover and let stand for 20 minutes. Strain through cheesecloth-lined sieve into clean saucepan.

Stir in sugar; bring to full rolling boil over high heat, stirring often. Boil for 1 minute, stirring constantly.

Remove from heat. Stir in pectin; stir and skim off any foam for 1 minute.

Fill hot ½-cup (125 mL) canning jars, leaving ¼-inch (5 mm) headspace. Cover with prepared discs. Screw on bands until resistance is met; increase to fingertip tight. Boil in boiling water canner for 10 minutes. (See Canning Basics, page 10.)

Turn off heat. Uncover and let jars stand in canner for 5 minutes. Lift up rack. With canning tongs, transfer jars to cooling rack; let cool undisturbed for 24 hours.

MAKES ABOUT 4 CUPS. PER 1 TBSP: about 47 cal, 0 g pro, 0 g total fat (0 g sat. fat), 11 g carb, 0 g fibre, 0 mg chol, 0 mg sodium.

Variation
Gewürztraminer Wine Jelly: Replace Cabernet Franc with Gewürztraminer or Riesling, and vinegar with freshly squeezed lemon juice. Replace thyme with 1 strip each lime zest and Granny Smith apple peel, and 2 dried apricots, halved.

Jellies

Rosemary Peppercorn Wine Jelly

Crystal clear with sharp peppery notes, this jelly is an ideal companion to roast lamb or chicken. Or serve with aged cheese, such as manchego or Gruyère.

3 cups **granulated sugar**

1 cup **white wine**

¾ cup **cider vinegar**

2 sprigs (each 6 inches/15 cm) **fresh rosemary**

1 pkg (85 mL) **liquid fruit pectin**

1½ tsp **pink peppercorns** and/or **green peppercorns,** crushed

In large saucepan, bring sugar, white wine, vinegar and rosemary sprigs to boil over medium heat; boil for 5 minutes.

Discard rosemary. Stir in pectin, then peppercorns.

Remove from heat. Skim off foam.

Fill hot ½-cup (125 mL) canning jars, leaving ¼-inch (5 mm) headspace. Cover with prepared discs. Screw on bands until resistance is met; increase to fingertip tight. Boil in boiling water canner for 10 minutes. (See Canning Basics, page 10.)

Turn off heat. Uncover and let jars stand in canner for 5 minutes. Lift up rack. With canning tongs, transfer jars to cooling rack; let cool undisturbed for 24 hours.

MAKES ABOUT SIX ½-CUP (125 mL) JARS. PER 1 TBSP: about 49 cal, 0 g pro, 0 g total fat (0 g sat. fat), 13 g carb, 0 g fibre, 0 mg chol, 0 mg sodium. % RDI: 1% iron.

tip
To help evenly suspend the peppercorns throughout the jelly, gently twist or tilt the jars (do not invert) occasionally during cooling.

Jellies

Rhubarb Orange Jelly

Sharp yet sweet, this jelly is delicious on toast or as an accompaniment to poultry or pork. Use the pinkest rhubarb you can find for vibrant colour.

1 **orange**

10 cups chopped **fresh rhubarb**

1 pkg (49 g) **light fruit pectin crystals**

3¼ cups **granulated sugar**

Scrub orange; cut in half. Squeeze juice into large Dutch oven. Cut peel into wedges; add to pan. Add rhubarb and 1½ cups water; bring to boil, stirring occasionally. Reduce heat, cover and simmer until rhubarb is tender, about 10 minutes.

Using potato masher, crush any chunks. Spoon rhubarb mixture into damp jelly bag suspended over large glass measure or bowl. Let drip, without squeezing bag, until juice measures 4 cups, about 2 hours. (See Tip, page 90.)

Mix pectin with ¼ cup of the sugar. In clean Dutch oven, stir pectin mixture with juice; bring to full rolling boil over high heat. Stir in remaining sugar; return to full rolling boil, stirring often. Boil hard, stirring constantly, for 1 minute.

Remove from heat. Skim off any foam.

Fill hot 1-cup (250 mL) canning jars, leaving ¼-inch (5 mm) headspace. Cover with prepared discs. Screw on bands until resistance is met; increase to fingertip tight. Boil in boiling water canner for 10 minutes. (See Canning Basics, page 10.)

Turn off heat. Uncover and let jars stand in canner for 5 minutes. Lift up rack. With canning tongs, transfer jars to cooling rack; let cool undisturbed for 24 hours.

MAKES ABOUT 6 CUPS. PER 1 TBSP: about 30 cal, trace pro, 0 g total fat (0 g sat. fat), 8 g carb, 0 g fibre, 0 mg chol, 1 mg sodium. % RDI: 1% calcium, 3% vit C.

Jellies

Clockwise from bottom right: Rhubarb Orange Jelly (opposite), Strawberry Balsamic Black Pepper Jam (page 33) and Strawberry Vanilla Jam (page 31)

Cranberry Riesling Jelly

Tart cranberries are a nice counterpoint to the slightly sweet wine in this glistening jelly. Serve this jewel-toned beauty with roast poultry, pork or cheese.

8 cups **cranberries** (2 lb/900 g)

1 cup **Riesling wine,** Sauternes or other medium-dry or medium white wine

6 cups **granulated sugar**

2 pkg (each 85 mL) **liquid fruit pectin**

In large Dutch oven, combine cranberries and 5 cups water. Bring to boil over high heat, stirring often. Cover, reduce heat to low and simmer, crushing with potato masher and stirring often, until cranberries are very soft and well mashed and some liquid remains, 10 minutes.

Scoop cranberries into damp jelly bag suspended over large glass measure or bowl. Let drip, without squeezing bag, until juice measures 3 cups, 4 hours. (See Tip, page 90.) If juice measures less, pour boiling water slowly over cranberries and let drip until correct amount.

In clean Dutch oven, bring juice, wine and sugar to boil over high heat, stirring often. Boil hard, stirring constantly, for 1 minute.

Remove from heat; stir in pectin. Let stand for 5 minutes. Skim off foam.

Fill hot 1-cup (250 mL) canning jars, leaving ¼-inch (5 mm) headspace. Cover with prepared discs. Screw on bands until resistance is met; increase to fingertip tight. Boil in boiling water canner for 10 minutes. (See Canning Basics, page 10.)

Turn off heat. Uncover and let jars stand in canner for 5 minutes. Lift up rack. With canning tongs, transfer jars to cooling rack; let cool undisturbed for 24 hours.

MAKES ABOUT FIVE 1-CUP (250 ML) JARS. PER 1 TBSP: about 61 cal, 0 g pro, 0 g total fat (0 g sat. fat), 15 g carb, 0 g fibre, 0 mg chol, 1 mg sodium, 6 mg potassium.

tip

The fresh cranberries create a lot of foam. Be sure to wait the full five minutes and let the foam settle on top before patiently skimming off as much as possible. Foam left in the jelly can make it cloudy, and can cause it to expand and leak out in the canner. Use the skimmed-off foam as a glaze for roast chicken, whisk it into gravy or beat it into softened cream cheese for a spread.

Jellies

Pork Loin

Get this roast ready a day ahead to enjoy the full effects of the soy-lime marinade. Sweet plum sauce or jam is brushed on at the last minute so that it won't char.

2 tbsp **soy sauce**

2 tbsp **lime juice**

2 tsp minced **fresh ginger**

2 cloves **garlic,** minced

½ tsp **pepper**

3 lb (1.35 kg) **pork loin centre-cut roast** (single loin)

¼ cup **plum sauce** or Apricot Jam (page 56)

In glass bowl, whisk together soy sauce, lime juice, ginger, garlic and pepper.

Add pork roast, turning to coat. Cover and refrigerate for 8 hours. *(Make-ahead: Refrigerate for up to 24 hours, turning pork occasionally.)*

Reserving marinade, place roast on greased grill over medium heat; brush with reserved marinade. Close lid and grill, turning occasionally, for 1½ hours.

Brush with plum sauce; grill, turning occasionally, until thermometer inserted in centre registers 160°F (71°C) and just a hint of pink remains inside, about 10 minutes.

Transfer to cutting board. Tent with foil; let stand for 10 minutes before carving.

MAKES 8 SERVINGS. PER SERVING: about 186 cal, 25 g pro, 7 g total fat (2 g sat. fat), 4 g carb, trace fibre, 68 mg chol, 313 mg sodium. % RDI: 3% calcium, 6% iron, 2% vit C, 3% folate.

Pomegranate Wine Jelly

This deep crimson jelly partners deliciously with chicken, goose or quail, but is just as much at home on a cheese plate alongside old Cheddar or goat cheese.

3 cups **pomegranate juice**

1 cup **red wine**

1 pkg (49 g) **light fruit pectin crystals**

3½ cups **granulated sugar**

In large saucepan, stir pomegranate juice with red wine. Mix pectin with ¼ cup of the sugar; stir into pan. Bring to full rolling boil over medium-high heat, stirring constantly.

Add remaining sugar; return to full rolling boil. Boil hard, stirring constantly, for 1 minute.

Remove from heat. Skim off foam.

Fill hot 1-cup (250 mL) canning jars, leaving ¼-inch (5 mm) headspace. Cover with prepared discs. Screw on bands until resistance is met; increase to fingertip tight. Boil in boiling water canner for 10 minutes. (See Canning Basics, page 10.)

Turn off heat. Uncover and let jars stand in canner for 5 minutes. Lift up rack. With canning tongs, transfer jars to cooling rack; let cool undisturbed for 24 hours.

MAKES ABOUT FIVE 1-CUP (250 ML) JARS. PER 1 TBSP: about 42 cal, 0 g pro, 0 g total fat (0 g sat. fat), 11 g carb, 0 g fibre, 0 mg chol, 1 mg sodium.

Jellies

Lemon, Lime and Rosemary Jelly

Rosemary is very easy to grow, and this simple refrigerator jelly is a delicious way to make the most of your crop. Serve a dollop with grilled meats or fish.

4 **limes**

2 **lemons**

2½ cups cold **water**

6 sprigs (each 4 inches/ 10 cm) **fresh rosemary**

3¾ cups **granulated sugar**

1 pkg (85 mL) **liquid fruit pectin**

Scrub 1 each of the limes and lemons; thinly slice. Squeeze remaining limes and lemon to make about ½ cup juice.

In saucepan, combine cold water, lime and lemon slices, juice and 2 of the rosemary sprigs; bring to boil. Reduce heat and simmer until reduced to 2 cups, about 10 minutes. Strain through dampened jelly bag into clean saucepan. (See Tip, below.)

Stir in sugar; bring to full rolling boil over high heat, stirring constantly. Add pectin; boil hard, stirring constantly, for 1 minute.

Remove from heat. Skim off foam.

Divide remaining rosemary sprigs among 4 hot 1-cup (250 mL) canning jars; pour in jelly, leaving ⅛-inch (3 mm) headspace.

Seal and refrigerate for up to 2 months.

MAKES 4 CUPS. PER 1 TBSP: about 46 cal, 0 g pro, 0 g total fat (0 g sat. fat), 12 g carb, 0 g fibre, 0 mg chol, 1 mg sodium, 4 mg potassium. % RDI: 2% vit C.

tip

To make your own jelly bag, you need porous yet tightly woven fabric, such as unbleached cotton. Before using, rinse in water and wring dry. Line sieve suspended over large measuring cup with fabric. Pour in mixture; bring up corners of fabric and tie to form bag. Let drip at room temperature.

Fresh Mint Jelly

Fresh mint and white wine vinegar create a sweet, tangy jelly that's much nicer than store-bought ones. Once you try it, you'll see it goes with more than just lamb. Try it on zippy cheese canapés, in vinaigrettes or tossed with fruit.

2 cups lightly packed **fresh mint leaves**

½ cup **white wine vinegar**

1 pkg (57 g) **fruit pectin crystals**

4 cups **granulated sugar**

In saucepan, combine mint with 3½ cups water; bring to boil over high heat, gently mashing with wooden spoon. Remove from heat. Cover; let stand for 15 minutes.

Pour mint mixture into damp jelly bag suspended over large glass measure or bowl. Let drip, without squeezing bag, until mint infusion measures 3 cups, about 2 hours. (See Tip, page 90.)

In large Dutch oven, stir together mint infusion, vinegar and pectin. Bring to boil over high heat, stirring often. Gradually stir in sugar; return to full rolling boil over high heat, stirring often. Boil hard, stirring constantly, for 1 minute.

Remove from heat. Stir and skim off foam for 5 minutes.

Fill hot 1-cup (250 mL) canning jars, leaving ¼-inch (5 mm) headspace. Cover with prepared discs. Screw on bands until resistance is met; increase to fingertip tight. Boil in boiling water canner for 10 minutes. (See Canning Basics, page 10.)

Turn off heat. Uncover and let jars stand in canner for 5 minutes. Lift up rack. With canning tongs, transfer jars to cooling rack; let cool undisturbed for 24 hours.

MAKES ABOUT 5 CUPS. PER 1 TBSP: about 42 cal, 0 g pro, 0 g total fat (0 g sat. fat), 11 g carb, 0 g fibre, 0 mg chol, 1 mg sodium, 1 mg potassium.

tip

You can use any mint for this jelly; spearmint is milder, while peppermint is stronger. Or try lemon mint, pineapple mint, even chocolate mint – or a blend. Just do a taste-test of a small batch of the infusion first.

Jellies

Clockwise from top: Tequila Sunset Pepper Jelly, Jalapeño Jelly and Red Hot Pepper Jelly

Tequila Sunset Pepper Jelly

This sparkling blend of sweet and fiery brightly coloured peppers suspended in a tequila-flavoured jelly will dazzle your taste buds. It's sensational with cheese and crackers.

3 cups **granulated sugar**

⅓ cup each finely diced **sweet red, orange** and **yellow peppers**

¾ cup **white wine vinegar**

1 tsp minced **red hot pepper**

¼ cup **tequila**

1 pkg (85 mL) **liquid fruit pectin**

In large saucepan, combine sugar; red, orange and yellow peppers; vinegar; and hot pepper. Bring to full rolling boil over medium-high heat, stirring. Boil for 5 minutes.

Stir in tequila and pectin. Remove from heat. Skim off foam.

Fill hot ½-cup (125 mL) canning jars, leaving ¼-inch (5 mm) headspace. Cover with prepared discs. Screw on bands until resistance is met; increase to fingertip tight. Boil in boiling water canner for 10 minutes. (See Canning Basics, page 10.)

Turn off heat; let water stop boiling before removing jars. Lift up rack. With canning tongs, transfer jars to cooling rack; let cool for 30 minutes.

Wearing oven mitts, grasp each jar without disturbing screw band or disc; invert, twist or turn to distribute peppers throughout jelly.

Let jars cool on cooling rack for 24 hours, repeating inverting as necessary until solids are suspended in jelly.

MAKES ABOUT 3 CUPS. PER 1 TBSP: about 38 cal, 0 g pro, 0 g total fat (0 g sat. fat), 10 g carb, 0 g fibre, 0 mg chol, 0 mg sodium. % RDI: 7% vit C.

Variations

Jalapeño Jelly: Omit sweet and hot peppers and tequila. Substitute 1 cup finely chopped sweet green pepper, 1 tbsp minced jalapeño pepper, and ¼ tsp jalapeño or regular hot sauce.

Red Hot Pepper Jelly: Omit sweet and hot peppers, white wine vinegar and tequila. Substitute 1 cup finely chopped sweet red pepper, 1 tbsp minced red hot pepper, ¼ tsp hot pepper sauce and ¾ cup cider vinegar.

Jellies

Honey Lavender Jelly

One taste of this powerful floral jelly, accented with honey and lemon, will conjure up images of the lavender fields of Provence. It has an intense herbal flavour that is intriguing with goat cheese on crackers or baguette slices.

½ cup **dried culinary lavender**

¼ cup freshly squeezed **lemon juice**

1 pkg (57 g) **fruit pectin crystals**

3½ cups **granulated sugar**

½ cup **liquid honey**

In saucepan, bring 3½ cups water to boil over high heat. Stir in lavender; return to boil. Remove from heat; cover and let stand for 20 minutes.

Pour lavender mixture into damp jelly bag suspended over large glass measure or bowl. Let drip, without squeezing bag, until infusion measures 3 cups, about 2 hours. (See Tip, page 90.)

In large Dutch oven, stir together lavender infusion, lemon juice and pectin. Bring to boil over high heat, stirring often.

Gradually stir in sugar and honey; return to full rolling boil over high heat, stirring often. Boil hard, stirring constantly, for 1 minute.

Remove from heat. Stir and skim off foam for 5 minutes.

Fill hot 1-cup (250 mL) canning jars, leaving ¼-inch (5 mm) headspace. Cover with prepared discs. Screw on bands until resistance is met; increase to fingertip tight. Boil in boiling water canner for 10 minutes. (See Canning Basics, page 10.)

Turn off heat. Uncover and let jars stand in canner for 5 minutes. Lift up rack. With canning tongs, transfer jars to cooling rack; let cool undisturbed for 24 hours.

MAKES ABOUT 5 CUPS. PER 1 TBSP: about 43 cal, 0 g pro, 0 g total fat (0 g sat. fat), 11 g carb, 0 g fibre, 0 mg chol, 1 mg sodium, 2 mg potassium.

Tips
• If you prefer a milder flavour, decrease lavender to ¼ or ⅓ cup.

• Be sure to use lavender labelled for culinary use. Lavender sold at gift and flower shops is often treated with inedible preservatives.

Jellies

chapter four

Pickles
& Relishes

Garlic Dill Spears

Soaking the cucumbers in an ice-water brine helps them stay crunchy and delicious.

6 lb (2.7 kg) **small pickling cucumbers** (4 inches/10 cm)

12 cups **ice cubes**

⅓ cup **pickling salt**

3 tbsp **mustard seeds**

9 heads **fresh dill**

9 cloves **garlic**

PICKLING LIQUID:

4 cups **white vinegar**

½ cup **pickling salt**

2 tbsp **mixed pickling spices**

tip

Whole dill that has the dill head, or flowers, attached is available in season in some farmer's markets or grocery stores. If unavailable, you can substitute four sprigs fresh dill for each dill head.

Scrub cucumbers. Cut ⅛ inch (3 mm) off ends. Layer cucumbers and ice in large deep glass or stainless-steel container.

Dissolve salt in 3 cups cold water; pour over cucumbers. Add enough cold water to just cover cucumbers. Fill resealable bags with water; place over cucumbers to keep submerged. Refrigerate for 4 hours. *(Make-ahead: Refrigerate for up to 8 hours.)*

Drain cucumbers. Trim to 3½ inches (9 cm); cut each cucumber lengthwise into 6 spears.

PICKLING LIQUID: In large saucepan, bring vinegar, 4 cups water, salt and pickling spices to boil; reduce heat and simmer for 15 minutes. Strain.

Into each of 9 hot 2-cup (500 mL) canning jars, place 1 tsp mustard seeds, 1 head dill and 1 clove garlic.

Tightly pack in cucumbers to within ¾ inch (2 cm) of rim. Divide hot pickling solution among jars to cover cucumbers, leaving ½-inch (1 cm) headspace. Remove any air bubbles.

Cover with prepared discs. Screw on bands until resistance is met; increase to fingertip tight. Boil in boiling water canner for 10 minutes. (See Canning Basics, page 10.)

Turn off heat. Uncover and let jars stand in canner for 5 minutes. Lift up rack. With canning tongs, transfer jars to cooling rack; let cool for 24 hours.

Let jars stand for 3 weeks before opening.

MAKES NINE 2-CUP (500 mL) JARS.
PER PICKLE: about 3 cal, 0 g pro, 0 g total fat (0 g sat. fat), 1 g carb, trace fibre, 0 mg chol, 318 mg sodium. % RDI: 2% vit C, 1% folate.

Dill Pickles

Fragrant dill heads give this old-fashioned pickle its classic flavour. Dill grows very well in backyard gardens, and this recipe is great for using up the bountiful flower heads.

4 lb (1.8 kg) **small pickling cucumbers** (3 to 4 inches/ 8 to 10 cm)

Fresh dill heads

Garlic cloves

2 cups **white vinegar**

¼ cup **pickling salt**

Scrub cucumbers. Cut off and discard blossom ends.

Place 1 dill head and 1 garlic clove in bottoms of hot 2-cup (500 mL) canning jars. Tightly pack in cucumbers to within ¾ inch (2 cm) of rim; top with another dill head and more garlic (if desired).

Meanwhile, in large saucepan, bring 6 cups water, vinegar and salt to boil. Divide hot liquid among jars to cover cucumbers, leaving ½-inch (1 cm) headspace. Remove any air bubbles.

Cover with prepared discs. Screw on bands until resistance is met; increase to fingertip tight. Boil in boiling water canner for 10 minutes. (See Canning Basics, page 10.)

Turn off heat. Uncover and let jars stand in canner for 5 minutes. Lift up rack. With canning tongs, transfer jars to cooling rack; let cool for 24 hours.

Let jars stand for 4 to 6 weeks before opening.

MAKES ABOUT 16 CUPS. PER PICKLE: about 16 cal, 1 g pro, trace total fat (0 g sat. fat), 4 g carb, 1 g fibre, 0 mg chol, 716 mg sodium, 135 mg potassium. % RDI: 1% calcium, 2% iron, 7% vit C, 4% folate.

tip

The blossom end of a cucumber contains an enzyme that can make pickles go limp. Cut about ⅛ inch (1.5 mm) off blossom end and discard to prevent the problem.

Bread-and-Butter Pickles

This classic golden-green picnic pickle is well spiced and has a pleasing tension between salty and sweet flavours.

4 lb (1.8 kg) **pickling cucumbers**

2 cups sliced **shallots**

2 **red hot peppers,** seeded and cut in rings

8 cups **ice cubes**

⅓ cup **pickling salt**

PICKLING LIQUID:

2½ cups **cider vinegar**

1 cup **granulated sugar**

2 tbsp **mustard seeds**

1 tbsp **pickling salt**

1 tbsp **celery seeds**

1 tsp **ground coriander**

½ tsp **turmeric**

Pinch **ground cloves**

Scrub cucumbers. Cut ⅛ inch (3 mm) off ends. Using knife or crinkle cutter, cut crosswise into ¼-inch (5 mm) thick slices. Layer cucumbers, shallots, hot peppers and ice cubes in large deep glass or stainless-steel container.

Dissolve salt in 12 cups cold water; pour over cucumber mixture, adding more water if necessary to cover. Place plate on top; weigh down to keep cucumbers submerged. Let stand for 30 minutes or for up to 1 hour.

Drain and rinse well; drain again, gently pressing. Tightly pack cucumber mixture into 6 hot 2-cup (500 mL) canning jars to within 1 inch (2.5 cm) of rim.

PICKLING LIQUID: In saucepan, bring vinegar, 2 cups water, sugar, mustard seeds, salt, celery seeds, coriander, turmeric and cloves to boil, stirring until sugar is dissolved.

Divide among jars, leaving ½-inch (1 cm) headspace. Remove any air bubbles.

Cover with prepared discs. Screw on bands until resistance is met; increase to fingertip tight. Boil in boiling water canner for 10 minutes. (See Canning Basics, page 10.)

Turn off heat. Uncover and let jars stand in canner for 5 minutes. Lift up rack. With canning tongs, transfer jars to cooling rack; let cool for 24 hours.

Let jars stand for 1 week before opening.

MAKES SIX 2-CUP (500 ML) JARS.
PER 2 TBSP: about 12 cal, trace pro, trace total fat (0 g sat. fat), 3 g carb, trace fibre, 0 mg chol, 232 mg sodium, 45 mg potassium. % RDI: 1% calcium, 1% iron, 1% vit A, 3% vit C, 1% folate.

Pickles & Relishes

Peppery Hamburger Pickle Slices

Sweet and sour, peppery and piquant, these pickles are an ideal hamburger topping and a relish tray star.

3 lb (1.35 kg) **pickling cucumbers**

1 **large sweet onion,** quartered and thinly sliced

2 **hot banana peppers,** hot shepherd peppers or other hot peppers, seeded and sliced in thin rings

Half **sweet green pepper,** diced

⅓ cup **pickling salt**

24 **ice cubes**

2 tbsp **black peppercorns**

2 tbsp **mustard seeds**

2 tsp **celery seeds**

½ tsp **turmeric**

Generous pinch **ground cloves**

1½ cups **cider vinegar**

1¼ cups **granulated sugar**

Scrub cucumbers. Cut ⅛ inch (3 mm) off ends. Slice cucumbers lengthwise into ¼-inch (5 mm) thick slices.

In large stainless-steel or glass bowl, toss together cucumber slices, onion, hot peppers, green pepper, salt and half of the ice cubes. Sprinkle remaining ice cubes over top; let stand for 3 hours.

Drain cucumbers well; rinse and drain well again, pressing gently to remove excess liquid. Return to bowl. Add peppercorns, mustard seeds, celery seeds, turmeric and cloves; mix well. Pack into 4 hot 2-cup (500 mL) canning jars to within ¾ inch (2 cm) of rim.

Meanwhile, in saucepan, bring vinegar and sugar to boil, stirring until sugar is dissolved.

Divide hot liquid among jars, leaving ½-inch (1 cm) headspace. Remove any air bubbles.

Cover with prepared discs. Screw on bands until resistance is met; increase to fingertip tight. Boil in boiling water canner for 10 minutes. (See Canning Basics, page 10.)

Turn off heat. Uncover and let jars stand in canner for 5 minutes. Lift up rack. With canning tongs, transfer jars to cooling rack; let cool for 24 hours.

Let jars stand for 1 week before opening.

MAKES FOUR 2-CUP (500 mL) JARS.
PER PICKLE SLICE: about 4 cal, 0 g pro, 0 g total fat (0 g sat. fat), 1 g carb, trace fibre, 0 mg chol, 115 mg sodium, 11 mg potassium.

Pickles & Relishes

Freezer Pickle Slices

For quick, last-minute pickling, try these easy freezer bread-and-butter pickles. Save the liquid to use in coleslaw or potato salad.

9 **small field cucumbers**
  (about 3 lb/1.35 kg)

2 **onions**

2 tbsp **pickling salt**

1½ cups **granulated sugar**

1 cup **white vinegar**

2 tbsp **mixed pickling spices**

1 tsp **celery seeds**

½ tsp **hot pepper flakes**
  (optional)

Scrub cucumbers; trim off ends. Thinly slice cucumbers and onions; place in large glass or stainless-steel bowl. Sprinkle with salt; toss to coat. Let stand for 2 hours.

Drain cucumber mixture but do not rinse. Pack into airtight freezer containers.

In saucepan, bring sugar, vinegar, pickling spices, celery seeds, and hot pepper flakes (if using) to boil; reduce heat and simmer for 5 minutes. Strain and pour over vegetables to cover; let cool.

Seal with lids and freeze for up to 2 months. Thaw in refrigerator.

MAKES ABOUT 8 CUPS. PER 2 TBSP: about 21 cal, trace pro, 0 g total fat (0 g sat. fat), 5 g carb, trace fibre, 0 mg chol, 5 mg sodium. % RDI: 1% iron, 2% vit C, 1% folate.

tip
To thinly slice the cucumbers and onions, use a mandoline or food processor.

Pickles & Relishes

Sweet Cucumber Mustard Pickles

These pickles are inspired by the spiced sweet vegetable marrow pickles served with cold and roast meats, pâtés and sandwiches in Denmark. Use large, thick-fleshed field cucumbers or slightly overgrown ones from your garden.

4 lb (1.8 kg) **field cucumbers**

1 **large red onion,** chopped

7 tsp **salt**

2¼ cups **malt vinegar** or cider vinegar

¾ cup **granulated sugar**

⅓ cup **dry mustard**

3 tbsp **ground ginger**

2 tsp **turmeric**

½ tsp **ground allspice**

½ tsp **cayenne pepper**

¼ tsp **ground cloves**

1 **sweet red pepper,** chopped

Peel, halve lengthwise and core cucumbers; cut into about 1-inch (2.5 cm) pieces. Toss together cucumbers, onion and 6 tsp of the salt until well combined; place in colander over bowl. Top with plate and weigh down for 4 to 8 hours. Discard liquid.

Bring vinegar, sugar, ⅔ cup water, mustard, ginger, turmeric, remaining salt, allspice, cayenne pepper and cloves to boil. Add cucumber mixture and red pepper; return to boil. Remove from heat.

Fill 4 hot 2-cup (500 mL) canning jars, leaving ½-inch (1 cm) headspace. Remove any air bubbles.

Cover with prepared discs. Screw on bands until resistance is met; increase to fingertip tight. Boil in boiling water canner for 10 minutes. (See Canning Basics, page 10.)

Turn off heat. Uncover and let jars stand in canner for 5 minutes. Lift up rack. With canning tongs, transfer jars to cooling rack; let cool for 24 hours.

Let jars stand for 3 days before opening.

MAKES FOUR 2-CUP (500 ML) JARS.
PER 1 TBSP: about 7 cal, trace pro, trace total fat (0 g sat. fat), 2 g carb, trace fibre, 0 mg chol, 43 mg sodium, 24 mg potassium. % RDI: 1% iron, 1% vit A, 3% vit C.

Clockwise from top left: Banana Pepper
Hot Sauce (page 276), Apple Raisin
Chutney (page 213) and Sweet
Cucumber Mustard Pickles (opposite)

Quick Zucchini Pickles

Fast to make and delicious with roast pork or on sandwiches, these pickles are a great way to use up an abundant zucchini harvest in the garden.

6 **zucchini** (yellow or green, or a combination)

4 cloves **garlic**

4 tsp **mustard seeds**

2 tsp **hot pepper flakes**

3 cups **white vinegar**

1 cup **granulated sugar**

¼ cup **pickling salt**

Cut each zucchini into six 4- x ½- x ½-inch (10 x 1 x 1 cm) sticks, retaining some skin on each.

In each of 4 hot 2-cup (500 mL) canning jars, place 1 clove garlic, 1 tsp mustard seeds and ½ tsp hot pepper flakes. Pack zucchini sticks tightly into jars.

Meanwhile, in small saucepan, bring vinegar, 1 cup water, sugar and salt to boil; boil for 10 minutes. Divide hot liquid among jars to cover zucchini.

Seal jars with lids; let cool. Refrigerate for 1 week before opening.

Refrigerate for up to 1 month.

MAKES FOUR 2-CUP (500 mL) JARS, EACH WITH 9 PICKLES. PER PICKLE: about 17 cal, trace pro, 0 g total fat (0 g sat. fat), 5 g carb, trace fibre, 0 mg chol, 419 mg sodium. % RDI: 1% iron, 3% vit A, 2% vit C, 2% folate.

Pickles & Relishes

Zucchini Bread-and-Butter Pickles

Zucchini stands in for traditional cucumbers in this tasty, sweet-tart sliced pickle recipe.

4 **green zucchini**

3 **yellow zucchini**

1 **small sweet red pepper,** cut into julienne

2 **small onions,** thinly sliced

¼ cup **pickling salt**

24 **ice cubes**

1½ cups **white vinegar**

¾ cup **granulated sugar**

1 tbsp **mustard seeds**

¼ tsp **turmeric**

¼ tsp **celery seeds**

Trim ends off green and yellow zucchini; slice thinly. In large glass or stainless-steel bowl, toss together zucchini, red pepper, onions and salt until well combined. Add ice cubes; pour in enough cold water to cover. Let stand for 1 to 2 hours. Drain and rinse; drain again.

In large saucepan, bring vinegar, sugar, mustard seeds, turmeric and celery seeds to boil. Add zucchini mixture and return to boil; reduce heat and simmer until vegetables are tender-crisp, about 3 minutes.

Fill hot 1-cup (250 mL) canning jars, leaving ½-inch (1 cm) headspace. Remove any air bubbles.

Cover with prepared discs. Screw on bands until resistance is met; increase to fingertip tight. Boil in boiling water canner for 10 minutes. (See Canning Basics, page 10.)

Turn off heat. Uncover and let jars stand in canner for 5 minutes. Lift up rack. With canning tongs, transfer jars to cooling rack; let cool for 24 hours.

MAKES ABOUT 4 CUPS. PER 2 TBSP: about 26 cal, trace pro, trace total fat (0 g sat. fat), 6 g carb, 1 g fibre, 0 mg chol, 256 mg sodium, 101 mg potassium. % RDI: 1% calcium, 1% iron, 5% vit A, 8% vit C, 3% folate.

Pickled
Hot Peppers

Fiery-food lovers, now you can pickle your own hot peppers to enjoy on, well, everything! This recipe is a great base for experimentation with other pepper varieties.

4 cups **white vinegar**

4 cloves **garlic,** smashed

4 tsp **pickling salt**

1 tbsp **mixed pickling spices**

8 cups sliced seeded **hot banana peppers** (about 1½ lb/675 g)

8 cups sliced seeded **red Hungarian peppers** (about 1½ lb/675 g)

In large saucepan, bring vinegar, 4 cups water, garlic, salt and pickling spices to boil. Reduce heat and simmer for 15 minutes; strain.

Toss banana peppers with Hungarian peppers. Tightly pack into 6 hot 2-cup (500 mL) canning jars to within ¾ inch (2 cm) of rim. Strain hot liquid into jars to cover peppers, leaving ½-inch (1 cm) headspace. Remove any air bubbles.

Cover with prepared discs. Screw on bands until resistance is met; increase to fingertip tight. Boil in boiling water canner for 10 minutes. (See Canning Basics, page 10.)

Turn off heat. Uncover and let jars stand in canner for 5 minutes. Lift up rack. With canning tongs, transfer jars to cooling rack; let cool for 24 hours.

MAKES SIX 2-CUP (500 mL) JARS.
PER ¼ CUP: about 18 cal, 1 g pro, trace total fat (0 g sat. fat), 4 g carb, 1 g fibre, 0 mg chol, 108 mg sodium, 146 mg potassium. % RDI: 1% calcium, 3% iron, 3% vit A, 80% vit C, 5% folate.

Quick Pickled Beans With Hot Peppers

These simple pickles make a refreshing side for grilled meat, a crunchy garnish for Bloody Marys or Caesars, and a piquant addition to a pickle tray.

1 lb (450 g) **green beans,** trimmed

3 **red hot peppers**

10 cloves **garlic,** halved

2 cups **cider vinegar**

½ cup **granulated sugar**

2 tbsp **salt**

2 tsp **mustard seeds**

1 tsp **black peppercorns**

In large pot of boiling salted water, cook beans for 3 minutes. Drain and chill under cold water; drain well and place in large jar.

Slit peppers lengthwise almost but not all the way through. In saucepan, bring peppers, garlic, vinegar, 1½ cups water, sugar, salt, mustard seeds and peppercorns to boil; pour over beans. Let cool.

Cover and refrigerate for 3 days before opening.

Refrigerate for up to 1 week.

MAKES 6 CUPS. PER ¼ CUP: about 12 cal, trace pro, 0 g total fat (0 g sat. fat), 3 g carb, trace fibre, 0 mg chol, 212 mg sodium. % RDI: 1% calcium, 2% iron, 1% vit A, 3% vit C, 2% folate.

tip
If you have any leftover pickling liquid, add a splash to your favourite homemade salad dressing.

Pickles & Relishes

French-Style Sour Pickled Gherkins

These pickles are preserved in pure white wine vinegar, as they are in France. Their sour bite is wonderful with cured or roasted meats or pâtés. Use gherkin cucumbers or the smallest pickling cucumbers you can find.

8 cups **gherkins** or tiny pickling cucumbers (2½ lb/1.125 kg)

⅓ cup **pickling salt** or kosher salt

4¼ cups **white wine vinegar**

4 **fresh grape leaves** (optional)

12 sprigs **fresh tarragon**

4 **small bay leaves**

4 **shallots,** cut in rounds

2 small cloves **garlic,** each cut in 4 slices

24 **black peppercorns**

12 **whole allspice**

4 **whole cloves**

Scrub gherkins in 2 changes of cold water, rubbing off any prickles or blemishes. Trim off blossom ends.

Pat gherkins dry; in large glass or stainless-steel bowl, toss gherkins with salt. Let stand for 4 to 6 hours, stirring often. Drain and rinse under cold water. Return to bowl; cover with cold water and soak for 8 minutes. Drain well; pat dry.

Meanwhile, in saucepan, bring vinegar to boil.

Into each of 4 hot 2-cup (500 mL) canning jars, place 1 grape leaf (if using), 3 tarragon sprigs, 1 bay leaf, one-eighth of the shallots, 1 slice garlic, 6 peppercorns, 3 allspice and 1 clove.

Pack gherkins into jars to within ¾ inch (2 cm) of rim; top with remaining shallots and garlic. Divide hot vinegar among jars to cover gherkins, leaving ½-inch (1 cm) headspace. Remove any air bubbles.

Cover with prepared discs. Screw on bands until resistance is met; increase to fingertip tight. Boil in boiling water canner for 12 minutes. (See Canning Basics, page 10.)

Turn off heat. Uncover and let jars stand in canner for 5 minutes. Lift up rack. With canning tongs, transfer jars to cooling rack; let cool for 24 hours.

MAKES FOUR 2-CUP (500 mL) JARS.
PER GHERKIN: about 8 cal, trace pro, trace total fat (0 g sat. fat), 1 g carb, trace fibre, 0 mg chol, 289 mg sodium, 55 mg potassium. % RDI: 1% calcium, 1% iron, 2% vit C, 2% folate.

Tip

The grape leaves are a traditional addition to help the pickles stay crisp; either cultivated or wild grape leaves are fine to use. We cut off the blossom ends of the cucumbers, which contain a softening enzyme, so the grape leaves are not absolutely necessary.

Pickles & Relishes

Pickled Asparagus Spears

Don't let the asparagus trimmings go to waste after cutting the stalks to fit in the jars. Discard the woody ends and use the trimmings in omelettes, soups and stir-fries.

4 lb (1.8 kg) **asparagus** (about 4 bunches)

12 sprigs **fresh dill**

6 cloves **garlic**

1 tbsp **mustard seeds**

2 cups **white vinegar**

2 tbsp **granulated sugar**

1 tbsp **pickling salt**

Trim asparagus spears to fit into 2-cup (500 mL) wide-mouth canning jars, leaving ¾-inch (2 cm) headspace.

Into each of 3 hot 2-cup (500 mL) canning jars, pack 4 sprigs dill, 2 cloves garlic and 1 tsp mustard seeds. Tightly pack in asparagus, tips down.

Meanwhile, in saucepan, bring vinegar, 2 cups water, sugar and salt to boil; reduce heat and simmer for 3 minutes. Divide hot liquid among jars to cover asparagus, leaving ½-inch (1 cm) headspace. Remove any air bubbles.

Cover with prepared discs. Screw on bands until resistance is met; increase to fingertip tight. Boil in boiling water canner for 10 minutes. (See Canning Basics, page 10.)

Turn off heat. Uncover and let jars stand in canner for 5 minutes. Lift up rack. With canning tongs, transfer jars to cooling rack; let cool for 24 hours.

MAKES THREE 2-CUP (500 ᴍʟ) JARS.
PER SPEAR: about 3 cal, trace pro, 0 g total fat (0 g sat. fat), 1 g carb, trace fibre, 0 mg chol, 33 mg sodium. % RDI: 1% iron, 1% vit A, 2% vit C, 7% folate.

Hot Pickled Okra

Even if you've never liked okra before, give this spicy, crunchy pickle a try. It has a completely different texture than cooked okra.

1½ lb (675 g) **okra**

4 **Scotch bonnet peppers** or habanero peppers

8 cloves **garlic,** halved

2 tsp **dillseed**

2 tsp **mustard seeds**

1 tsp **coriander seeds**

3 cups **white vinegar**

3 tbsp **pickling salt**

1 tbsp **granulated sugar**

Trim okra stems to just above caps; trim off any brown at tips. Cut peppers in half. Divide peppers, garlic, dillseed, mustard seeds and coriander seeds evenly among 4 hot 2-cup (500 mL) canning jars; pack with okra.

Meanwhile, in saucepan, bring vinegar, 1½ cups water, salt and sugar to boil.

Divide hot liquid among jars to cover okra, leaving ½-inch (1 cm) headspace. Remove any air bubbles.

Cover with prepared discs. Screw on bands until resistance is met; increase to fingertip tight. Boil in boiling water canner for 15 minutes. (See Canning Basics, page 10.)

Turn off heat. Uncover and let jars stand in canner for 5 minutes. Lift up rack. With canning tongs, transfer jars to cooling rack; let cool for 24 hours.

Let jars stand for 2 weeks before opening.

MAKES FOUR 2-CUP (500 mL) JARS.
PER OKRA POD: about 5 cal, trace pro, 0 g total fat (0 g sat. fat), 1 g carb, trace fibre, 0 mg chol, 171 mg sodium, 43 mg potassium. % RDI: 1% calcium, 1% iron, 1% vit A, 3% vit C, 3% folate.

tip
If you don't have fiery Scotch bonnet peppers, substitute eight Thai bird's-eye peppers or cayenne hot peppers. Or use eight small dried hot peppers to get the mildest heat. Whichever you use, simply slit lengthwise down the side instead of halving.

Pickles & Relishes

Cheese and Antipasto Plates

Pickles and preserves partner well with cheeses and cured meats of all kinds. Here are some pointers on creating delicious cheese and antipasto plates for entertaining.

CREATING A CHEESE PLATE

• Serve three or more kinds of cheese chosen from different categories.

• Vary types and strengths, and contrast colours and textures. For example, try a soft blue cheese; a firm, drier aged cheese; and a semisoft, full-flavoured washed-rind cheese.

• Always serve cheese at room temperature. Take it out of the fridge at least one hour before serving.

• Hard cheeses can share a knife or cheese plane. Supply separate knives for each soft and semisoft cheese.

• For appetizer or after-dinner cheese plates, offer three to six choices, with a little less than 1 oz (30 g) of each type per person.

CHEESE PLATE COMPLEMENTS

• Cheese and bread are a natural match, but the bread shouldn't overpower the cheese. For most cheeses, a plain crusty bread, such as a baguette, is perfect.

• Pair strong blue cheeses with nut and fruit breads or whole grain crackers. Rye bread also pairs well with strong cheeses, such as very old Cheddar or raclette.

• Fresh fruit is always welcome. Grapes, pears and apples go well with cheeses. Or try figs, strawberries, melons or peaches.

• Dried fruits, such as figs, apricots, dates and raisins, are lovely with cheese, as are walnuts, hazelnuts and pecans.

• Chutneys and fruit preserves, especially plum and apricot, are good with sharp, aged cheeses.

CREATING AN ANTIPASTO PLATE

• Scour farmer's markets for tasty offerings from local cheesemongers and butchers selling house-made salami, prosciutto, pepperoni and other dry sausages.

• For six servings, plan on 12 oz (340 g) assorted sliced cured meats and 10 oz (280 g) assorted cheeses, cubed or sliced.

• Complement meats and cheeses with homemade pickles. Try Antipasto Pickles (page 142) or Vegetarian Antipasto (page 144).

• Marinated olives are a must-have. Just toss together 1 cup mixed brined olives (such as Niçoise, Kalamata and green), ¼ tsp grated lemon zest and ¼ tsp each dried oregano and hot pepper flakes; let stand for 30 minutes. *(Make-ahead: Refrigerate in airtight container for up to 1 week.)*

Pickles & Relishes

Spicy Dilled Beans

Spicy beans like these make a tasty garnish for cocktails. If you can't get fresh hot peppers and dill heads, substitute dried hot peppers and four sprigs fresh dill for each dill head.

1 lb (450 g) **green beans**

1 lb (450 g) **yellow wax beans**

4 **small red hot peppers**

4 heads **fresh dill**

4 cloves **garlic**

4 tsp **mustard seeds**

2½ cups **white vinegar**

2 tbsp **pickling salt**

Cut green and yellow beans into 3½-inch (9 cm) lengths, discarding stem ends. Cut slit lengthwise in each hot pepper.

Into each of 4 hot 2-cup (500 mL) canning jars, place 1 hot pepper, 1 dill head, 1 clove garlic and 1 tsp mustard seeds. Tightly pack in beans, cut side up.

Meanwhile, in saucepan, bring 2½ cups water, vinegar and salt to boil; reduce heat and simmer for 3 minutes. Divide liquid among jars to cover beans, leaving ½-inch (1 cm) headspace. Remove any air bubbles.

Cover with prepared discs. Screw on bands until resistance is met; increase to fingertip tight. Boil in boiling water canner for 10 minutes. (See Canning Basics, page 10.)

Turn off heat. Uncover and let jars stand in canner for 5 minutes. Lift up rack. With canning tongs, transfer jars to cooling rack; let cool for 24 hours.

MAKES FOUR 2-CUP (500 mL) JARS.
PER BEAN: about 5 cal, trace pro, 0 g total fat (0 g sat. fat), 1 g carb, trace fibre, 0 mg chol, 29 mg sodium. % RDI: 1% iron, 1% folate.

Horseradish Pickled Beans

Bean pickles flavoured with horseradish make a lively side dish or drink garnish. Try them with grilled steak for a taste-of-summertime treat.

2 lb (900 g) **green beans** or yellow beans

3-inch (8 cm) piece **horseradish root**

8 sprigs **fresh dill,** thick stems trimmed and discarded

4 cloves **garlic,** halved

2 tbsp **mustard seeds**

2½ cups **white vinegar**

2 tbsp **pickling salt**

Cut beans into 3½-inch (9 cm) lengths, discarding stem ends. Peel horseradish; cut crosswise into 20 slices. Divide dill, garlic and mustard seeds evenly among 4 hot 2-cup (500 mL) canning jars; tightly pack in beans, cut side up, and horseradish slices.

Meanwhile, in saucepan, bring vinegar, 2½ cups water and salt to boil. Divide hot liquid among jars to cover beans, leaving ½-inch (1 cm) headspace. Remove any air bubbles.

Cover with prepared discs. Screw on bands until resistance is met; increase to fingertip tight. Boil in boiling water canner for 10 minutes. (See Canning Basics, page 10.)

Turn off heat. Uncover and let jars stand in canner for 5 minutes. Lift up rack. With canning tongs, transfer jars to cooling rack; let cool for 24 hours.

Let jars stand for 1 week before opening.

MAKES FOUR 2-CUP (500 mL) JARS.
PER BEAN: about 1 cal, trace pro, 0 g total fat (0 g sat. fat), trace carb, trace fibre, 0 mg chol, 25 mg sodium, 6 mg potassium.

tips
•Use the cylindrical top part, not the gnarled root end, of the horseradish root. Wrap leftover horseradish in wet towels, cover in plastic wrap and store in your refrigerator's crisper.

•For a little extra bite, add a halved red or green hot pepper to each jar.

Pickles & Relishes

Caesar Beans

Like all pickled beans, these go well with cocktails. Try them instead of olives in a classic martini. Their flavour is inspired by the seasonings used in a Bloody Caesar.

2 lb (900 g) **green string beans** or yellow string beans

3-inch (8 cm) piece **horseradish root**

2 **red hot peppers,** halved

8 sprigs **fresh dill**

4 cloves **garlic**

2 tbsp **mustard seeds**

2 tsp **celery seeds**

2½ cups **white vinegar**

2 tbsp **pickling salt**

1 tsp **Worcestershire sauce**

Cut beans into 3½-inch (9 cm) lengths, discarding stem ends. Peel horseradish; cut crosswise into 20 slices. Divide horseradish, hot peppers, dill, garlic, mustard seeds and celery seeds evenly among 4 hot 2-cup (500 mL) canning jars; tightly pack in beans, cut side up.

In saucepan, bring vinegar, 2½ cups water, salt and Worcestershire sauce to boil. Divide hot liquid among jars to cover beans, leaving ½-inch (1 cm) headspace. Remove any air bubbles.

Cover with prepared discs. Screw on bands until resistance is met; increase to fingertip tight. Boil in boiling water canner for 10 minutes. (See Canning Basics, page 10.)

Turn off heat. Uncover and let jars stand in canner for 5 minutes. Lift up rack. With canning tongs, transfer jars to cooling rack; let cool for 24 hours.

Let jars stand for 1 week before opening.

MAKES FOUR 2-CUP (500 mL) JARS.
PER BEAN: about 2 cal, trace pro, 0 g total fat (0 g sat. fat), 1 g carb, trace fibre, 0 mg chol, 36 mg sodium, 8 mg potassium. % RDI: 2% vit C, 1% folate.

Antipasto Pickles

These colourful vegetables look best when uniformly cut. Look for a white wine vinegar, such as Maille brand, that says it is six per cent acetic acid on the label.

2½ cups **white wine vinegar**

1½ cups **white wine**

¼ cup **granulated sugar**

4 tsp **pickling salt**

3 cups diced peeled **eggplant**

3 cups **cauliflower florets**

2½ cups cut **green beans**
  (¼-inch/5 mm pieces)

2 cups chopped **onions**

2 cups each chopped **sweet red** and **green peppers**

1½ cups chopped **carrots**

1½ cups chopped **celery**

1½ tsp **dried oregano**

¾ tsp **hot pepper flakes**

SPICE BAG:

4 cloves **garlic,** smashed

3 **bay leaves**

1 tbsp **coriander seeds**

2 tsp **fennel seeds**

1 tsp **black peppercorns**

SPICE BAG: Tie garlic, bay leaves, coriander seeds, fennel seeds and peppercorns in cheesecloth square to form bag.

In large saucepan or Dutch oven, combine vinegar, wine, 1½ cups water, sugar, salt and spice bag. Bring to boil; boil until sugar and salt are dissolved, about 5 minutes.

Add eggplant, cauliflower, green beans, onions, red peppers, green peppers, carrots and celery. Return to boil; boil, stirring occasionally, until vegetables are softened, about 5 minutes. Remove from heat. Remove spice bag.

Into each of 6 hot 2-cup (500 mL) canning jars, place ¼ tsp oregano and pinch hot pepper flakes. Using slotted spoon, fill jars with vegetables to within ¾ inch (2 cm) of rim.

Strain liquid through fine sieve; divide among jars to cover vegetables, leaving ½-inch (1 cm) headspace. Remove any air bubbles.

Cover with prepared discs. Screw on bands until resistance is met; increase to fingertip tight. Boil in boiling water canner for 10 minutes. (See Canning Basics, page 10.)

Turn off heat. Uncover and let jars stand in canner for 5 minutes. Lift up rack. With canning tongs, transfer jars to cooling rack; let cool for 24 hours.

MAKES SIX 2-CUP (500 mL) JARS.
PER 1 TBSP: about 5 cal, trace pro, 0 g total fat (0 g sat. fat), 1 g carb, trace fibre, 0 mg chol, 50 mg sodium. % RDI: 1% iron, 2% vit A, 8% vit C, 1% folate.

Pickles & Relishes

Vegetarian Antipasto

Antipasto usually contains low-acid foods such as fish and olives, and must be canned using a pressure canner. This higher-acid version, adapted from one by Bernardin, can be safely canned in a boiling water canner.

2 cups **red wine vinegar**

1¾ cups packed **brown sugar**

3 cans (each 5½ oz/156 mL) **tomato paste**

¼ cup **Worcestershire sauce**

3 tbsp **pickling salt**

2 tsp **hot pepper sauce**

2½ cups cut **green beans** (½-inch/1 cm pieces)

2½ cups **cauliflower florets**

2 cups chopped **onions**

2 cups each chopped **sweet red** and **green peppers**

2 cups diced peeled **eggplant** or diced zucchini

1½ cups chopped **carrots**

1½ cups chopped **celery**

4 cloves **garlic,** minced

1 tbsp **dried basil**

In Dutch oven, stir together red wine vinegar, sugar, tomato paste, Worcestershire sauce, salt and hot pepper sauce; bring to boil, stirring occasionally.

Add beans, cauliflower, onions, red and green peppers, eggplant, carrots, celery and garlic. Bring to boil; boil, stirring often, until vegetables are softened, about 5 minutes. Remove from heat. Stir in basil.

Fill hot 2-cup (500 mL) canning jars, leaving ½-inch (1 cm) headspace. Remove any air bubbles.

Cover with prepared discs. Screw on bands until resistance is met; increase to fingertip tight. Boil in boiling water canner for 25 minutes. (See Canning Basics, page 10.)

Turn off heat. Uncover and let jars stand in canner for 5 minutes. Lift up rack. With canning tongs, transfer jars to cooling rack; let cool for 24 hours.

MAKES 13 CUPS. PER 1 TBSP: about 12 cal, 0 g pro, 0 g total fat (0 g sat. fat), 3 g carb, 0 g fibre, 0 mg chol, 74 mg sodium. % RDI: 1% iron, 3% vit A, 7% vit C, 1% folate.

Pickles & Relishes

Classic Baguette

To make the flavourful dough for this bread (which is great with Antipasto Pickles, page 142), a starter ferments for 18 hours ahead of time. It's more work than other loaves, but the taste and texture are worth it.

½ cup warm **water**

½ tsp **active dry yeast**

2½ cups **all-purpose flour**

1½ tsp **sea salt**

STARTER:

¼ tsp **active dry yeast**

¾ cup room-temperature **water**

1 cup **all-purpose flour**

tips

• **To test for doneness, a digital rapid-read thermometer should register 200°F (100°C) when inserted into centre of bread.**

• **This bread makes delicious crostini. Simply cut loaf into ½-inch (1 cm) slices; brush both sides with olive oil and broil, turning once, until golden on both sides, two to three minutes.**

STARTER: In large bowl, sprinkle yeast over water; let stand for 1 minute. Stir in flour until smooth and slightly elastic, 2 minutes. Scrape down side of bowl. Cover with plastic wrap; set aside for 18 hours or for up to 24 hours.

Mix warm water and yeast into starter until broken up and slightly foaming, 2 minutes. Stir in flour and salt to form ragged soft dough. Transfer to floured surface. Knead until smooth and elastic, 6 minutes. Shape into ball.

Place in greased bowl, turning to grease all over. Cover with plastic wrap; let rise in warm place until doubled in bulk and indentation remains after pressing finger into dough, about 1½ hours.

Punch down dough; divide in half and shape into balls. Cover with plastic wrap and let rest for 15 minutes.

Press balls to flatten; roll into logs. Roll each until 15 inches (38 cm) long. Place on lightly floured tea towel, pleating towel between loaves. Cover with greased plastic wrap; let rise until doubled in bulk, 45 to 60 minutes.

Place loaves, 3 inches (8 cm) apart, on large flour-dusted baking sheet. Using sharp knife, score top of each loaf 7 times diagonally at 2-inch (5 cm) intervals.

Place in 450°F (230°C) oven. Spritz cold water on wall and floor of oven (avoid oven lightbulb) until steam fills oven, about 10 seconds. Immediately close oven door. Repeat spraying in 3 minutes. Bake loaves until golden and hollow sounding when tapped on bottoms, 20 minutes. Let cool on rack.

MAKES 2 LOAVES, 8 SERVINGS EACH.
PER SERVING: about 100 cal, 3 g pro, trace total fat (0 g sat. fat), 21 g carb, 1 g fibre, 0 mg chol, 146 mg sodium. % RDI: 9% iron, 27% folate.

Pickles & Relishes

Jardinière

Enjoy this vinegar-laced mix of summer vegetables with cheese and cold meats.

3 cups **pearl onions**

4 cups **white vinegar**

2 cups **granulated sugar**

1 tbsp **pickling salt**

1 tbsp each **celery seeds** and **mustard seeds**

1 tsp **black peppercorns**

3 **bay leaves**

1 lb (450 g) **green beans,** cut in 2-inch (5 cm) lengths

2 **zucchini,** sliced

3 cups **cauliflower florets**

2 cups thickly sliced **carrots**

In saucepan of boiling water, blanch onions for 30 seconds. Immerse in cold water; drain and peel. Set aside.

In saucepan, bring vinegar, sugar, salt, celery seeds, mustard seeds, peppercorns and bay leaves to boil; boil for 5 minutes.

Add beans, zucchini, cauliflower, carrots and onions; return to boil. Remove from heat. Discard bay leaves.

Using slotted spoon, tightly pack vegetables into 6 hot 2-cup (500 mL) canning jars to within ¾ inch (2 cm) of rim. Pour in hot vinegar mixture to cover vegetables, leaving ½-inch (1 cm) headspace. Remove any air bubbles.

Cover with prepared discs. Screw on bands until resistance is met; increase to fingertip tight. Boil in boiling water canner for 10 minutes. (See Canning Basics, page 10.)

Turn off heat. Uncover and let jars stand in canner for 5 minutes. Lift up rack. With canning tongs, transfer jars to cooling rack; let cool for 24 hours.

MAKES ABOUT SIX 2-CUP (500 mL) JARS. PER ¼ CUP: about 31 cal, 1 g pro, trace total fat (0 g sat. fat), 8 g carb, 1 g fibre, 0 mg chol, 90 mg sodium. % RDI: 1% calcium, 1% iron, 9% vit A, 7% vit C, 4% folate.

Pickles & Relishes

Pickled Garlic

This garlic stays nice and crunchy, and isn't as strong as raw garlic. It can be used in pasta sauces, antipasto platters and salads.

12 heads **garlic** (1¾ lb/790 g)

2½ cups **white vinegar**

1 cup **dry white wine**

1 tbsp **pickling salt**

1 tbsp **granulated sugar**

1 tbsp **dried oregano,** basil or thyme

5 **dried hot peppers**

Separate garlic into cloves. Blanch in boiling water for 30 seconds. Immediately immerse in cold water; drain and peel.

In large saucepan, bring vinegar, wine, salt, sugar and oregano to boil; boil for 1 minute. Remove from heat. Add garlic; stir constantly for 1 minute.

With slotted spoon, divide garlic and hot peppers evenly among each of 5 hot 1-cup (250 mL) canning jars to within ¾ inch (2 cm) of rim. Pour in hot vinegar mixture to cover garlic, leaving ½-inch (1 cm) headspace. Remove any air bubbles.

Cover with prepared discs. Screw on bands until resistance is met; increase to fingertip tight. Boil in boiling water canner for 10 minutes. (See Canning Basics, page 10.)

Turn off heat. Uncover and let jars stand in canner for 5 minutes. Lift up rack. With canning tongs, transfer jars to cooling rack; let cool for 24 hours.

MAKES 6 CUPS. PER 1 TBSP: about 18 cal, 1 g pro, 0 g total fat (0 g sat. fat), 4 g carb, 0 g fibre, 0 mg chol, 24 mg sodium. % RDI: 2% calcium, 1% iron, 1% vit A, 7% vit C.

Pickles & Relishes

Pearl Onion Pickles

With a fresh, gingery undertone, these quick refrigerator pickles are delicious with all kinds of grilled or cured meats.

2 pkg (each 10 oz/284 g) **pearl onions,** peeled, trimmed and halved

3 slices **fresh ginger**

PICKLING LIQUID:

1½ tsp **black peppercorns**

1½ tsp **coriander seeds**

1½ cups **unseasoned rice vinegar**

1 cup **granulated sugar**

¼ cup **fish sauce**

PICKLING LIQUID: Tie peppercorns and coriander seeds in cheesecloth square to form bag. In saucepan, bring vinegar, sugar, 1 cup water, fish sauce and spice bag to boil; boil until sugar is dissolved.

Add pearl onions and ginger. Return to boil; boil for 1 minute.

Spoon into large jar(s), discarding spice bag; let cool to room temperature.

Seal with lid(s); refrigerate for 2 days before opening.

Refrigerate for up to 2 weeks.

MAKES 6 CUPS. PER ¼ CUP: about 21 cal, trace pro, 0 g total fat (0 g sat. fat), 5 g carb, trace fibre, 0 mg chol, 85 mg sodium, 34 mg potassium. % RDI: 1% iron, 2% vit C, 1% folate.

Dilled Pearl Onions

It takes a little time to peel pearl onions, but these excellent, dill-scented pickles are worth the work.

8 cups **pearl onions,** peeled (about 1¾ lb/790 g)

¼ cup **pickling salt**

2 cups **white vinegar**

2 tbsp **granulated sugar**

2 tsp **mixed pickling spices**

6 heads **fresh dill** or sprigs fresh tarragon

6 **black peppercorns**

In large glass or stainless-steel bowl, mix onions with salt; pour in enough cold water to cover. Let stand in cool spot in kitchen for 2 hours; drain. Rinse under cold water; drain well.

In large saucepan, bring vinegar, 2 cups water, sugar and pickling spices to boil.

Meanwhile, place 2 dill heads and 2 peppercorns in each of 3 hot 2-cup (500 mL) canning jars. Pack onions into jars to within ¾ inch (2 cm) of rim. Divide hot vinegar mixture among jars to cover onions, leaving ½-inch (1 cm) headspace. Remove any air bubbles.

Cover with prepared discs. Screw on bands until resistance is met; increase to fingertip tight. Boil in boiling water canner for 10 minutes. (See Canning Basics, page 10.)

Turn off heat. Uncover and let jars stand in canner for 5 minutes. Lift up rack. With canning tongs, transfer jars to cooling rack; let cool for 24 hours.

MAKES ABOUT 6 CUPS. PER 1 TBSP: about 3 cal, trace pro, 0 g total fat (0 g sat. fat), 1 g carb, trace fibre, 0 mg chol, 26 mg sodium, 10 mg potassium.

Pickles & Relishes

Spicy Pearl Onion Sours

Two unusual spices – green peppercorns and juniper berries – are combined with the more typical mix of cinnamon and cloves that seasons these tiny pearl onions.

9 cups **pearl onions** (2 lb/900 g)

¼ cup **pickling salt**

3 cups **white vinegar**

2 tbsp **granulated sugar**

1 tbsp **juniper berries**

1 **cinnamon stick**

2 tsp **whole cloves**

2 tsp **green peppercorns**

3 sprigs **fresh tarragon**

In heatproof bowl, cover onions with boiling water; let stand for 1 minute. Drain and peel.

In large bowl, mix onions with salt; add enough cold water to cover. Let stand for 8 hours or overnight. Drain and rinse well under cold water; drain well.

In large saucepan, bring vinegar, sugar, juniper berries, cinnamon stick, cloves and green peppercorns to boil. Remove from heat; cover and let stand for 30 minutes or for up to 2 hours.

Reserving vinegar mixture in saucepan, strain out and discard spices. Return vinegar mixture to boil.

Place 1 tarragon sprig in each of 3 hot 2-cup (500 mL) canning jars. Pack onions into jars to within ¾ inch (2 cm) of rim. Divide hot vinegar mixture among jars to cover onions, leaving ½-inch (1 cm) headspace. Remove any air bubbles.

Cover with prepared discs. Screw on bands until resistance is met; increase to fingertip tight. Boil in boiling water canner for 10 minutes. (See Canning Basics, page 10.)

Turn off heat. Uncover and let jars stand in canner for 5 minutes. Lift up rack. With canning tongs, transfer jars to cooling rack; let cool for 24 hours.

MAKES ABOUT 6 CUPS. PER 1 TBSP: about 4 cal, trace pro, 0 g total fat (0 g sat. fat), 1 g carb, trace fibre, 0 mg chol, 23 mg sodium, 12 mg potassium.

tip
Look for green peppercorns and juniper berries in specialty stores or in well-stocked spice sections of supermarkets.

Pickles & Relishes

Pickled Fiddleheads

Fiddleheads should be well cleaned and cooked before pickling. These are attractive and tasty pickles for a condiment tray and a puckery side with juicy grilled steak.

3 lb (1.35 kg) **fresh fiddleheads**

16 **white pearl onions**

2 cups **white vinegar**

¼ cup **granulated sugar**

1 tbsp **pickling salt,** kosher salt or noniodized sea salt

4 tsp **mustard seeds**

2 tsp **coriander seeds**

16 **whole allspice**

4 **dried hot peppers**

8 cloves **garlic,** halved

Clean fiddleheads under cold running water, rinsing off any brown membranes; trim off any brown ends. In large pot of boiling water, cook fiddleheads for 7 minutes. Drain and chill under cold water; drain well.

Peel onions (do not blanch), leaving bases intact but trimming off any brown bits. Cut each in half lengthwise.

In saucepan, bring vinegar, 1⅔ cups water, sugar and salt to boil.

Divide mustard seeds, coriander seeds, allspice and hot peppers evenly among 4 hot 2-cup (500 mL) canning jars. Pack fiddleheads, onions and garlic into jars to within ¾ inch (2 cm) of rim.

Divide vinegar mixture among jars to cover fiddleheads, leaving ½-inch (1 cm) headspace. Remove any air bubbles.

Cover with prepared discs. Screw on bands until resistance is met; increase to fingertip tight. Boil in boiling water canner for 10 minutes. (See Canning Basics, page 10.)

Turn off heat. Uncover and let jars stand in canner for 5 minutes. Lift up rack. With canning tongs, transfer jars to cooling rack; let cool for 24 hours.

MAKES FOUR 2-CUP (500 mL) JARS.
PER 1 TBSP: about 7 cal, 1 g pro, trace total fat (0 g sat. fat), 1 g carb, trace fibre, 0 mg chol, 33 mg sodium, 54 mg potassium. % RDI: 1% iron, 5% vit A, 3% vit C.

Pickles & Relishes

Sweet-and-Sour Cauliflower Pickles

Cauliflower is surprisingly delicious pickled. These florets have just a touch of heat and a nice mix of spices.

10 oz (280 g) **red pearl onions** or white pearl onions

1 large head **cauliflower** (2½ to 3 lb/1.125 to 1.35 kg)

2 **sweet red peppers,** seeded and cut in chunks

4 **hot banana peppers,** seeded and cut in 1-inch (2.5 cm) thick rings

3 cloves **garlic,** halved

6 **whole cloves**

2 tbsp **coriander seeds**

4 cups **cider vinegar**

1⅓ cups **granulated sugar**

¼ cup **pickling salt**

¼ cup **mustard seeds**

Trim and peel pearl onions (do not blanch). Cut cauliflower into florets to make about 12 cups.

Tightly pack onions, cauliflower, red peppers and banana peppers into 3 hot 4-cup (1 L) canning jars to within ¾ inch (2 cm) of rim. Divide garlic and whole cloves evenly between jars.

In saucepan over medium-low heat, lightly toast coriander seeds until fragrant and slightly darkened; add vinegar, 2 cups water, sugar, salt and mustard seeds. Bring to boil; reduce heat and simmer for 3 minutes. Divide among jars to cover vegetables, leaving ½-inch (1 cm) headspace. Remove any air bubbles.

Cover with prepared discs. Screw on bands until resistance is met; increase to fingertip tight. Boil in boiling water canner for 15 minutes. (See Canning Basics, page 10.)

Turn off heat. Uncover and let jars stand in canner for 5 minutes. Lift up rack. With canning tongs, transfer jars to cooling rack; let cool for 24 hours.

Let jars stand for 5 days before opening.

MAKES THREE 4-CUP (1 L) JARS.
PER ¼ CUP: about 22 cal, 1 g pro, trace total fat (0 g sat. fat), 5 g carb, 1 g fibre, 0 mg chol, 301 mg sodium, 67 mg potassium. % RDI: 1% calcium, 1% iron, 2% vit A, 35% vit C, 5% folate.

Pickles & Relishes

Pickled Turnips and Beets

These vibrant pink Middle Eastern–style pickles add the ultimate tangy crunch to sandwiches or falafels. They're also wonderful as a side to grilled kabobs.

3 **turnips** (about 1 lb/450 g)
3 **beets** (about 1 lb/450 g)
1¼ cups **cider vinegar**
1 cup **granulated sugar**
1 tsp **mustard seeds**
2 **bay leaves**

Peel and cut turnips into about 1-inch (2.5 cm) chunks; divide between two 2-cup (500 mL) canning jars.

In large pot of boiling salted water, cover and cook beets until tender but firm, about 40 minutes. Drain and let cool slightly. Slip off skins; cut into 1-inch (2.5 cm) chunks. Divide between jars.

In saucepan, bring vinegar, sugar, ¾ cup water, mustard seeds and bay leaves to boil; boil gently for 5 minutes. Remove bay leaves.

Divide liquid between jars to cover vegetables; seal with lids and let cool. Refrigerate for 24 hours before opening.

Refrigerate for up to 1 month.

MAKES 4 CUPS. PER ¼ CUP: about 45 cal, 1 g pro, 0 g total fat (0 g sat. fat), 11 g carb, 1 g fibre, 0 mg chol, 64 mg sodium. % RDI: 1% calcium, 2% iron, 10% vit C, 10% folate.

Pickled Beets and Pearl Onions

Look for equal-size beets that are about 1 inch (2.5 cm) in diameter. Otherwise, halve or quarter larger ones.

4 lb (1.8 kg) **baby beets**

4 cups **pearl onions** (about two 10 oz/284 g pkg)

1¾ cups **granulated sugar**

1⅔ cups **white vinegar**

1 tbsp **salt**

2 tsp **mustard seeds**

1 tsp **caraway seeds**

6 **bay leaves**

Scrub beets, leaving root end and ½ inch (1 cm) of stem intact. In large saucepan of boiling salted water, cover and cook beets just until tender, 15 to 20 minutes. Drain and chill in cold water. Trim off root ends and stems; slip off skins.

Meanwhile, in heatproof bowl, pour boiling water over pearl onions; let stand for 2 minutes. Drain and chill in cold water; peel.

In large saucepan, bring sugar, vinegar, 1⅔ cups water, salt, mustard seeds, caraway seeds and bay leaves to boil. Add beets and pearl onions; return to boil.

With slotted spoon, pack beets and onions into 6 hot 2-cup (500 mL) canning jars to within ¾ inch (2 cm) of rim, gently pressing to fit. Add 1 bay leaf to each jar.

Divide hot vinegar mixture among jars to cover vegetables, leaving ½-inch (1 cm) headspace. Remove any air bubbles.

Cover with prepared discs. Screw on bands until resistance is met; increase to fingertip tight. Boil in boiling water canner for 30 minutes. (See Canning Basics, page 10.)

Turn off heat. Uncover and let jars stand in canner for 5 minutes. Lift up rack. With canning tongs, transfer jars to cooling rack; let cool for 24 hours.

MAKES ABOUT 12 CUPS. PER 1 EACH BEET AND ONION: about 39 cal, 1 g pro, trace total fat (0 g sat. fat), 10 g carb, 1 g fibre, 0 mg chol, 199 mg sodium. % RDI: 1% calcium, 2% iron, 3% vit C, 12% folate.

Hot and Spicy Carrot Pickles

In India, spicy pickled carrots preserved in oil are served as a tasty side dish. Similar in flavour, these use North American preserving methods for safekeeping.

3 lb (1.35 kg) **carrots**

12 **green hot peppers** (such as finger, serrano or jalapeño)

¼ cup **pickling salt**

3 tbsp **black mustard seeds**

1 tbsp **coriander seeds**

2 tsp **cumin seeds**

4 tsp **Indian hot pepper powder** or cayenne pepper

1 tsp **turmeric**

1 tsp **fenugreek seeds** (optional)

4 cloves **garlic,** sliced

1½-inch (4 cm) piece **fresh ginger,** thinly sliced

4 strips (each 2 inches/ 5 cm long) **lemon zest**

1⅓ cups **white vinegar**

½ cup packed **brown sugar**

1 cup freshly squeezed **lemon juice**

tip
If you need to top off jars to achieve the specified headspace, use more lemon juice.

Peel or scrub carrots; trim off ends. Cut into 3½-inch (9 cm) long sticks. Halve hot peppers lengthwise; seed. Stir together carrots, hot peppers and salt. Let stand, stirring a few times, until carrots are tender, about 1½ hours. Rinse under cold running water; drain well.

In dry skillet over medium-low heat, toast mustard seeds until grey. Using mortar and pestle, crush coarsely. In same pan, separately toast coriander seeds and cumin seeds until fragrant.

Mix together mustard, coriander and cumin seeds, hot pepper powder, turmeric, and fenugreek (if using). Divide spice mixture, garlic, ginger and lemon zest evenly among 4 hot 2-cup (500 mL) canning jars.

Pack carrots and 6 hot pepper halves into each jar. In saucepan, bring vinegar and sugar to boil; add lemon juice and return to boil. Divide among jars, leaving ½-inch (1 cm) headspace. Remove any air bubbles.

Cover with prepared discs. Screw on bands until resistance is met; increase to fingertip tight. Boil in boiling water canner for 15 minutes. (See Canning Basics, page 10.)

Turn off heat. Uncover and let jars stand in canner for 5 minutes. Lift up rack. With canning tongs, transfer jars to cooling rack; let cool for 24 hours.

When cool, shake jars to distribute spices. Let stand for 10 days before opening.

MAKES FOUR 2-CUP (500 mL) JARS.
PER CARROT STICK: about 6 cal, trace pro, 0 g total fat (0 g sat. fat), 1 g carb, trace fibre, 0 mg chol, 118 mg sodium, 25 mg potassium. % RDI: 1% iron, 15% vit A, 2% vit C.

Pickles & Relishes

Pickled Beets

These spices are intense enough to stand up to robust beets, and they add a touch of exotic flavour. Use a vinegar that is at least five per cent acetic acid.

3½ lb (1.5 kg) **small beets**
2½ cups **cider vinegar**
½ cup **granulated sugar**
2½ tsp **pickling salt**
4 tsp **mustard seeds**
4 whole **star anise**
4 whole **cloves**
2 tsp **black peppercorns**
2 tsp **coriander seeds**

In large saucepan of boiling water, cook beets until tender, 30 to 35 minutes. Drain; let cool. Trim off ends and roots; slip off skins. If beets are larger than 1½ inches (4 cm), cut in half or quarters. Set aside.

In large saucepan, bring vinegar, 1 cup water, sugar and salt to boil; boil until sugar and salt are dissolved, about 5 minutes.

Divide mustard seeds, star anise, cloves, peppercorns and coriander seeds evenly among 4 hot 2-cup (500 mL) wide-mouth canning jars; tightly pack beets in jars to within ¾ inch (2 cm) of rim.

Divide hot vinegar mixture among jars to cover beets, leaving ½-inch (1 cm) headspace. Remove any air bubbles.

Cover with prepared discs. Screw on bands until resistance is met; increase to fingertip tight. Boil in boiling water canner for 30 minutes. (See Canning Basics, page 10.)

Turn off heat. Uncover and let jars stand in canner for 5 minutes. Lift up rack. With canning tongs, transfer jars to cooling rack; let cool for 24 hours.

MAKES FOUR 2-CUP (500 mL) JARS.
PER BEET: about 20 cal, 1 g pro, 0 g total fat (0 g sat. fat), 5 g carb, 1 g fibre, 0 mg chol, 105 mg sodium. % RDI: 2% iron, 2% vit C, 11% folate.

Carrot Pickles

Crunchy and zesty, these deliciously spiced carrots have just the right balance between sweet and sour.

3 lb (1.35 kg) **carrots**

4 **small red hot peppers**

¼ cup **pickling salt**

2 tbsp **black mustard seeds**

1 tbsp **coriander seeds**

1 tbsp **cumin seeds**

8 thin slices **fresh ginger**

4 cloves **garlic,** peeled

1½ cups **white vinegar**

½ cup **granulated sugar**

2 tbsp **black peppercorns**

2 tbsp freshly squeezed **lemon juice**

Peel and trim carrots; cut into 3½-inch (9 cm) sticks. Cut slit lengthwise in each hot pepper.

Place half each of the carrots and hot peppers in large bowl. Sprinkle with 1 tbsp of the salt. Layer remaining carrots and hot peppers on top. Pour in enough cold water to cover. Place plate on top; weigh down to keep carrots submerged. Let stand for 30 minutes or for up to 1 hour. Drain; rinse well. Set aside.

In dry skillet over medium heat, toast mustard, coriander and cumin seeds until fragrant, about 1 minute.

Divide hot peppers, ginger, garlic and carrot sticks evenly among 4 hot 2-cup (500 mL) canning jars.

Meanwhile, in saucepan, bring vinegar, 1½ cups water, sugar, toasted seeds, remaining salt, peppercorns and lemon juice to boil; boil for 5 minutes. Strain into jars, leaving ½-inch (1 cm) headspace. Remove any air bubbles.

Cover with prepared discs. Screw on bands until resistance is met; increase to fingertip tight. Boil in boiling water canner for 10 minutes. (See Canning Basics, page 10.)

Turn off heat. Uncover and let jars stand in canner for 5 minutes. Lift up rack. With canning tongs, transfer jars to cooling rack; let cool for 24 hours.

Let jars stand for 2 weeks before opening.

MAKES FOUR 2-CUP (500 mL) JARS.
PER CARROT STICK: about 4 cal, 0 g pro, 0 g total fat (0 g sat. fat), 1 g carb, trace fibre, 0 mg chol, 93 mg sodium, 15 mg potassium. % RDI: 11% vit A.

Pickles & Relishes

Carrot and Daikon Pickles

These Asian-inspired refrigerator pickles are a delicious side dish with spicy curries.

2 cups each **carrot sticks** and **daikon radish sticks** (2 x ¼ inch/5 cm x 5 mm)

1 cup **English cucumber sticks** (2 x ¼ inch/5 cm x 5 mm)

1 **red hot pepper,** thinly sliced

1 clove **garlic,** minced

PICKLING LIQUID:

1½ tsp **black peppercorns**

1½ tsp **coriander seeds**

1½ cups **unseasoned rice vinegar**

1 cup **granulated sugar**

¼ cup **fish sauce**

In large bowl, stir together carrots, daikon, cucumber, hot pepper and garlic; transfer to 6-cup (1.5 L) jar.

PICKLING LIQUID: Tie peppercorns and coriander seeds in cheesecloth square to form bag. Add to jar. In saucepan, bring vinegar, sugar, 1 cup water and fish sauce to boil; boil until sugar is dissolved.

Pour into jar; let cool until room temperature. Seal with lid. Refrigerate for 2 days before opening.

Refrigerate for up to 2 weeks.

MAKES 6 CUPS. PER ¼ CUP: about 25 cal, trace pro, trace total fat (0 g sat. fat), 6 g carb, 1 g fibre, 0 mg chol, 127 mg sodium, 77 mg potassium. % RDI: 1% calcium, 1% iron, 18% vit A, 8% vit C, 2% folate.

Pickles & Relishes

Riesling and Ginger Pickled Sugar Pears

Diminutive sugar pears are commonly found in urban gardens. They are green but sweet and full of flavour.

8 cups **sugar pears**

3 cups **Riesling wine**

2½ cups **granulated sugar**

1¼ cups **white wine vinegar,** cider vinegar or white vinegar

2-inch (5 cm) piece **fresh ginger,** thinly sliced

4 tsp **black peppercorns**

½ tsp **salt**

Peel pears; trim off and discard blossom ends, keeping stem ends whole.

In saucepan, bring wine, sugar, vinegar, ginger, peppercorns and salt to boil. Add pears; return to boil. Reduce heat, cover and simmer just until tender, 9 to 12 minutes.

Pack pears and ginger into 5 hot 2-cup (500 mL) canning jars. Divide wine mixture among jars, leaving ½-inch (1 cm) headspace. Remove any air bubbles.

Cover with prepared discs. Screw on bands until resistance is met; increase to fingertip tight. Boil in boiling water canner for 10 minutes. (See Canning Basics, page 10.)

Turn off heat. Uncover and let jars stand in canner for 5 minutes. Lift up rack. With canning tongs, transfer jars to cooling rack; let cool for 24 hours.

Let jars stand for 3 days before opening.

MAKES FIVE 2-CUP (500 mL) JARS.
PER PEAR: about 52 cal, trace pro, 0 g total fat (0 g sat. fat), 13 g carb, 1 g fibre, 0 mg chol, 18 mg sodium, 47 mg potassium. % RDI: 1% iron, 1% vit C.

tip
When choosing sugar pears, make sure they are ripe yet still pretty firm (not mushy) so that they will hold together.

Clockwise from bottom left:
Riesling and Ginger Pickled Sugar
Pears (opposite), Spiced Apple Mint
Jelly (page 93) and Spicy Crab
Apple Pickles (page 164)

Anise Spiced Crab Apple Pickles

With their brilliant colour and sharp sweet-and-sour taste, pickled crab apples are a fabulous traditional garnish for roast ham, pork, turkey, goose or duck.

8 cups **crab apples**

Six 2-inch (5 cm) pieces **cinnamon stick**

24 **whole cloves**

2 tsp **coriander seeds**

6 **whole star anise**

3⅓ cups **granulated sugar**

3 cups **cider vinegar**

1 tsp **salt**

Trim off and discard blossom ends of crab apples, keeping stem ends whole. Using needle or toothpick, prick each crab apple several times. Tie cinnamon, cloves, coriander seeds and star anise in cheesecloth square to form spice bag.

Bring sugar, vinegar, 1½ cups water and salt to boil; add spice bag and crab apples. Return to boil. Reduce heat and simmer until crab apples are slightly tender and skins just begin to split, 2 to 6 minutes depending on ripeness and variety.

With slotted spoon, remove crab apples and spice bag. Divide crab apples evenly among 6 hot 2-cup (500 mL) canning jars.

Untie spice bag; divide spices evenly among jars. Divide hot liquid among jars to cover crab apples, leaving ½-inch (1 cm) headspace. Remove any air bubbles.

Cover with prepared discs. Screw on bands until resistance is met; increase to fingertip tight. Boil in boiling water canner for 10 minutes. (See Canning Basics, page 10.)

Turn off heat. Uncover and let jars stand in canner for 5 minutes. Lift up rack. With canning tongs, transfer jars to cooling rack; let cool for 24 hours.

Let stand for 3 days before opening.

MAKES SIX 2-CUP (500 mL) JARS.
PER CRAB APPLE: about 53 cal, trace pro, trace total fat (0 g sat. fat), 14 g carb, 1 g fibre, 0 mg chol, 26 mg sodium, 61 mg potassium. % RDI: 1% calcium, 1% iron, 3% vit C.

Tip
The tender, tiny apples can break down easily, so watch them carefully and remove them as soon as the skins begin to split. Do not overcook or they will become mushy and fall apart.

Pickles & Relishes

Cinnamon Clove Crab Apples

These spicy, tangy crab apples stay supercrisp because they are packed raw and whole into jars, then bathed in hot pickling liquid.

2 **cinnamon sticks,** broken in pieces

2 tsp **whole cloves**

1 tsp **black peppercorns**

4½ cups **granulated sugar**

2½ cups **cider vinegar**

8 cups **crab apples**

Tie cinnamon, cloves and peppercorns in cheesecloth square to form spice bag.

In large saucepan, bring sugar, 3 cups water, vinegar and spice bag to boil; boil for 10 minutes. Discard spice bag.

Meanwhile, using needle or toothpick, prick each crab apple several times. Remove stems if desired. Pack tightly into 7 hot 2-cup (500 mL) canning jars to within ¾ inch (2 cm) of rim.

Divide hot liquid among jars to cover crab apples, leaving ½-inch (1 cm) headspace. Remove any air bubbles.

Cover with prepared discs. Screw on bands until resistance is met; increase to fingertip tight. Boil in boiling water canner for 20 minutes. (See Canning Basics, page 10.)

Turn off heat. Uncover and let jars stand in canner for 5 minutes. Lift up rack. With canning tongs, transfer jars to cooling rack; let cool for 24 hours.

MAKES SEVEN 2-CUP (500 ML) JARS.
PER CRAB APPLE: about 21 cal, 0 g pro, 0 g total fat (0 g sat. fat), 5 g carb, trace fibre, 0 mg chol, 0 mg sodium. % RDI: 1% iron, 2% vit C.

Pickles & Relishes

Choosing and Storing Summer Vegetables

Pickles and savoury preserves are best when made with the ripest produce you can find. Check out farmer's markets and local farm stands for the best selection. Here's how to choose and store your main ingredients.

TOMATOES

Look for firm, unblemished, colourful tomatoes. Avoid any with soft spots. Keep at room temperature in a single layer, without touching, to discourage spoilage.

CUCUMBERS

Choose cucumbers with firm, crisp flesh and dark green skin. Avoid any that are overly large, and those that have soft spots or discolourations. Wrap individually in paper towels and store in a loose plastic bag for up to five days in the crisper drawer of the fridge.

BEETS

Choose firm, ruby-coloured, tight-skinned beets. The greens, if attached, should be crisp and bright. Before storing, cut off tops, leaving 1½ inches (4 cm) attached. Store beets and tops separately in refrigerator – two weeks for beets, two to three days for tops.

EGGPLANTS

Eggplants should be firm, glossy and richly coloured, with no blemishes or soft spots. Wrap in paper towels and enclose in a plastic bag. Store in the refrigerator for up to four days.

HOT OR SWEET PEPPERS

Look for brightly coloured, glossy skins without dark or soft spots. Store whole and unwashed in a plastic bag in the fridge for up to five days. Green peppers keep longer than other colours.

CORN

Choose cobs with bright green husks and dark, moist silk. The kernels should feel plump and fully developed through the husk. Corn is best eaten as soon as it's picked, but if you must store it, wrap unhusked cobs in paper towels and enclose in a plastic bag for no longer than two days.

CARROTS

Look for bright orange, crisp carrots. If the tops are attached, they should look green and fresh. Twist off tops to keep carrots moist; wrap loosely in paper towels and store inside plastic bag or airtight container. They should last a week or more.

BEANS

Pick firm, slim beans that are deep green or deep yellow, depending on variety. Avoid any that are wrinkly, spotty or lumpy. Store in a loose plastic bag in the crisper drawer for three to four days.

ZUCCHINI

Look for deep green or deep yellow zucchini with glossy skin. Avoid any that are bruised or soft. Wrap zucchini in paper towel and place in plastic bag; refrigerate for up to three days.

Thai Cabbage Refrigerator Pickles

Thai seasonings of lime, ginger, lemongrass and fish sauce flavour layers of cabbage, green onions and hot peppers in this fabulous side to grilled fish, poultry or meat.

2 **green onions**

1 lb (450 g) **napa cabbage** (about half head)

1 **hot red pepper** or hot green pepper

1 tbsp **pickling salt**

1 stalk **fresh lemongrass**

1 tbsp grated **fresh ginger**

2 cloves **garlic,** minced

1 cup **unseasoned rice vinegar**

⅓ cup **granulated sugar**

2 tbsp **lime juice**

1 tbsp **fish sauce**

¾ tsp **turmeric**

½ tsp **hot pepper sauce**

Cut green onions into ½-inch (1 cm) lengths. Cut cabbage crosswise into 1-inch (2.5 cm) wide pieces. Halve and seed hot pepper; cut into thin strips. In large bowl, combine onions, cabbage and hot pepper; sprinkle with salt and toss to combine.

Place plate on mixture; weigh down and let stand for 1 hour. Rinse well; drain, pressing out liquid. Return to bowl.

Cut bottom third from lemongrass; discard remainder. Remove tough outer layer; cut into 1-inch (2.5 cm) pieces and add to vegetables. Add ginger and garlic.

In saucepan, bring vinegar, 1 cup water, sugar, lime juice, fish sauce, turmeric and hot pepper sauce to boil, stirring until sugar is dissolved. Pour over vegetables; mix well. Let cool.

Pack vegetables with liquid into canning jars. Seal with lids and refrigerate for 2 days before opening.

Refrigerate for up to 3 weeks.

MAKES 4 CUPS. PER 2 TBSP: about 14 cal, 0 g pro, 0 g total fat (0 g sat. fat), 3 g carb, 0 g fibre, 0 mg chol, 262 mg sodium. % RDI: 1% calcium, 1% iron, 2% vit A, 8% vit C, 6% folate.

Cut Cabbage Kimchi

This kimchi is synonymous with Korean cuisine. It's the most popular type of kimchi and is widely consumed in Korean households – even for breakfast.

1 **large napa cabbage**
   (5 lb/2.25 kg)

1 cup **Korean fine sea salt**

SPICE MIX:

2 tsp **sweet rice powder**

1 cup thinly sliced **Korean radishes** or daikon radish

1 **small onion,** chopped

5 **red finger hot peppers,** chopped

5 **Thai bird's-eye peppers,** chopped

⅓ cup chopped **garlic**

1 tbsp chopped **fresh ginger**

1 tbsp **granulated sugar**

2 tsp **Korean fine sea salt**

⅓ cup **Korean coarse red pepper powder**

¼ cup **fish sauce**

5 **green onions,** halved lengthwise and cut in 1-inch (2.5 cm) pieces

Peel leaves off cabbage. Cut leaves in half lengthwise; cut into 1¼-inch (3 cm) squares. Spread one-eighth of the cabbage in large wide bowl; sprinkle with 2 tbsp of the salt and 3 tbsp water. Repeat layers 7 more times. Cover and let stand, stirring every 30 minutes, until wilted and toughest leaf is consistency of a dill pickle, about 2 hours. Drain.

Fill same bowl with cold water; rinse cabbage twice. Drain in large colander for 30 minutes; return to bowl.

SPICE MIX: Meanwhile, in small saucepan, bring rice powder and ¾ cup water to boil over high heat; boil, stirring, until thickened, about 2 minutes. Transfer to bowl; let cool.

In food processor, purée together radishes, onion, finger peppers, Thai bird's-eye peppers, garlic, ginger, sugar and salt until smooth, about 30 seconds. Stir into rice powder mixture along with red pepper powder, fish sauce and green onions. Pour over cabbage. Wearing rubber gloves, mix thoroughly with hands.

Transfer to large airtight container, pressing firmly and leaving 2-inch (5 cm) headspace. Seal with lid. Let stand at room temperature for 24 hours before opening.

Refrigerate for up to 1 month.

MAKES ABOUT 12 CUPS. PER ¼ CUP: about 14 cal, 1 g pro, trace total fat (0 g sat. fat), 3 g carb, 1 g fibre, 0 mg chol, 361 mg sodium, 142 mg potassium. % RDI: 4% calcium, 2% iron, 5% vit A, 27% vit C, 17% folate.

tip

Korean sea salt has a pronounced saltiness that's needed in kimchi. Find the salt, sweet rice powder, radishes and red pepper powder at Korean markets or some Asian grocery stores.

Pickles & Relishes

Cut Radish Kimchi

These radish cubes are another favourite in Korean cuisine. The sweet and spicy flavours paired with the bitterness of radish is sheer perfection – all in one crunchy bite.

4½ lb (2.025 kg) **Korean radishes** or daikon radishes, peeled and cut in 1-inch (2.5 cm) chunks

3 tbsp **Korean fine sea salt** (approx)

4 tsp **granulated sugar**

2 tbsp **Korean coarse red pepper powder**

1 tbsp minced **salted shrimp**

1 tbsp **fish sauce**

3 **green onions,** halved lengthwise and cut in 1-inch (2.5 cm) pieces

SAUCE:

1 **small onion,** chopped

3 **red finger hot peppers,** chopped

2 **Thai bird's-eye peppers,** chopped

4 cloves **garlic,** chopped

1 tbsp chopped **fresh ginger**

In large bowl, sprinkle radishes with salt and sugar; toss to coat. Let stand for 30 minutes, stirring twice. Reserving ¼ cup of the liquid, drain. Mix red pepper powder into radishes.

SAUCE: In food processor, purée together onion, finger peppers, Thai bird's-eye peppers, garlic and ginger until smooth, about 30 seconds; transfer to bowl.

Stir reserved radish liquid into sauce; stir in shrimp and fish sauce. Pour over radish mixture. Wearing rubber gloves, mix thoroughly with hands, rubbing in mixture. Sprinkle with 2 tsp more salt (if desired); stir in green onions.

Transfer to large airtight container, pressing firmly and leaving 1-inch (2.5 cm) headspace. Seal with lid. Let stand at room temperature for 24 hours before opening.

Refrigerate for up to 1 month.

MAKES ABOUT 10 CUPS. PER ¼ CUP: about 14 cal, 1 g pro, trace total fat (trace sat. fat), 3 g carb, 1 g fibre, 1 mg chol, 512 mg sodium, 126 mg potassium. % RDI: 1% calcium, 2% iron, 2% vit A, 20% vit C, 7% folate.

Zippy Zucchini Relish

This sweet, tangy, spicy zucchini relish adds a zing to everything from hamburgers to tuna sandwiches.

3 lb (1.35 kg) **zucchini,** cut in 1-inch (2.5 cm) chunks

3 **onions,** chopped

2 **sweet red peppers,** diced

¼ cup **pickling salt**

2½ cups **granulated sugar**

1½ cups **cider vinegar**

1 tbsp **dry mustard**

1 tsp **celery seeds**

½ tsp **ground ginger**

½ tsp **turmeric**

½ tsp **hot pepper flakes**

1 tbsp **cornstarch**

In food processor, pulse zucchini, a few pieces at a time, until size of rice with a few larger pieces. Transfer to large stainless-steel or glass bowl. Add onions, red peppers and salt to bowl; stir to blend. Let stand for 1 hour, stirring occasionally. Drain well; rinse and drain again, pressing out moisture.

In large heavy shallow saucepan, combine sugar, vinegar, mustard, celery seeds, ginger, turmeric and hot pepper flakes; bring to boil.

Add drained vegetables; reduce heat and simmer, stirring often, until vegetables are tender, about 15 minutes.

Mix cornstarch with 1 tbsp water; stir into relish. Simmer, stirring, until spoon pulled across bottom leaves trail that fills in slowly, 5 minutes.

Pack into hot 2-cup (500 mL) canning jars, leaving ½-inch (1 cm) headspace. Remove any air bubbles.

Cover with prepared discs. Screw on bands until resistance is met; increase to fingertip tight. Boil in boiling water canner for 15 minutes. (See Canning Basics, page 10.)

Turn off heat. Uncover and let jars stand in canner for 5 minutes. Lift up rack. With canning tongs, transfer jars to cooling rack; let cool for 24 hours.

MAKES ABOUT 8 CUPS. PER 1 TBSP: about 19 cal, 0 g pro, 0 g total fat (0 g sat. fat), 5 g carb, 0 g fibre, 0 mg chol, 0 mg sodium, 142 mg potassium. % RDI: 1% iron, 1% vit A, 7% vit C, 1% folate.

Zippy Zucchini Relish

From top: Pickled Beets and
Pearl Onions (page 156) and
Zippy Zucchini Relish (opposite)

Zucchini Pepper Relish

For hotdogs or any kind of sausage, this is the tangy, golden-hued relish of choice.

9 **zucchini** (3 lb/1.35 kg), finely chopped

3 **onions,** finely chopped

2 **sweet red peppers,** finely chopped

¼ cup **pickling salt**

2½ cups **granulated sugar**

1½ cups **white vinegar**

1½ tsp **dry mustard**

1 tsp **celery seeds**

½ tsp **coarsely ground pepper**

½ tsp **turmeric**

2 tsp **cornstarch**

In large bowl, combine zucchini, onions and red peppers. Sprinkle with salt; stir to blend. Let stand for 1 hour, stirring occasionally. Drain and rinse well under cold running water; drain well, pressing out excess moisture.

In large heavy Dutch oven, bring sugar, vinegar, mustard, celery seeds, pepper and turmeric to boil.

Add drained vegetables; return to boil, stirring frequently. Reduce heat and simmer, stirring often, until vegetables are tender and liquid is thickened, about 15 minutes.

Stir cornstarch with 1 tbsp water; stir into relish. Cook, stirring, until liquid clears and thickens, about 5 minutes.

Pack into hot 2-cup (500 mL) canning jars, leaving ½-inch (1 cm) headspace. Remove any air bubbles.

Cover with prepared discs. Screw on bands until resistance is met; increase to fingertip tight. Boil in boiling water canner for 15 minutes. (See Canning Basics, page 10.)

Turn off heat. Uncover and let jars stand in canner for 5 minutes. Lift up rack. With canning tongs, transfer jars to cooling rack; let cool for 24 hours.

MAKES ABOUT 8 CUPS. PER 1 TBSP: about 19 cal, trace pro, trace total fat (0 g sat. fat), 5 g carb, trace fibre, 0 mg chol, 0 mg sodium. % RDI: 1% iron, 1% vit A, 7% vit C, 1% folate.

Pickles & Relishes

Small-Batch Zucchini Mustard Relish

Mustard relish is a barbecue must-eat. This bright yellow condiment adds that addictive sweet-and-sour tang to burgers, pork chops and sausages.

4 cups chopped **zucchini**

2 **onions,** chopped

½ cup each chopped **sweet red** and **green peppers**

1 tbsp **pickling salt**

1⅓ cups cold **water**

1 cup **granulated sugar**

1 cup **white vinegar**

3 tbsp **all-purpose flour**

1 tbsp **dry mustard**

½ tsp **turmeric**

½ tsp each **mustard seeds** and **celery seeds**

In bowl, combine zucchini, onions, red pepper and green pepper; sprinkle with salt. Pour in 1 cup of the cold water; stir well. Let stand for 1 hour, stirring occasionally. Drain and rinse well under cold running water; drain well, pressing out excess moisture.

In heavy saucepan, bring sugar, vinegar, remaining cold water, flour, mustard, turmeric, mustard seeds and celery seeds to boil.

Add drained vegetables; return to boil, stirring often. Reduce heat to medium-low and simmer, stirring occasionally, until thickened but vegetables are still crunchy, 20 to 25 minutes.

Pack into hot 1-cup (250 mL) canning jars, leaving ½-inch (1 cm) headspace. Remove any air bubbles.

Cover with prepared discs. Screw on bands until resistance is met; increase to fingertip tight. Boil in boiling water canner for 10 minutes. (See Canning Basics, page 10.)

Turn off heat. Uncover and let jars stand in canner for 5 minutes. Lift up rack. With canning tongs, transfer jars to cooling rack; let cool for 24 hours.

MAKES ABOUT 5 CUPS. PER 1 TBSP: about 14 cal, trace pro, 0 g total fat (0 g sat. fat), 4 g carb, trace fibre, 0 mg chol, 67 mg sodium, 22 mg potassium. % RDI: 1% iron, 1% vit A, 3% vit C, 1% folate.

Pickles & Relishes

Hamburger Relish

Like many relishes, this one tastes better after it has mellowed for three weeks. Serve with burgers, of course, or leftover roast beef or pork.

2 cups chopped (unpeeled) **cucumbers**

1 cup each chopped **sweet red, yellow** and **green peppers**

1 cup chopped **celery**

1 cup chopped **onion**

¼ cup **pickling salt**

4 cups chopped seeded peeled **tomatoes**

3 cups **white vinegar**

1 tbsp **mustard seeds**

1 tsp **turmeric**

½ tsp **cinnamon**

½ tsp **ground allspice**

¼ tsp **cayenne pepper**

2 cups **granulated sugar**

¼ cup **tomato paste**

In large bowl, combine cucumbers, red pepper, yellow pepper, green pepper, celery, onion and salt; pour in enough boiling water to cover. Let stand for 1 hour. Drain and rinse well under cold running water; drain well. Set aside.

In large heavy saucepan, combine tomatoes, vinegar, mustard seeds, turmeric, cinnamon, allspice and cayenne pepper; bring to boil, stirring often. Reduce heat to medium and simmer until tomatoes are softened, about 30 minutes.

Stir in sugar and drained vegetables; bring to boil, stirring often. Reduce heat to medium and boil gently, stirring often, for 15 minutes.

Stir in tomato paste; cook, stirring often, until thickened, about 5 minutes.

Pack into hot 1-cup (250 mL) canning jars, leaving ½-inch (1 cm) headspace. Remove any air bubbles.

Cover with prepared discs. Screw on bands until resistance is met; increase to fingertip tight. Boil in boiling water canner for 10 minutes. (See Canning Basics, page 10.)

Turn off heat. Uncover and let jars stand in canner for 5 minutes. Lift up rack. With canning tongs, transfer jars to cooling rack; let cool for 24 hours.

Let jars stand for 3 weeks before opening.

MAKES ABOUT 7 CUPS. PER 1 TBSP: about 20 cal, trace pro, trace total fat (0 g sat. fat), 5 g carb, trace fibre, 0 mg chol, 69 mg sodium, 54 mg potassium. % RDI: 1% iron, 2% vit A, 12% vit C, 1% folate.

Pickles & Relishes

Dill Pickle Relish

For those who prefer a savoury pickle relish, this tastes like chopped dill pickles. It's delicious in tuna or salmon salad.

4 lb (1.8 kg) **pickling cucumbers**

¼ cup **pickling salt**

½ tsp **turmeric**

1 cup cold **water**

2 cups **white vinegar**

⅓ cup **granulated sugar**

4 cloves **garlic,** minced

1 tbsp **dillseed**

2 tsp **mustard seeds**

1½ cups finely chopped **onions**

Scrub cucumbers and trim off ends; cut into chunks. In batches in food processor, pulse cucumbers 8 to 10 times to cut into ⅛- to ¼-inch (3 to 5 mm) pieces.

In large bowl, sprinkle cucumbers with salt and turmeric. Stir in cold water; let stand for 1 hour, stirring occasionally. Drain and rinse well under cold running water; drain well, pressing out excess moisture.

In Dutch oven, bring vinegar, sugar, garlic, dillseed and mustard seeds to boil. Add cucumber mixture and onions; return to boil, stirring often. Reduce heat and simmer, stirring occasionally, until thickened, about 30 minutes.

Pack into hot 1-cup (250 mL) canning jars, leaving ½-inch (1 cm) headspace. Remove any air bubbles.

Cover with prepared discs. Screw on bands until resistance is met; increase to fingertip tight. Boil in boiling water canner for 10 minutes. (See Canning Basics, page 10.)

Turn off heat. Uncover and let jars stand in canner for 5 minutes. Lift up rack. With canning tongs, transfer jars to cooling rack; let cool for 24 hours.

MAKES ABOUT SIX 1-CUP (250 mL) JARS. PER 1 TBSP: about 7 cal, trace pro, 0 g total fat (0 g sat. fat), 2 g carb, trace fibre, 0 mg chol, 2 mg sodium. % RDI: 1% iron, 2% vit C, 1% folate.

Lady Ross Relish

Canadian Living reader Janet Vernon of Langley, B.C., shared this recipe for a zippy, golden relish that won first prize at the Cloverdale, B.C., fair in the early 1950s. It's delicious on grilled meats, especially sausage.

5 cups chopped **cauliflower** (half head)

4 cups chopped **field cucumbers**

4 cups chopped **onions** (about 4 large)

3 cups chopped **celery**

2 **apples,** cored and chopped

1 **sweet red pepper,** chopped

½ cup **pickling salt**

4 cups packed **brown sugar**

2 cups **white vinegar**

⅓ cup **mustard seeds**

¾ cup **dry mustard**

½ cup cold **water**

⅓ cup **all-purpose flour**

1 tbsp **turmeric**

In food processor, in batches, pulse together cauliflower, cucumbers, onions, celery, apples and red pepper until finely chopped; transfer to large bowl. Stir in 4 cups water and pickling salt; cover and let stand for 12 hours or for up to 24 hours.

Drain well and rinse under cold running water. Drain well again, pressing out excess moisture.

In large Dutch oven, bring sugar, vinegar and mustard seeds to boil. Add vegetables and return to boil; reduce heat and simmer until tender, about 10 minutes.

Whisk together dry mustard, cold water, flour and turmeric; whisk into pan. Simmer, stirring, until liquid is thick enough to coat back of spoon, about 5 minutes.

Pack into hot 2-cup (500 mL) canning jars, leaving ½-inch (1 cm) headspace. Remove any air bubbles.

Cover with prepared discs. Screw on bands until resistance is met; increase to fingertip tight. Boil in boiling water canner for 10 minutes. (See Canning Basics, page 10.)

Turn off heat. Uncover and let jars stand in canner for 5 minutes. Lift up rack. With canning tongs, transfer jars to cooling rack; let cool for 24 hours.

MAKES 11 CUPS. PER 1 TBSP: about 27 cal, trace pro, trace total fat (0 g sat. fat), 6 g carb, trace fibre, 0 mg chol, 13 mg sodium. % RDI: 1% calcium, 1% iron, 5% vit C, 1% folate.

Pickles & Relishes

Thousand Island Relish

This sweet golden relish, which is wonderful with hamburgers, hotdogs and cold meats, gets its yellow hue from flavourful turmeric and mustard seeds.

6 **large cucumbers,** peeled, seeded and finely chopped

6 **large onions,** finely chopped

1 each **sweet red** and **green pepper,** finely chopped

¼ cup **pickling salt**

3 cups **granulated sugar**

½ cup **all-purpose flour**

3 tbsp **dry mustard**

1½ tsp **turmeric**

1½ tsp each **mustard seeds** and **celery seeds**

3 cups **white vinegar**

In large bowl, combine cucumbers, onions, red pepper and green pepper; sprinkle with salt. Pour in enough cold water to cover. Let stand for 1 hour; drain well.

In large heavy saucepan, stir together sugar, flour, dry mustard, turmeric, mustard seeds and celery seeds; gradually stir in vinegar and 1 cup water.

Add drained vegetables; bring to boil. Simmer, stirring often, until liquid is thickened but still covers vegetables, about 30 minutes.

Pack into hot 1-cup (250 mL) canning jars, leaving ½-inch (1 cm) headspace. Remove any air bubbles.

Cover with prepared discs. Screw on bands until resistance is met; increase to fingertip tight. Boil in boiling water canner for 10 minutes. (See Canning Basics, page 10.)

Turn off heat. Uncover and let jars stand in canner for 5 minutes. Lift up rack. With canning tongs, transfer jars to cooling rack; let cool for 24 hours.

MAKES ABOUT 12 CUPS. PER 1 TBSP: about 17 cal, trace pro, trace total fat (0 g sat. fat), 4 g carb, trace fibre, 0 mg chol, 69 mg sodium, 20 mg potassium. % RDI: 1% iron, 3% vit C, 1% folate.

Horseradish Beet Relish

This is the simplest relish to make, and it can be delightfully nose-tingling, thanks to the fresh horseradish. Serve with fish, roast beef or poultry.

¾ cup finely grated peeled **horseradish root**

½ cup **cider vinegar**

⅓ cup finely grated peeled **beet**

2 tbsp **granulated sugar**

¼ tsp **salt**

Stir together grated horseradish, vinegar, beet, sugar and salt.

Seal in airtight container. Refrigerate for up to 1 month.

MAKES ABOUT 1 CUP. PER 1 TBSP: about 13 cal, trace pro, 0 g total fat (0 g sat. fat), 3 g carb, trace fibre, 0 mg chol, 38 mg sodium, 44 mg potassium. % RDI: 1% calcium, 1% iron, 7% vit C, 1% folate.

Thousand Island Dressing

This all-purpose dressing suits any salad mix, but is just as delicious on simple wedges of lettuce.

1 cup **light mayonnaise**

2 tbsp finely chopped **sweet pickles** (such as Bread-and-Butter Pickles, page 123)

2 tbsp finely chopped drained **capers**

2 tbsp finely chopped **green olives**

2 tbsp **ketchup** or chili sauce

1 tbsp **cider vinegar**

Pinch **pepper**

Whisk together mayonnaise, pickles, capers, green olives, ketchup, 2 tbsp water, vinegar and pepper. *(Make-ahead: Refrigerate in airtight container for up to 1 week.)*

MAKES ABOUT 1½ CUPS. PER 1 TBSP: about 36 cal, trace pro, 3 g total fat (1 g sat. fat), 2 g carb, 0 g fibre, 3 mg chol, 121 mg sodium. % RDI: 1% iron, 1% vit A.

Pepper Relish

Peppers of all varieties have a home in this tasty harvest relish. It's a great one to make at the end of the gardening season to preserve summer's bounty.

6 cups coarsely chopped peeled **tomatoes**

4 cups chopped **sweet onions**

4 cups chopped **shepherd peppers**

2 cups chopped **sweet green peppers**

1¾ cups **cider vinegar**

1 cup chopped **Anaheim peppers,** sweet banana peppers or Cubanelle peppers

1 cup chopped seeded **hot banana peppers**

1 cup finely chopped seeded **jalapeño peppers**

4 **red hot peppers,** seeded and finely chopped

8 cloves **garlic,** minced

¼ cup **granulated sugar**

1 tbsp **pickling salt**

In large heavy stockpot, combine tomatoes, onions, shepherd peppers, green peppers, vinegar, Anaheim peppers, banana peppers, jalapeño peppers, red hot peppers, garlic, sugar and salt. Bring to boil, stirring often. Reduce heat to medium-low and simmer, stirring often, until thickened, 1½ to 2 hours.

Pack into hot 2-cup (500 mL) canning jars, leaving ½-inch (1 cm) headspace. Remove any air bubbles.

Cover with prepared discs. Screw on bands until resistance is met; increase to fingertip tight. Boil in boiling water canner for 20 minutes. (See Canning Basics, page 10.)

Turn off heat. Uncover and let jars stand in canner for 5 minutes. Lift up rack. With canning tongs, transfer jars to cooling rack; let cool for 24 hours.

MAKES FOUR 2-CUP (500 mL) JARS.
PER 1 TBSP: about 9 cal, trace pro, trace total fat (0 g sat. fat), 2 g carb, trace fibre, 0 mg chol, 55 mg sodium, 54 mg potassium. % RDI: 1% iron, 3% vit A, 23% vit C, 2% folate.

tip
If you prefer a spicier relish, include the hot pepper seeds.

CORN
RELISH

Quick Corn Relish

Sweet and a little crunchy, corn relish tastes marvelous on grilled sausages. This version is a quick refrigerator relish, which does not require processing in boiling water.

2 cups **fresh corn kernels**

½ cup diced **sweet red pepper**

½ cup diced **white onion**

⅓ cup **cider vinegar**

3 tbsp **granulated sugar**

¾ tsp **salt**

½ tsp **mustard seeds**

¼ tsp **celery seeds**

¼ tsp **hot pepper flakes**

¼ tsp **turmeric**

1 tbsp **cornstarch**

In saucepan, combine corn, red pepper and onion. Stir in vinegar, sugar, salt, mustard seeds, celery seeds, hot pepper flakes and turmeric; bring to boil, stirring often. Reduce heat, cover and simmer for 3 minutes.

Stir cornstarch with 1 tbsp cold water until dissolved; stir into pan and cook until thickened, about 1 minute.

Ladle into 2-cup (500 mL) canning jar. Seal with lid and let stand for 30 minutes. Refrigerate until cold before opening, about 1 hour.

Refrigerate for up to 1 month.

MAKES ABOUT 2 CUPS. PER 1 TBSP: about 17 cal, trace pro, trace total fat (0 g sat. fat), 4 g carb, trace fibre, 0 mg chol, 55 mg sodium. % RDI: 1% iron, 1% vit A, 7% vit C, 2% folate.

Corn Relish

When tender, local sweet corn is at its peak, make a double batch of this sweet-tart relish to enjoy all year round.

2 cups **white vinegar**

1 cup **granulated sugar**

1 tbsp **salt**

1 tbsp **dry mustard**

2 tsp **celery seeds**

½ tsp **turmeric**

½ tsp **hot pepper sauce**

5 cups **fresh corn kernels**

1½ cups finely chopped **onions**

1 cup finely chopped **celery**

3 tbsp **all-purpose flour**

3 tbsp **cold water**

1 cup each diced **sweet red** and **green peppers**

In large Dutch oven, bring vinegar, sugar, salt, dry mustard, celery seeds, turmeric and hot pepper sauce to boil. Stir in corn, onions and celery; reduce heat and simmer, stirring often, until softened, about 20 minutes.

Whisk flour with cold water; whisk into pan. Add red and green peppers; bring to boil and cook, stirring often, until thickened, about 5 minutes.

Pack into hot 1-cup (250 mL) canning jars, leaving ½-inch (1 cm) headspace. Remove any air bubbles.

Cover with prepared discs. Screw on bands until resistance is met; increase to fingertip tight. Boil in boiling water canner for 10 minutes. (See Canning Basics, page 10.)

Turn off heat. Uncover and let jars stand in canner for 5 minutes. Lift up rack. With canning tongs, transfer jars to cooling rack; let cool for 24 hours.

MAKES ABOUT SIX 1-CUP (250 mL) JARS. PER 1 TBSP: about 20 cal, trace pro, trace total fat (0 g sat. fat), 5 g carb, trace fibre, 0 mg chol, 75 mg sodium. % RDI: 1% iron, 1% vit A, 7% vit C, 2% folate.

Pickles & Relishes

Cranberry-Orange Relish

This tart and chunky fresh relish is perfect with turkey, whether it's hot out of the oven or cold in sandwiches.

1½ cups **fresh cranberries**

1 **tart apple,** peeled and cored

⅔ cup **granulated sugar**

½ cup chopped **pecans,** toasted

¼ cup **raisins**

¼ cup **orange marmalade**
(such as Seville Orange Marmalade, page 68)

1 tbsp grated **lemon zest**

1 tbsp **lemon juice**

Pinch **cinnamon** (optional)

In food processor or grinder, grind cranberries with apple. Transfer to bowl.

Stir in sugar, pecans, raisins, orange marmalade, lemon zest, lemon juice, and cinnamon (if using).

Transfer to jar; seal with lid. Refrigerate for 8 hours before opening.

Refrigerate for up to 1 week.

MAKES ABOUT 2 CUPS. PER 1 TBSP: about 42 cal, trace pro, 1 g total fat (trace sat. fat), 8 g carb, 1 g fibre, 0 mg chol, 2 mg sodium, 26 mg potassium. % RDI: 1% iron, 2% vit C.

tip
To toast pecans, spread on a baking sheet and bake in 350°F (180°C) oven until golden, about five minutes.

Peach and Red Pepper Relish

This colourful relish is a puckery match for pork, chicken or sharp cheese. It's also a no-fuss topping to spread over pork or chicken in the last five minutes of cooking.

6 cups chopped peeled **fresh peaches**

6 **sweet red peppers,** finely chopped

1 **jalapeño pepper,** seeded and finely chopped

1 **lemon,** cut in half

1½ cups **cider vinegar**

3 cups **granulated sugar**

In large Dutch oven, combine peaches, red peppers, jalapeño pepper, lemon and vinegar; bring to boil. Reduce heat and simmer until peaches and peppers are tender, 20 minutes.

Discard lemon. Stir in sugar; return to boil. Reduce heat to medium; cook, stirring often, until thickened, about 40 minutes.

Pack into hot 1-cup (250 mL) canning jars, leaving ½-inch (1 cm) headspace. Remove any air bubbles.

Cover with prepared discs. Screw on bands until resistance is met; increase to fingertip tight. Boil in boiling water canner for 10 minutes. (See Canning Basics, page 10.)

Turn off heat. Uncover and let jars stand in canner for 5 minutes. Lift up rack. With canning tongs, transfer jars to cooling rack; let cool for 24 hours.

MAKES ABOUT 9 CUPS. PER 1 TBSP: about 21 cal, 0 g pro, 0 g total fat (0 g sat. fat), 5 g carb, trace fibre, 0 mg chol, 0 mg sodium. % RDI: 2% vit A, 15% vit C.

Pickles & Relishes

Classic Chili Sauce

This spicy fall relish is a must on burgers or meat loaves. Make it during the harvest or freeze bags of measured chopped tomatoes to simmer up a batch later on.

8 cups chopped peeled **tomatoes** (about 4½ lb/ 2.025 kg)

1½ cups chopped **onions**

1½ cups chopped **sweet red pepper**

1½ cups **white vinegar**

1 cup chopped **sweet green pepper**

1 cup chopped **celery**

¾ cup **granulated sugar** (approx)

1 tbsp finely chopped **hot pepper**

1 clove **garlic,** minced

1 tsp **salt**

1 tsp **mustard seeds**

½ tsp each **celery seeds, ground cloves** and **cinnamon**

¼ tsp each **ground ginger** and **pepper**

Pinch **cayenne pepper** (approx)

In large heavy saucepan, combine tomatoes, onions, red pepper, vinegar, green pepper, celery, sugar, hot pepper, garlic, salt, mustard seeds, celery seeds, cloves, cinnamon, ginger, pepper and cayenne pepper.

Bring to boil, stirring often; reduce heat and simmer briskly, stirring often, until thickened, about 1 hour. Taste and add up to ¼ cup more sugar and a little more cayenne, if desired.

Pack into hot 1-cup (250 mL) canning jars, leaving ½-inch (1 cm) headspace. Remove any air bubbles.

Cover with prepared discs. Screw on bands until resistance is met; increase to fingertip tight. Boil in boiling water canner for 10 minutes. (See Canning Basics, page 10.)

Turn off heat. Uncover and let jars stand in canner for 5 minutes. Lift up rack. With canning tongs, transfer jars to cooling rack; let cool for 24 hours.

MAKES ABOUT 6 CUPS. PER 1 TBSP: about 12 cal, trace pro, trace total fat (0 g sat. fat), 3 g carb, trace fibre, 0 mg chol, 26 mg sodium, 50 mg potassium. % RDI: 1% iron, 2% vit A, 12% vit C, 1% folate.

Chili Fruit Sauce

Late-summer fruits, such as pears and plums, give a mild sweetness to this chili sauce. Ripe, in-season field tomatoes are the best choice for a rich taste.

5 cups chopped peeled **tomatoes** (2 lb/900 g)

3 cups chopped peeled **pears** (about 3 large)

3 cups chopped **onions**

2 cups **cider vinegar**

1½ cups chopped peeled **plums**

1 cup chopped **celery**

1 cup each finely chopped **sweet red** and **green peppers**

1 cup packed **brown sugar**

½ cup finely chopped seeded **jalapeño peppers**

2 tsp **salt**

SPICE BAG:

1 **cinnamon stick, broken in half**

2 tbsp **mixed pickling spices**

2 tsp **mustard seeds**

1 tsp **celery seeds**

½ tsp each **whole cloves** and **black peppercorns**

SPICE BAG: Tie cinnamon, pickling spices, mustard seeds, celery seeds, cloves and peppercorns in cheesecloth square to form bag.

In large saucepan, combine tomatoes, pears, onions, vinegar, plums, celery, red pepper, green pepper, sugar, jalapeño peppers, salt and spice bag.

Bring to boil, stirring occasionally. Reduce heat and simmer for 45 minutes.

Using potato masher, mash any large pieces; cook until thickened and translucent, 15 to 30 minutes. Discard spice bag.

Pack into hot 2-cup (500 mL) canning jars, leaving ½-inch (1 cm) headspace. Remove any air bubbles.

Cover with prepared discs. Screw on bands until resistance is met; increase to fingertip tight. Boil in boiling water canner for 20 minutes. (See Canning Basics, page 10.)

Turn off heat. Uncover and let jars stand in canner for 5 minutes. Lift up rack. With canning tongs, transfer jars to cooling rack; let cool for 24 hours.

MAKES ABOUT FOUR 2-CUP (500 mL) JARS. PER 1 TBSP: about 14 cal, trace pro, 0 g total fat (0 g sat. fat), 4 g carb, trace fibre, 0 mg chol, 38 mg sodium. % RDI: 1% iron, 1% vit A, 7% vit C, 1% folate.

Pickles & Relishes

Traditional Scotch Pies

Enjoy these hearty meat pies – hot or cold – with your favourite homemade chili sauce. They travel well, which makes them ideal for potlucks.

3 **hard-cooked eggs,** halved lengthwise

1 **egg**

HOT MILK PASTRY:

1¼ cups **milk**

⅔ cup **lard**

3½ cups **all-purpose flour**

¾ tsp **salt**

FILLING:

1 tsp **vegetable oil**

1 **onion,** minced

2 lb (900 g) **lean ground lamb,** beef or veal

3 cloves **garlic,** chopped

1½ tsp **pepper**

1 tsp **salt**

1 tsp **dried savory**

1 tsp **dried sage**

½ tsp **ground allspice**

tip

To make ahead, let baked pies cool for 30 minutes; refrigerate until cold. Wrap and refrigerate for up to 24 hours. Or overwrap in heavy-duty foil and freeze for up to two weeks; thaw in refrigerator. Unwrap and reheat in 375°F (190°C) oven until hot, 20 minutes.

HOT MILK PASTRY: In saucepan, heat milk with lard over medium heat until almost boiling. In food processor, blend flour with salt. Add milk mixture; pulse until pastry forms ball. Shape into disc; cover and let rest on floured surface for 20 minutes. *(Make-ahead: Wrap and refrigerate for up to 2 days. Let come to room temperature before using.)*

FILLING: Meanwhile, in skillet, heat oil over medium heat; fry onion, stirring, until golden, about 15 minutes. Transfer to bowl; let cool. Mix in lamb, garlic, pepper, salt, savory, sage and allspice.

Divide pastry into 6 pieces; shape into balls. Cut off one-third of each; set aside for tops. On floured surface, roll out remaining balls into 8-inch (20 cm) circles; press into six 5-inch (12 cm) foil pie plates.

Divide meat mixture into 12 portions; press 1 into each pie shell. Place 1 hard-cooked egg half, cut side down, in centre of each. Press 1 remaining meat portion over top of each to cover.

Beat egg with 1 tbsp water. Roll out remaining pastry into 5-inch (12 cm) circles; cut ½-inch (1 cm) hole in centre of each. Brush edge of bottom pastry with egg wash. Place pastry circle on top; trim. Crimp edges to seal.

Brush with egg wash. Bake in bottom third of 325°F (160°C) oven until meat thermometer inserted in centre registers 160°F (71°C), about 1 hour. Let stand for 15 minutes before serving.

MAKES 6 SERVINGS. PER SERVING: about 903 cal, 41 g pro, 54 g total fat (22 g sat. fat), 60 g carb, 3 g fibre, 255 mg chol, 824 mg sodium. % RDI: 11% calcium, 46% iron, 8% vit A, 3% vit C, 59% folate.

Pickles & Relishes

English Brown Pickle

Commercially available as Branston Pickle, this is a favourite sweet-and-sour condiment in Britain, especially on bread with Cheddar or blue cheese.

4 cups diced peeled **rutabaga** (1 medium)

3 cups minced **cauliflower**

3 **carrots,** peeled and diced

2 **onions,** finely diced

2 cups finely diced **zucchini**

2 **Granny Smith apples,** peeled and finely diced

1 cup packed **brown sugar**

1 cup chopped **dates**

12 **sweet gherkin pickles,** finely diced

5 cloves **garlic,** minced

2⅔ cups **malt vinegar**

⅓ cup freshly squeezed **lemon juice**

¼ cup **Worcestershire sauce**

2 tsp each **salt** and **mustard seeds**

1½ tsp **ground allspice**

¼ tsp **cayenne pepper**

2 tsp **browning** (optional)

1 tbsp **all-purpose flour**

In Dutch oven, combine rutabaga, cauliflower, carrots, onions, zucchini, apples, brown sugar, dates, gherkins and garlic. Stir in vinegar, 2½ cups water, lemon juice, Worcestershire sauce, salt, mustard seeds, allspice and cayenne pepper; bring to boil.

Reduce heat and simmer, stirring occasionally, until reduced by about half, about 1½ hours. Stir in browning (if using).

Whisk flour with 2 tbsp water; whisk into vegetable mixture. Boil for 3 minutes.

Pack into hot 2-cup (500 mL) canning jars, leaving ½-inch (1 cm) headspace. Remove any air bubbles.

Cover with prepared discs. Screw on bands until resistance is met; increase to fingertip tight. Boil in boiling water canner for 15 minutes. (See Canning Basics, page 10.)

Turn off heat. Uncover and let jars stand in canner for 5 minutes. Lift up rack. With canning tongs, transfer jars to cooling rack; let cool for 24 hours.

MAKES ABOUT FIVE 2-CUP (500 mL) JARS. PER 1 TBSP: about 16 cal, trace pro, 0 g total fat (0 g sat. fat), 4 g carb, trace fibre, 0 mg chol, 53 mg sodium. % RDI: 1% calcium, 1% iron, 3% vit A, 3% vit C, 1% folate.

tip

If you choose to use the browning, be sure to use an unflavoured one, such as Kitchen Bouquet, which will impart only colour and not a beefy taste.

Pickles & Relishes

Three-Pepper Chili Sauce

Thick and chunky, this tangy sauce is versatile enough to go from a burger to a baked potato.

5 lb (2.25 kg) **ripe plum tomatoes** (about 18)

4 cups chopped **sweet red peppers**

2 cups chopped **Anaheim peppers** or Cubanelle peppers

1 cup chopped **onion**

¼ cup chopped seeded **jalapeño peppers**

1½ cups **granulated sugar**

1½ cups **cider vinegar**

1 tsp **salt**

1 **bay leaf**

½ tsp **celery seeds**

½ tsp **cinnamon**

¼ tsp **ground ginger**

¼ tsp **nutmeg**

¼ tsp **pepper**

Pinch **ground cloves**

Using tip of knife, score X on bottom of each tomato. In large pot of boiling water, blanch tomatoes just until skins start to loosen, 1 to 2 minutes. Drain and plunge into cold water. Slip off skins; chop tomatoes to make about 9 cups.

In large heavy saucepan, combine tomatoes, red peppers, Anaheim peppers, onion and jalapeño peppers; add sugar, vinegar, salt, bay leaf, celery seeds, cinnamon, ginger, nutmeg, pepper and cloves. Bring to boil, stirring often. Reduce heat and simmer briskly, stirring often, until thickened, 1¼ hours.

Discard bay leaf. Transfer 3 cups of mixture to food processor or blender; purée until smooth. Return to pan and simmer for 15 minutes.

Pack into hot 1-cup (250 mL) canning jars, leaving ½-inch (1 cm) headspace. Remove any air bubbles.

Cover with prepared discs. Screw on bands until resistance is met; increase to fingertip tight. Boil in boiling water canner for 20 minutes. (See Canning Basics, page 10.)

Turn off heat. Uncover and let jars stand in canner for 5 minutes. Lift up rack. With canning tongs, transfer jars to cooling rack; let cool for 24 hours.

MAKES 8 CUPS. PER 1 TBSP: about 14 cal, trace pro, 0 g total fat (0 g sat. fat), 4 g carb, 0 g fibre, 0 mg chol, 19 mg sodium. % RDI: 1% iron, 5% vit A, 18% vit C, 1% folate.

Pickles & Relishes

Apricot Jalapeño Cheese Topper

This fruity topping is divine with cream cheese on crackers. Or spoon it over a round of Brie cheese and bake just until cheese melts for an easy entertaining appetizer.

1 cup **white wine**

1 cup chopped **dried apricots**

½ cup **granulated sugar**

1 **jalapeño pepper,** seeded and minced

½ tsp freshly squeezed **lemon juice**

In large glass measure, microwave wine at high until hot, about 1 minute. Add apricots; let stand for 1 hour.

Strain into saucepan, pressing apricots to release any liquid; set apricots aside.

Add sugar and ½ cup water to pan; bring to boil over medium-high heat, stirring until sugar is dissolved. Boil until syrupy, about 10 minutes.

Add reserved apricots and jalapeño pepper; simmer until as thick as corn syrup, about 10 minutes. Stir in lemon juice. Let cool.

Spoon into decorative jars; seal with lids. Refrigerate for up to 1 month.

MAKES ABOUT 1 CUP. PER 1 TBSP: about 49 cal, trace pro, 0 g total fat (0 g sat. fat), 12 g carb, 1 g fibre, 0 mg chol, 2 mg sodium. % RDI: 1% calcium, 2% iron, 3% vit A.

chapter five

Chutneys, Salsas & Conserves

Peppy Salsa

Put up a whole season's supply of this favourite salsa –
one of *Canadian Living*'s most requested recipes.

8 cups coarsely chopped
    peeled **tomatoes**

3 cups chopped **Cubanelle
    peppers,** Anaheim peppers
    or sweet banana peppers

2 cups chopped **onions**

2 cups **cider vinegar**

1 cup each chopped **sweet
    red** and **yellow peppers**

1 cup finely chopped seeded
    jalapeño peppers

4 cloves **garlic,** minced

1 can (5½ oz/156 mL)
    tomato paste

2 tbsp **granulated sugar**

1 tbsp **salt**

2 tsp **sweet paprika**

1 tsp **dried oregano**

¼ cup chopped **fresh cilantro**

In large heavy nonaluminum
pot, combine tomatoes,
Cubanelle peppers, onions,
vinegar, red pepper, yellow
pepper, jalapeños, garlic,
tomato paste, sugar, salt,
paprika and oregano; bring
to boil, stirring often.

Reduce heat to medium-low;
simmer, stirring often, until
thick enough that 1 tbsp
dropped onto chilled plate
flows slowly in single stream
when plate is tilted, 1 hour.

Add cilantro; simmer, stirring
occasionally, for 5 minutes.

Fill hot 2-cup (500 mL)
canning jars, leaving ½-inch
(1 cm) headspace. Remove
any air bubbles.

Cover with prepared discs.
Screw on bands until
resistance is met; increase
to fingertip tight. Boil in
boiling water canner for
20 minutes. (See Canning
Basics, page 10.)

Turn off heat. Uncover and
let jars stand in canner for
5 minutes. Lift up rack.
With canning tongs, transfer
jars to cooling rack; let cool
for 24 hours.

MAKES 11 CUPS. PER 1 TBSP: about
6 cal, trace pro, 0 g total fat
(0 g sat. fat), 1 g carb, trace fibre,
0 mg chol, 41 mg sodium. % RDI:
1% iron, 2% vit A, 17% vit C, 1% folate.

tip

**Don't chop hot peppers with bare hands unless you like them to burn
for hours afterward. A pair of inexpensive kitchen gloves will keep
the spicy chili oil off your fingers. Just remember not to touch your
face while you're wearing the gloves.**

Chutneys, Salsas & Conserves

Fresh Salsas

Canned salsas are great to have on hand, but sometimes you want to whip up something fresh in the moment. Here are three simple serve-right-away salsas to enjoy.

PINEAPPLE SALSA

Stir together half fresh pineapple, peeled, cored and cubed; 1 green onion, thinly sliced; ¼ cup diced red onion and 2 tsp lime juice.

If you like some heat, stir in 1 Thai bird's-eye pepper, thinly sliced.

Serve with grilled pork.

MAKES 4 CUPS. PER 1 TBSP: about 4 cal, 0 g pro, 0 g total fat (0 g sat. fat), 1 g carb, trace fibre, 0 mg chol, 0 mg sodium, 9 mg potassium. % RDI: 7% vit C, 1% folate.

TOMATO TOMATILLO SALSA

In saucepan of boiling water, blanch 2 tomatoes just long enough to loosen skins, about 30 seconds. Immediately plunge into ice water. Peel, seed and chop to make about 1 cup; let drain for 5 minutes.

Chop 2 canned tomatillos to make about ½ cup.

Toss together tomatoes; tomatillos; half small red onion, diced; 1 jalapeño pepper, minced; 1 clove garlic, minced; ⅓ cup chopped fresh cilantro; 2 tbsp orange juice; 2 tbsp extra-virgin olive oil; and pinch each salt and pepper.

Serve with grilled or baked trout fillets.

MAKES 2¼ CUPS. PER 1 TBSP: about 9 cal, trace pro, 1 g total fat (trace sat. fat), 1 g carb, trace fibre, 0 mg chol, 1 mg sodium, 23 mg potassium. % RDI: 1% vit A, 3% vit C, 1% folate.

AVOCADO GREEN TOMATO SALSA

Stir together 1 green tomato, diced; ⅓ cup finely diced sweet onion; 2 tbsp minced fresh cilantro; 1 tbsp lime juice; 1 jalapeño pepper, seeded and minced; and ½ tsp salt. Gently stir in 1 avocado, peeled and diced.

Serve with nachos, or grilled chicken or shrimp.

MAKES ABOUT 2⅓ CUPS, OR 4 TO 6 SERVINGS. PER EACH OF 6 SERVINGS: about 63 cal, 1 g pro, 5 g total fat (1 g sat. fat), 5 g carb, 3 g fibre, 0 mg chol, 197 mg sodium. % RDI: 1% calcium, 2% iron, 2% vit A, 17% vit C, 15% folate.

Chutneys, Salsas & Conserves

Chipotle Salsa

Smoky and with a spicy zing, this big-batch salsa brightens up everything from tacos to scrambled eggs.

1 can (7 oz/198 g) **chipotle peppers in adobo sauce**

16 cups coarsely chopped peeled **tomatoes**

6 cups chopped **Cubanelle peppers,** Anaheim peppers or sweet banana peppers

4 cups chopped **onions**

4 cups chopped **sweet green peppers**

4 cups **cider vinegar**

1 cup finely chopped seeded **jalapeño peppers**

8 cloves **garlic,** minced

2 cans (each 5½ oz/156 mL) **tomato paste**

¼ cup **granulated sugar**

5 tsp **salt**

2 tsp **dried oregano**

¾ cup chopped **fresh cilantro**

Reserving sauce, remove chipotle peppers from adobo sauce; seed if desired and chop.

In large heavy stock pot, combine chipotle peppers, reserved adobo sauce, tomatoes, Cubanelle peppers, onions, green peppers, vinegar, jalapeño peppers, garlic, tomato paste, sugar, salt and oregano. Bring to boil, stirring often. Reduce heat to medium-low; simmer, stirring often, until thickened, 2 to 2¼ hours.

Stir in cilantro; simmer, stirring occasionally, for 10 minutes.

Fill hot 2-cup (500 mL) canning jars, leaving ½-inch (1 cm) headspace. Remove any air bubbles.

Cover with prepared discs. Screw on bands until resistance is met; increase to fingertip tight. Boil in boiling water canner for 20 minutes. (See Canning Basics, page 10.)

Turn off heat. Uncover and let jars stand in canner for 5 minutes. Lift up rack. With canning tongs, transfer jars to cooling rack; let cool for 24 hours.

MAKES ABOUT EIGHT 2-CUP (500 mL) JARS. PER 1 TBSP: about 8 cal, trace pro, 0 g total fat (0 g sat. fat), 2 g carb, trace fibre, 0 mg chol, 55 mg sodium. % RDI: 1% iron, 2% vit A, 10% vit C, 1% folate.

Chutneys, Salsas & Conserves

Green Garden Salsa

You can make this salsa with either tomatillos or green tomatoes, whichever are on hand. It's a great way to use up end-of-the-garden tomatoes that aren't likely to ripen.

3 cups chopped **tomatillos** or seeded green tomatoes

3 cups chopped **sweet green peppers** (such as Cubanelle or bell peppers)

3 cups finely diced cored (unpeeled) **pickling cucumbers** or English cucumbers

2 cups chopped **white onions**

2 cups diced seeded **green hot peppers**

4 cloves **garlic,** minced

½ cup **white wine vinegar** or cider vinegar

3½ tsp **salt**

1 tbsp **granulated sugar**

1 tsp **ground coriander**

1 tsp **ground cumin**

¼ tsp **pepper**

¾ cup finely chopped **fresh cilantro**

½ cup finely chopped **fresh parsley**

¼ cup freshly squeezed **lime juice** or lemon juice

In large saucepan over medium-high heat, bring tomatillos, sweet green peppers, cucumbers, onion, hot peppers, garlic, vinegar, salt, sugar, coriander, cumin and pepper to boil, stirring.

Reduce heat to medium, cover and simmer for 5 minutes. Uncover and continue simmering, stirring occasionally, until no longer watery, about 20 minutes.

Stir in cilantro, parsley and lime juice; simmer for 3 minutes.

Fill hot 2-cup (500 mL) canning jars, leaving ½-inch (1 cm) headspace. Remove any air bubbles.

Cover with prepared discs. Screw on bands until resistance is met; increase to fingertip tight. Boil in boiling water canner for 20 minutes. (See Canning Basics, page 10.)

Turn off heat. Uncover and let jars stand in canner for 5 minutes. Lift up rack. With canning tongs, transfer jars to cooling rack; let cool for 24 hours.

Let stand for 1 week before opening.

MAKES FOUR 2-CUP (500 mL) JARS.
PER 1 TBSP: about 5 cal, trace pro, 0 g total fat (0 g sat. fat), 1 g carb, trace fibre, 0 mg chol, 60 mg sodium, 29 mg potassium. % RDI: 1% iron, 1% vit A, 8% vit C, 1% folate.

Fish Tacos

Fish is a healthy, delicious taco filling that you can feel good about. Top these with Green Garden Salsa (opposite) for an extra hit of fresh, tangy flavour.

½ cup shredded **carrot**

¼ cup thinly sliced **red onion**

1 tsp **lime juice**

¼ cup **light sour cream** or plain yogurt

1 tbsp minced **fresh cilantro**

1 **green onion,** minced

8 **small flour tortillas** or corn tortillas

1 **plum tomato,** diced

Half **avocado,** peeled and diced

FISH:

1 lb (450 g) **tilapia fillets** or rainbow trout fillets

1 tbsp **vegetable oil**

1 tsp **chili powder**

½ tsp **dried oregano**

¼ tsp each **salt** and **pepper**

FISH: Pat fish dry; place on foil-lined or greased rimmed baking sheet. Brush with oil. Stir together chili powder, oregano, salt and pepper; sprinkle over fish. Broil until fish flakes easily when tested, about 5 minutes.

Meanwhile, in small bowl, combine carrot, red onion and lime juice. In separate small bowl, stir together sour cream, cilantro and green onion.

Break fish into chunks; divide among tortillas. Top with sour cream mixture, carrot mixture, tomato and avocado.

MAKES 4 SERVINGS. PER SERVING: about 417 cal, 27 g pro, 15 g total fat (3 g sat. fat), 42 g carb, 4 g fibre, 54 mg chol, 570 mg sodium. % RDI: 7% calcium, 20% iron, 56% vit A, 13% vit C, 49% folate.

Tomatillo Salsa

Their name makes them sound like they're mini-tomatoes, but tomatillos are actually relatives of the cape gooseberry. Look for them in farmer's markets from late summer to early fall.

4 **sweet green peppers**

6 **jalapeño peppers**

6 cups chopped **fresh tomatillos** (about 2 lb/900 g)

2 cups chopped **white onions**

4 cloves **garlic,** minced

⅔ cup **white wine vinegar**

3½ tsp **salt**

1 tbsp **granulated sugar**

1 tsp **ground coriander**

1 tsp **ground cumin**

¼ tsp **pepper**

¾ cup finely chopped **fresh cilantro**

½ cup finely chopped **fresh parsley**

¼ cup **lime juice**

On baking sheet, roast green peppers with jalapeño peppers in 475°F (240°C) oven, turning once, until charred, 30 minutes. Let cool. Peel, seed and chop.

In large saucepan, combine green peppers, jalapeño peppers, tomatillos, onion, garlic, vinegar, salt, sugar, coriander, cumin and pepper; bring to boil, stirring.

Reduce heat to medium; cover and simmer for 5 minutes. Uncover and simmer, stirring occasionally, until no longer watery, about 30 minutes.

Stir in cilantro, parsley and lime juice; simmer for 3 minutes.

Fill hot 1-cup (250 mL) canning jars, leaving ½-inch (1 cm) headspace. Remove any air bubbles.

Cover with prepared discs. Screw on bands until resistance is met; increase to fingertip tight. Boil in boiling water canner for 20 minutes. (See Canning Basics, page 10.)

Turn off heat. Uncover and let jars stand in canner for 5 minutes. Lift up rack. With canning tongs, transfer jars to cooling rack; let cool for 24 hours.

MAKES 8 CUPS. PER 1 TBSP: about 5 cal, trace pro, trace total fat (0 g sat. fat), 1 g carb, trace fibre, 0 mg chol, 63 mg sodium, 31 mg potassium. % RDI: 1% iron, 1% vit A, 7% vit C, 1% folate.

Spanish Tomato Salsa

Inspired by Spanish flavours – including sherry vinegar, roasted peppers, rosemary and smoked paprika – this salsa is as good in hearty sandwiches as it is on tortilla chips.

4 **dried New Mexico hot peppers**

8 cups chopped seeded peeled **tomatoes**

2½ cups chopped **Spanish onion** or sweet onion

1¾ cups chopped peeled roasted **red peppers**

2 cloves **garlic,** minced

1 sprig (3 inches/8 cm) **fresh rosemary** (or 1 tsp dried)

⅓ cup + 1 tbsp **sherry vinegar**

1 tbsp **salt**

1 tbsp **granulated sugar**

1½ tsp **smoked paprika**

½ tsp **ground cumin**

2 tbsp freshly squeezed **lemon juice**

In dry skillet over medium heat, toast hot peppers until slightly darkened on all sides; transfer to plate and let cool. Break open; discard seeds. In spice grinder, grind to coarse powder.

In large saucepan, stir together ground hot peppers, tomatoes, onion, roasted red peppers, garlic, rosemary, vinegar, salt, sugar, paprika and cumin; bring to boil over medium-high heat, stirring. Reduce heat to medium and simmer, uncovered and stirring often, until no longer watery, 30 to 45 minutes.

Remove rosemary. Stir in lemon juice; simmer for 2 minutes.

Fill 4 hot 2-cup (500 mL) canning jars, leaving ½-inch (1 cm) headspace. Remove any air bubbles.

Cover with prepared discs. Screw on bands until resistance is met; increase to fingertip tight. Boil in boiling water canner for 20 minutes. (See Canning Basics, page 10.)

Turn off heat. Uncover and let jars stand in canner for 5 minutes. Lift up rack. With canning tongs, transfer jars to cooling rack; let cool for 24 hours.

Let jars stand for 1 week before opening.

MAKES FOUR 2-CUP (500 mL) JARS.
PER 1 TBSP: about 4 cal, trace pro, 0 g total fat (0 g sat. fat), 1 g carb, trace fibre, 0 mg chol, 52 mg sodium, 34 mg potassium. % RDI: 1% iron, 2% vit A, 8% vit C, 1% folate.

tip
Dried New Mexico hot peppers are large and not too hot, with a rich pepper flavour. If they're unavailable, use Mexican guajillo chilies, or 4 tsp ancho chili powder or hot paprika, such as Hungarian hot paprika.

Sassy Sweet Salsa

Nicely balanced with fruit and vegetables, this chunky, colourful condiment goes well with most anything. If you want to increase the heat, add a red hot pepper, seeded and minced. For even more fire, include the seeds.

4 cups chopped peeled **tomatoes**

2 cups finely chopped peeled **fresh peaches**

2 cups finely chopped peeled **fresh pears**

1 **sweet red pepper,** finely chopped

1 cup chopped **red onion**

¾ cup **cider vinegar**

½ cup minced seeded **jalapeño peppers**

⅓ cup **tomato paste**

2 tbsp **granulated sugar**

2¼ tsp **salt**

1 tsp **ancho chili powder**

½ cup chopped **fresh cilantro**

In large shallow Dutch oven, combine tomatoes, peaches, pears, red pepper, onion, vinegar, jalapeños, tomato paste, sugar, salt and chili powder. Bring to boil over high heat, stirring constantly.

Reduce heat to medium-low; simmer, stirring often, until fruit is tender and spoon leaves trail when pulled through sauce, about 12 minutes.

Add cilantro; simmer, stirring often, for 3 minutes.

Fill hot 1-cup (250 mL) canning jars, leaving ½-inch (1 cm) headspace. Remove any air bubbles.

Cover with prepared discs. Screw on bands until resistance is met; increase to fingertip tight. Boil in boiling water canner for 20 minutes. (See Canning Basics, page 10.)

Turn off heat. Uncover and let jars stand in canner for 5 minutes. Lift up rack. With canning tongs, transfer jars to cooling rack; let cool for 24 hours.

MAKES ABOUT 6 CUPS. PER 1 TBSP: about 9 cal, trace pro, 0 g total fat (0 g sat. fat), 2 g carb, trace fibre, 0 mg chol, 55 mg sodium. % RDI: 1% iron, 1% vit A, 7% vit C, 1% folate.

Chutneys, Salsas & Conserves

Yellow Tomato and Mango Salsa

Serve this spicy and fruity salsa with chips, crackers or crudités. It's also terrific with grilled fish or chicken.

4 cups chopped seeded peeled **yellow tomatoes** or orange tomatoes

4 cups diced **ripe semi-firm mangoes**

1 **large white onion,** chopped

6 **Scotch bonnet peppers** or habanero peppers, seeded and finely chopped

⅓ cup **palm sugar,** cane sugar or granulated sugar

⅓ cup **white vinegar**

1½ tsp **salt**

1 tsp grated **lime zest**

¾ tsp **ground cumin**

½ tsp **ground mace**

½ tsp **ground allspice**

½ cup finely chopped **fresh culantro** or cilantro

⅓ cup **lime juice**

In large saucepan over medium-high heat, bring tomatoes, mangoes, onion, Scotch bonnet peppers, sugar, vinegar, salt, lime zest, cumin, mace and allspice to boil, stirring. Boil for 2 minutes.

Reduce heat, cover and simmer, stirring occasionally, for 15 minutes. Stir in culantro and lime juice; simmer, uncovered, over medium heat until no longer watery, 5 to 10 minutes.

Fill 4 hot 2-cup (500 mL) canning jars, leaving ½-inch (1 cm) headspace. Remove any air bubbles.

Cover with prepared discs. Screw on bands until resistance is met; increase to fingertip tight. Boil in boiling water canner for 20 minutes. (See Canning Basics, page 10.)

Turn off heat. Uncover and let jars stand in canner for 5 minutes. Lift up rack. With canning tongs, transfer jars to cooling rack; let cool for 24 hours.

Let jars stand for 1 week before opening.

MAKES FOUR 2-CUP (500 ᴍʟ) JARS.
PER 1 TBSP: about 7 cal, trace pro, 0 g total fat (0 g sat. fat), 2 g carb, trace fibre, 0 mg chol, 27 mg sodium, 25 mg potassium. % RDI: 1% iron, 1% vit A, 5% vit C, 1% folate.

tip
Culantro is known by a number of names, including shado beni, thistle coriander, Mexican coriander and recao. It's not a relative of cilantro, but it does have a similar (yet slightly more bitter) flavour. Look for it in Asian and Latin American markets.

Chutneys, Salsas & Conserves

Tomato and Eggplant Salsa

This salsa tastes great on chips, bread or Italian-style subs, and makes a nice addition to an antipasto plate (see page 137). When they're in season, use red shepherd peppers; otherwise red bell peppers are fine.

8 cups diced peeled **eggplant** (½-inch/1 cm cubes)

3¼ tsp **salt**

1½ tsp **fennel seeds**

1½ tsp **hot pepper flakes**

5 cups chopped seeded peeled **tomatoes**

2 cups chopped peeled roasted **red peppers**

1½ cups finely chopped **onion**

½ cup **red wine vinegar**

3 cloves **garlic,** minced

1½ tsp **dried oregano**

1 tsp **granulated sugar**

¼ tsp **pepper**

Toss eggplant with 2 tsp of the salt; let stand for 2 hours. Squeeze out and discard liquid.

In dry large saucepan over medium-low heat, toast fennel seeds with hot pepper flakes until fragrant. Stir in eggplant, tomatoes, red peppers, onion, vinegar, garlic, oregano, remaining salt, sugar and pepper. Increase heat; bring to boil.

Reduce heat to medium, cover and simmer for 10 minutes. Uncover and continue simmering, stirring occasionally, until no longer watery, about 15 minutes.

Fill 4 hot 2-cup (500 mL) canning jars, leaving ½-inch (1 cm) headspace. Remove any air bubbles.

Cover with prepared discs. Screw on bands until resistance is met; increase to fingertip tight. Boil in boiling water canner for 20 minutes. (See Canning Basics, page 10.)

Turn off heat. Uncover and let jars stand in canner for 5 minutes. Lift up rack. With canning tongs, transfer jars to cooling rack; let cool for 24 hours.

Let jars stand for 1 week before opening.

MAKES FOUR 2-CUP (500 ML) JARS.
PER 1 TBSP: about 5 cal, trace pro, 0 g total fat (0 g sat. fat), 1 g carb, trace fibre, 0 mg chol, 39 mg sodium, 29 mg potassium. % RDI: 1% iron, 1% vit A, 6% vit C, 4% folate.

Chutneys, Salsas & Conserves

Green Tomato Chutney

This chutney is excellent for using up firm green unripened tomatoes still on the vine at the end of the growing season. Try it on scrambled eggs for breakfast.

4 lb (1.8 kg) **green tomatoes**

3 **large tart apples,** peeled and chopped

10 **jalapeño peppers,** seeded and chopped

1 **large Spanish onion,** sweet onion or white onion, chopped

1 cup **golden raisins**

1 tbsp **pickling salt**

2 cups **cider vinegar**

2½ cups packed **light brown sugar**

3 large cloves **garlic,** pressed, grated or pounded into paste

4 tsp **dry mustard**

2 tsp **ground ginger**

1 tsp **ground dried hot peppers** or ½ tsp cayenne pepper (approx)

½ tsp **ground cardamom** or cinnamon

Cut out and discard stem ends from tomatoes; cut tomatoes in half lengthwise. Cut crosswise into scant ½-inch (1 cm) thick slices.

In large heavy saucepan, combine tomatoes, apples, jalapeño peppers, onion, raisins and salt; stir in half of the vinegar. Bring to simmer. Reduce heat to medium-low, cover and simmer, stirring occasionally, until tomatoes and apples are tender, about 30 minutes.

Stir in sugar, garlic, mustard, ginger, ground hot peppers, cardamom and remaining vinegar; bring to boil.

Reduce heat to medium and simmer, uncovered and stirring often, until thick and almost no liquid remains, about 45 minutes. Taste during last 5 minutes; add more ground hot peppers, if desired.

Fill hot 2-cup (500 mL) canning jars, leaving ½-inch (1 cm) headspace. Remove any air bubbles.

Cover with prepared discs. Screw on bands until resistance is met; increase to fingertip tight. Boil in boiling water canner for 15 minutes. (See Canning Basics, page 10.)

Turn off heat. Uncover and let jars stand in canner for 5 minutes. Lift up rack. With canning tongs, transfer jars to cooling rack; let cool for 24 hours.

MAKES 11 CUPS. PER 1 TBSP: about 20 cal, trace pro, trace total fat (0 g sat. fat), 5 g carb, trace fibre, 0 mg chol, 29 mg sodium, 49 mg potassium. % RDI: 1% calcium, 1% iron, 1% vit A, 5% vit C.

tip

Ten jalapeños might seem like a lot, but their heat mellows during cooking. This chutney is medium to mild. If you want it milder, replace four or five of the jalapeños with sweet green peppers and halve or omit the ground hot peppers.

Tomato Apple Chutney

Rich, flavourful and full of chunky fruit and vegetables, this chutney is delicious with meats, breads and cheeses.

12 cups chopped peeled **tomatoes**

8 cups chopped peeled **apples**

4 cups packed **brown sugar**

3 cups chopped **onions**

2 cups **cider vinegar**

1 cup **dried currants**

2 tbsp minced **fresh ginger**

2 large cloves **garlic,** minced

2 tsp **salt**

1 tsp each **dry mustard** and **mustard seeds**

1 tsp **hot pepper flakes**

½ tsp each **cinnamon** and **ground allspice**

In large heavy nonaluminum saucepan, combine tomatoes, apples, brown sugar, onions, vinegar, currants, ginger, garlic, salt, dry mustard, mustard seeds, hot pepper flakes, cinnamon and allspice; bring to boil over medium-high heat.

Reduce heat to medium; simmer, stirring often, until thickened, about 2 hours.

Fill hot 1-cup (250 mL) canning jars, leaving ½-inch (1 cm) headspace. Remove any air bubbles.

Cover with prepared discs. Screw on bands until resistance is met; increase to fingertip tight. Boil in boiling water canner for 10 minutes. (See Canning Basics, page 10.)

Turn off heat. Uncover and let jars stand in canner for 5 minutes. Lift up rack. With canning tongs, transfer jars to cooling rack; let cool for 24 hours.

MAKES ABOUT 12 CUPS. PER 1 TBSP: about 26 cal, trace pro, 0 g total fat (0 g sat. fat), 7 g carb, trace fibre, 0 mg chol, 26 mg sodium, 61 mg potassium. % RDI: 1% calcium, 1% iron, 1% vit A, 3% vit C, 1% folate.

Chutneys, Salsas & Conserves

Apple Chutney

Dress up your favourite roasted pork or lamb recipe with a dollop of this fruity chutney. Or serve it with aged Gouda or smoked Cheddar.

1 tbsp **vegetable oil**

6 **small dried red hot peppers**

12 **whole cloves**

5 tsp **black mustard seeds** or yellow mustard seeds

6 **tart apples**

6 **sweet apples**

½ cup **cider vinegar**

1½ cups chopped **red onion**

1½ cups packed **light brown sugar**

2 tsp **ground ginger**

½ tsp **salt**

¼ tsp **pepper**

2 **cinnamon sticks**

In small skillet, heat oil over high heat; cook hot peppers, cloves and mustard seeds just until seeds start to pop and peppers darken, about 20 seconds. Set aside.

Peel and core tart and sweet apples; cut into ½-inch (1 cm) cubes to make 12 cups total, tossing with a little of the vinegar to prevent browning as you work.

In large saucepan, bring apples, remaining vinegar, onion, sugar, ginger, salt, pepper, cinnamon and hot pepper mixture to simmer over medium heat. Reduce heat to medium-low; simmer, stirring often, until liquid is reduced to maple-syrup-like consistency and apples are softened but still intact, 30 to 45 minutes. Discard cinnamon.

Fill hot 1-cup (250 mL) canning jars, placing 1 hot pepper in each and leaving ½-inch (1 cm) headspace. Remove any air bubbles.

Cover with prepared discs. Screw on bands until resistance is met; increase to fingertip tight. Boil in boiling water canner for 15 minutes. (See Canning Basics, page 10.)

Turn off heat. Uncover and let jars stand in canner for 5 minutes. Lift up rack. With canning tongs, transfer jars to cooling rack; let cool for 24 hours.

MAKES 5 CUPS. PER 1 TBSP: about 26 cal, trace pro, trace total fat (0 g sat. fat), 6 g carb, trace fibre, 0 mg chol, 16 mg sodium. % RDI: 1% calcium, 1% iron.

Chutneys, Salsas & Conserves

Apple Mint Chutney

Some chutneys benefit from a bit of mellowing before sampling, but this mint-flecked delight is ready to enjoy right away.

2 **large lemons**

6 cups chopped peeled **apples**

6 cups chopped **onions**

3 cups diced peeled **tomatoes**

2½ cups **granulated sugar**

2 cups **cider vinegar**

1½ cups **raisins**

⅔ cup lightly packed chopped **fresh mint** (or 2 tbsp dried)

¼ cup chopped **fresh parsley**

½ tsp each **salt** and **cinnamon**

Pinch **cayenne pepper**

Using zester, remove zest from lemons. (Or pare off thin outer rind from lemons; cut into thin strips.) Squeeze and strain lemon juice into large heavy saucepan.

Stir in lemon zest, apples, onions, tomatoes, sugar, vinegar, raisins, mint, parsley, salt, cinnamon and cayenne pepper; bring to boil. Reduce heat to low; simmer until thickened, about 1½ hours.

Fill hot 1-cup (250 mL) canning jars, leaving ½-inch (1 cm) headspace. Remove any air bubbles.

Cover with prepared discs. Screw on bands until resistance is met; increase to fingertip tight. Boil in boiling water canner for 10 minutes. (See Canning Basics, page 10.)

Turn off heat. Uncover and let jars stand in canner for 5 minutes. Lift up rack. With canning tongs, transfer jars to cooling rack; let cool for 24 hours.

MAKES 12 CUPS. PER 1 TBSP: about 19 cal, trace pro, 0 g total fat (0 g sat. fat), 5 g carb, trace fibre, 0 mg chol, 7 mg sodium, 32 mg potassium. % RDI: 1% iron, 2% vit C.

Apple Raisin Chutney

To keep this sweet-and-spicy chutney chunky, use apples that hold their shape when cooked. Some varieties to try include: Cortland, Northern Spy, Spartan, Idared or Crispin.

4 lb (1.8 kg) **apples,** peeled and chopped

3 cups chopped **Spanish onions**

2 cups **cider vinegar**

1⅓ cups **granulated sugar**

1 cup **golden raisins** or sultana raisins

1 cup packed **brown sugar**

7 tsp **salt**

2 tbsp grated **fresh ginger**

4 tsp **ground coriander**

1 to 2 tsp **cayenne pepper**

1 tsp **cinnamon**

¾ tsp **ground cardamom**

½ tsp **pepper**

¼ tsp **ground cloves**

In large saucepan, combine apples, onions, vinegar, granulated sugar, raisins, brown sugar, salt, ginger, coriander, cayenne pepper, cinnamon, cardamom, pepper and cloves; bring to simmer over medium heat. Simmer, stirring occasionally, until apples are soft, about 20 minutes.

Fill 6 hot 2-cup (500 mL) canning jars, leaving ½-inch (1 cm) headspace. Remove any air bubbles.

Cover with prepared discs. Screw on bands until resistance is met; increase to fingertip tight. Boil in boiling water canner for 15 minutes. (See Canning Basics, page 10.)

Turn off heat. Uncover and let jars stand in canner for 5 minutes. Lift up rack. With canning tongs, transfer jars to cooling rack; let cool for 24 hours.

Let jars stand for 3 days before opening.

MAKES SIX 2-CUP (500 mL) JARS.
PER 1 TBSP: about 17 cal, trace pro, 0 g total fat (0 g sat. fat), 4 g carb, trace fibre, 0 mg chol, 81 mg sodium, 23 mg potassium. % RDI: 1% iron.

Sweet Mango Chutney

Sweet-tart with just a hint of heat, this chutney is based on traditional Anglo-Indian chutneys, such as the legendary Major Grey's. The subtly assertive spicing and generous hit of lime and ginger give it a distinctive taste.

6 cups chopped peeled **mangoes** (about 6)

1¾ cups packed **light brown sugar**

1½ cups finely chopped **white onion** or Spanish onion

1½ cups **malt vinegar**

1 tsp finely grated **lime zest**

1 cup finely chopped peeled **limes** (pith removed)

¾ cup **golden raisins**

⅓ cup minced **fresh ginger**

2 tsp each **salt** and **mustard seeds**

1½ tsp **ground dried hot peppers** (or 1 tsp cayenne pepper)

1¼ tsp **cinnamon**

1 tsp **ground coriander**

½ tsp **turmeric**

¼ tsp each **ground cloves** and **pepper**

In saucepan, stir together mangoes, brown sugar, onion, vinegar, lime zest, limes, raisins, ginger, salt, mustard seeds, ground hot peppers, cinnamon, coriander, turmeric, cloves and pepper; bring to boil.

Reduce heat to medium-low, cover and simmer, stirring twice, for 20 minutes. Increase heat to medium and simmer, uncovered and stirring often, until mixture is consistency of thin applesauce, about 15 minutes.

Fill hot 1-cup (250 mL) or 2-cup (500 mL) canning jars, leaving ½-inch (1 cm) headspace. Remove any air bubbles.

Cover with prepared discs. Screw on bands until resistance is met; increase to fingertip tight. Boil in boiling water canner for 10 minutes for 1-cup (250 mL) jars or 15 minutes for 2-cup (500 mL) jars. (See Canning Basics, page 10.)

Turn off heat. Uncover and let jars stand in canner for 5 minutes. Lift up rack. With canning tongs, transfer jars to cooling rack; let cool for 24 hours.

MAKES ABOUT 4½ CUPS. PER 1 TBSP: about 38 cal, trace pro, trace total fat (0 g sat. fat), 10 g carb, 1 g fibre, 0 mg chol, 67 mg sodium, 69 mg potassium. % RDI: 1% calcium, 1% iron, 1% vit A, 7% vit C, 1% folate.

tip

For this chutney, look for mangoes that are ripe. They should be fragrant and soft to the touch but firm enough to cut without becoming mushy. Mangoes with sap dripping from the stem end are often the sweetest.

Chutneys, Salsas & Conserves

Kumquat Chutney

Kumquats are gorgeous little fruits commonly available in the winter months. They're often a component in jams, jellies and pickles, and they're the star in this flavourful refrigerator chutney, which doesn't require processing.

1 lb (450 g) **kumquats,** stemmed

1 tbsp **vegetable oil**

¾ tsp **mustard seeds**

8 **black peppercorns**

1 **whole star anise**

1 **cinnamon stick,** broken

1 cup finely chopped **sweet onion**

1½ tsp minced **fresh ginger**

Pinch **hot pepper flakes**

Pinch **salt**

⅓ cup **granulated sugar**

3 tbsp **cider vinegar**

½ cup **golden raisins**

Scrub kumquats; cut in half crosswise. Using toothpick or skewer, pick out seeds. Coarsely chop fruit; place in large bowl. Pour in 8 cups cold water; let stand for 1 hour. *(Make-ahead: Cover and refrigerate for up to 24 hours.)* Drain.

In large pot of boiling water, blanch kumquats until they float and water returns to boil; drain.

Meanwhile, in saucepan, heat oil over medium heat; cook mustard seeds, peppercorns, star anise and cinnamon until mustard seeds begin to pop, about 1 minute.

Add onion, ginger, hot pepper flakes and salt; cook over medium-low heat, stirring occasionally, until onion is softened but not browned, 8 to 10 minutes.

Stir in kumquats, sugar, vinegar and 3 tbsp water; bring to boil. Reduce heat, cover and simmer for 15 minutes.

Stir in raisins; simmer, uncovered and stirring often, until thickened, 7 to 8 minutes. Let cool. Discard star anise and cinnamon.

Fill airtight container; seal with lid. Refrigerate for up to 1 week.

MAKES ABOUT 2 CUPS. PER 1 TBSP: about 31 cal, trace pro, 1 g total fat (trace sat. fat), 7 g carb, 1 g fibre, 0 mg chol, 2 mg sodium, 52 mg potassium. % RDI: 1% calcium, 1% iron, 8% vit C, 1% folate.

Cranberry Fruit Chutney

Fresh and tangy yet sweet enough to satisfy, this rich red condiment pairs beautifully with turkey, ham, goose or duck. Save some for pork loin roasts and chops, too.

2 cups lightly packed **dried apricots**

2½ cups freshly squeezed **orange juice**

1 cup chopped **dates**

½ cup **golden raisins**

½ cup chopped **preserved ginger in syrup**

2 pkg (each 12 oz/340 g) **fresh cranberries**

1½ cups **granulated sugar**

1¼ cups finely chopped **onions**

¾ cup **corn syrup**

¾ cup **cider vinegar**

1½ tsp **mustard seeds**

¼ tsp **salt**

Cut apricots into ¼-inch (5 mm) wide strips. In heavy stainless-steel Dutch oven, combine apricots, orange juice, dates, raisins and ginger; cover and let stand for 8 hours. *(Make-ahead: Let stand for up to 24 hours.)*

Stir in cranberries, sugar, onions, corn syrup, vinegar, mustard seeds and salt; bring to gentle boil over medium heat, stirring often. Reduce heat and simmer, stirring almost constantly, until thick enough to mound on spoon and cranberries pop, about 20 minutes.

Fill hot 1-cup (250 mL) canning jars, leaving ¼-inch (5 mm) headspace. Remove any air bubbles.

Cover with prepared discs. Screw on bands until resistance is met; increase to fingertip tight. Boil in boiling water canner for 10 minutes. (See Canning Basics, page 10.)

Turn off heat. Uncover and let jars stand in canner for 5 minutes. Lift up rack. With canning tongs, transfer jars to cooling rack; let cool for 24 hours.

MAKES 9 CUPS. PER 1 TBSP: about 28 cal, trace pro, 0 g total fat (0 g sat. fat), 7 g carb, 1 g fibre, 0 mg chol, 7 mg sodium. % RDI: 1% iron, 1% vit A, 3% vit C.

Pear Chutney

One of the finest preserves to keep in your cupboard year round, this chutney – and its fruity variations – has a mildly piquant, exotic flavour that's lovely with creamy cheeses, cold meats and curries.

1 **seedless orange**

8 cups chopped peeled **firm ripe pears**

2¾ cups packed **brown sugar**

2 cups chopped **onions**

2 cloves **garlic,** minced

1 cup diced **sweet red pepper**

½ cup **raisins**

1 tbsp **mustard seeds**

1 tsp **salt**

1 tsp **ground cloves**

1 tsp **cinnamon**

1 tsp **curry powder**

1 tsp **ground ginger**

2 cups **cider vinegar**

Scrub orange. Cut in half lengthwise; cut crosswise into thin slices. In large shallow Dutch oven, bring orange and 1 cup water to boil; reduce heat, cover and simmer until rind is very soft and almost no liquid remains, about 15 minutes.

Add pears, sugar, onions, garlic, red pepper, raisins, mustard seeds, salt, cloves, cinnamon, curry powder and ginger to pot. Pour in vinegar; stir to combine. Bring to boil.

Reduce heat to medium and simmer, uncovered and stirring often, until chutney is reduced to 8 cups and thick enough to mound on spoon, about 1 hour.

Fill hot 1-cup (250 mL) canning jars, leaving ½-inch (1 cm) headspace. Remove any air bubbles.

Cover with prepared discs. Screw on bands until resistance is met; increase to fingertip tight. Boil in boiling water canner for 10 minutes. (See Canning Basics, page 10.)

Turn off heat. Uncover and let jars stand in canner for 5 minutes. Lift up rack. With canning tongs, transfer jars to cooling rack; let cool for 24 hours.

MAKES ABOUT 8 CUPS. PER 1 TBSP: about 29 cal, trace pro, trace total fat (0 g sat. fat), 7 g carb, trace fibre, 0 mg chol, 20 mg sodium, 46 mg potassium. % RDI: 1% calcium, 1% iron, 1% vit A, 5% vit C.

Variations
Peach Chutney: Substitute chopped peeled peaches for pears.

Apple Plum Chutney: Omit pears. Substitute 4 cups each coarsely chopped (unpeeled) red plums and coarsely chopped peeled cooking apples. Omit curry powder. Add ½ tsp ground coriander.

Vegetable Samosas

Inspired by street food in India, these potato-filled pastries make chic cocktail hors d'oeuvres. They're best fresh, but you can freeze them ahead if it's convenient. Serve with Tamarind Chutney (page 220).

3 cups **vegetable oil**

FILLING:

2 cups diced peeled **potatoes**

½ cup diced **carrots**

3 tbsp **vegetable oil**

1 tsp each **fennel seeds** and **cumin seeds**

1 tsp **brown mustard seeds** or black mustard seeds

½ tsp each **turmeric, ground coriander** and **fenugreek seeds**

¼ tsp **cayenne pepper**

1 **onion,** chopped

2 cloves **garlic,** minced

1 tbsp grated **fresh ginger**

½ tsp **salt**

½ cup **frozen peas**

3 tbsp freshly squeezed **lemon juice**

2 tbsp chopped **fresh cilantro**

DOUGH:

2 cups **all-purpose flour**

1 tsp **cumin seeds** (preferably black)

½ tsp **salt**

½ cup cold **butter,** cubed

½ cup **milk**

DOUGH: In food processor, mix flour, cumin seeds and salt; pulse in butter until in fine crumbs. Pulse in milk until ball begins to form. Press into disc; wrap and refrigerate for 30 minutes. *(Make-ahead: Refrigerate for up to 24 hours.)*

FILLING: In large saucepan of boiling salted water, cover and cook potatoes and carrots until tender, 10 minutes; drain. Meanwhile, in skillet, heat oil over medium heat; fry fennel, cumin, mustard, turmeric, coriander, fenugreek and cayenne just until cumin begins to pop, 1 minute. Add onion, garlic, ginger and salt; fry until onion is softened, 3 minutes. Stir in peas, potato mixture, lemon juice and cilantro; let cool.

Cut dough into 12 pieces; form each into flat round. On floured surface, roll out each into 6-inch (15 cm) circle; cut in half.

Working with 1 piece at a time, moisten half of the cut edge with water. Form cone shape by overlapping cut edges by ¼ inch (5 mm). Fill with rounded 1 tbsp potato mixture. Moisten top inside edges of pastry; press to seal. Trim jagged edges. Crimp with fork.

In wok, heat oil to 350°F (180°C). Fry samosas, in batches, until golden, about 4 minutes. Drain on paper towel–lined tray. (Or bake in 425°F/220°C oven for 15 minutes.) Serve warm. *(Make-ahead: Let cool. Cover and refrigerate for up to 24 hours. Or freeze on waxed paper–lined tray; transfer to airtight container and freeze for up to 2 weeks. Reheat in 350°F/180°C oven for 10 to 20 minutes.)*

MAKES 24 PIECES. PER PIECE: about 133 cal, 2 g pro, 9 g total fat (3 g sat. fat), 12 g carb, 1 g fibre, 12 mg chol, 200 mg sodium. % RDI: 2% calcium, 6% iron, 11% vit A, 5% vit C, 8% folate.

Chutneys, Salsas & Conserves

Tamarind Chutney

Think of this chutney as a dipping sauce for samosas and spring rolls, and as a condiment for fried fish or chicken, barbecued or roast pork, or ground lamb or beef kabobs.

1 pkg (1 lb/454 g) **seedless tamarind paste**

4 tsp **cumin seeds**

1 tbsp **coriander seeds**

2 tsp **fennel seeds**

¼ tsp **black peppercorns**

4 **whole cloves**

1½ cups pitted **dates**, chopped

Half **large sweet onion** or white onion, chopped

1 cup chopped **fresh cilantro** (leaves and stems)

½ cup chopped seeded **green hot peppers**

2 tbsp chopped **fresh ginger**

3 cloves **garlic,** smashed

2¼ cups packed **light brown sugar**

⅓ cup **unseasoned rice vinegar**

2 tsp **salt**

¾ tsp **cayenne pepper**

In saucepan, bring 5 cups water and tamarind paste to boil, breaking up with spoon. Reduce heat to low and simmer, stirring occasionally to loosen up, for 20 minutes.

Remove from heat. Press and shake pulp through fine-mesh sieve into large glass measure to make 3 cups (if not enough, pour a little warm water over solids; mash to extract more juice). Discard solids.

In dry skillet over medium-low heat, separately toast cumin, coriander and fennel seeds, peppercorns and cloves until fragrant and slightly darkened (do not overtoast). In spice grinder, grind spices to fine powder.

In food processor, purée together dates, onion, cilantro, hot peppers, ginger and garlic until smooth.

In saucepan, bring tamarind liquid, spices, date mixture, sugar, vinegar, salt and cayenne to boil; reduce heat and simmer, stirring, until sugar is dissolved. Cover and simmer over medium-low heat, stirring often, for 25 minutes.

Fill hot 1-cup (250 mL) canning jars, leaving ½-inch (1 cm) headspace. Cover with prepared discs. Screw on bands until resistance is met; increase to fingertip tight. Boil in boiling water canner for 15 minutes. (See Canning Basics, page 10.)

Turn off heat. Uncover and let jars stand in canner for 5 minutes. Lift up rack. With canning tongs, transfer jars to cooling rack; let cool for 24 hours.

MAKES 6 CUPS. PER 1 TBSP: about 40 cal, trace pro, trace total fat (0 g sat. fat), 10 g carb, trace fibre, 0 mg chol, 52 mg sodium, 76 mg potassium. % RDI: 1% calcium, 3% iron, 2% vit C, 1% folate.

tip

For a tarter, slightly thinner dipping sauce, stir in lime juice to taste just before serving.

Vegetable Samosas (page 219) with
Tamarind Chutney (opposite)

Peach and Raisin Chutney

Chutneys like this one add spice to cold meats, and their sweet-and-sour notes are rounded off nicely by cheese, especially cream cheese or a buttery Jarlsberg.

8 cups sliced peeled
 fresh peaches

2 cups packed **brown sugar**

2 cups chopped **onions**

2 cups **raisins**

2 cups **cider vinegar**

½ cup diced **sweet red pepper**

2 tsp **mustard seeds**

1 tsp **salt**

½ tsp **turmeric**

½ tsp **cinnamon**

½ tsp **curry powder**

½ tsp **ground cumin**

½ tsp **ground coriander**

Pinch **cayenne pepper**

In large heavy Dutch oven, combine peaches, sugar, onions, raisins, vinegar, red pepper, mustard seeds, salt, turmeric, cinnamon, curry powder, cumin, coriander, and cayenne; bring to boil. Reduce heat to medium and simmer, stirring often, until thickened and toffee-brown in colour, about 1 hour.

Fill hot 1-cup (250 mL) canning jars, leaving ½-inch (1 cm) headspace. Remove any air bubbles.

Cover with prepared discs. Screw on bands until resistance is met; increase to fingertip tight. Boil in boiling water canner for 10 minutes. (See Canning Basics, page 10.)

Turn off heat. Uncover and let jars stand in canner for 5 minutes. Lift up rack. With canning tongs, transfer jars to cooling rack; let cool for 24 hours.

MAKES 8 CUPS. PER 1 TBSP: about 26 cal, trace pro, trace total fat (0 g sat. fat), 7 g carb, trace fibre, 0 mg chol, 20 mg sodium, 61 mg potassium. % RDI: 1% calcium, 1% iron, 1% vit A, 3% vit C.

Nectarine Chutney

Nectarines make a wonderful chutney to serve with pork, poultry, cheese or Indian dishes. And they're easy to prepare: Unlike peaches, nectarines don't need to be peeled. Choose firm yet ripe or almost ripe fruit.

2 tsp **black mustard seeds**

1 tsp **hot pepper flakes**

½ tsp **cumin seeds**

6 **whole cloves**

2-inch (5 cm) piece **cinnamon stick**

2 tsp **ground coriander**

½ cup **cider vinegar**

⅓ cup **palm sugar** or jaggery

¼ cup freshly squeezed **lemon juice**

1 **white onion,** chopped

2 tsp grated **fresh ginger**

½ tsp **salt**

Pinch **pepper**

8 **fresh nectarines** (unpeeled), pitted and coarsely chopped

In dry saucepan over medium-low heat, toast mustard seeds, hot pepper flakes, cumin seeds, cloves and cinnamon, shaking pan, until fragrant and mustard seeds begin to pop. Add coriander; toast for 20 seconds.

Stir in vinegar, sugar, lemon juice, onion, ginger, salt and pepper. Bring to boil; reduce heat and simmer for 3 minutes. Cover and simmer over low heat for 5 minutes.

Stir in nectarines; return to simmer. Cover and cook, stirring occasionally, until nectarines are very soft, about 8 minutes.

Uncover; continue simmering, stirring, until mixture is thickened, 10 to 12 minutes. Remove cinnamon stick.

Fill 5 hot 2-cup (500 mL) canning jars, leaving ½-inch (1 cm) headspace. Remove any air bubbles.

Cover with prepared discs. Screw on bands until resistance is met; increase to fingertip tight. Boil in boiling water canner for 20 minutes. (See Canning Basics, page 10.)

Turn off heat. Uncover and let jars stand in canner for 5 minutes. Lift up rack. With canning tongs, transfer jars to cooling rack; let cool for 24 hours.

Let jars stand for 1 week before opening.

MAKES FIVE 2-CUP (500 mL) JARS.
PER 1 TBSP: about 13 cal, trace pro, trace total fat (0 g sat. fat), 3 g carb, trace fibre, 0 mg chol, 15 mg sodium, 42 mg potassium. % RDI: 1% iron, 1% vit A, 2% vit C.

tips

• If you plan to eat this chutney immediately, you don't have to can it. The chutney will keep in the refrigerator for up to four weeks.

• Look for palm sugar or jaggery in Southeast Asian or South Asian markets. If it's not available, substitute an equal amount of packed brown sugar.

Banana Fruit Chutney

Bananas might not jump to mind when you think of preserves, but they give wonderful fragrance and flavour to this chutney. Choose firm, slightly green bananas and pitted dates sold in tubs or loose in bulk-food stores.

1 large **orange**

1 large **lemon**

3 cups chopped peeled **apples**

3 cups **cider vinegar**

1 tsp **curry paste**

½ tsp **salt**

3 cups sliced **bananas**

2 cups pitted halved **dates**

2 cups **granulated sugar**

½ cup **raisins**

Using zester, remove zest from orange and lemon. Squeeze and strain juice into large heavy nonaluminum saucepan. Stir in orange and lemon zest, apples, vinegar, ½ cup water, curry paste and salt; bring to boil. Cover and reduce heat to medium-low; simmer until apples are softened, about 10 minutes.

Add bananas, dates, sugar and raisins; return to simmer. Cook, uncovered and stirring occasionally, until thick enough to mound on spoon, 1 to 1½ hours.

Fill hot 1-cup (250 mL) canning jars, leaving ½-inch (1 cm) headspace. Remove any air bubbles.

Cover with prepared discs. Screw on bands until resistance is met; increase to fingertip tight. Boil in boiling water canner for 10 minutes. (See Canning Basics, page 10.)

Turn off heat. Uncover and let jars stand in canner for 5 minutes. Lift up rack. With canning tongs, transfer jars to cooling rack; let cool for 24 hours.

MAKES 7 CUPS. PER 2 TBSP: about 64 cal, trace pro, trace total fat (0 g sat. fat), 17 g carb, 1 g fibre, 0 mg chol, 24 mg sodium. % RDI: 1% iron, 5% vit C, 1% folate.

Apricot Ginger Chutney

Truly gingery, and studded with apricots and apples, this chutney is adapted from a recipe by Madhur Jaffrey, Indian chef, TV personality, teacher and author.

6 cups coarsely chopped peeled **apples**

4 cups packed **dried apricots,** halved

3 cups **white wine vinegar**

1 cup **golden raisins**

½ cup grated **fresh ginger**

8 cloves **garlic,** slivered

½ tsp **salt**

¼ tsp **hot pepper flakes**

4 cups **granulated sugar**

In large heavy saucepan, combine apples, apricots, vinegar, raisins, ginger, garlic, salt and hot pepper flakes; bring to boil. Cover and reduce heat to low; simmer until apricots are plumped, about 10 minutes.

Stir in sugar and return to simmer; cook, uncovered and stirring almost constantly, until thickened, about 20 minutes.

Fill hot 1-cup (250 mL) canning jars, leaving ½-inch (1 cm) headspace. Remove any air bubbles.

Cover with prepared discs. Screw on bands until resistance is met; increase to fingertip tight. Boil in boiling water canner for 10 minutes. (See Canning Basics, page 10.)

Turn off heat. Uncover and let jars stand in canner for 5 minutes. Lift up rack. With canning tongs, transfer jars to cooling rack; let cool for 24 hours.

MAKES 8 CUPS. PER 1 TBSP: about 42 cal, trace pro, 0 g total fat (0 g sat. fat), 11 g carb, trace fibre, 0 mg chol, 10 mg sodium, 67 mg potassium. % RDI: 1% iron, 2% vit A.

Chutneys, Salsas & Conserves

Apricot and Golden Raisin Chutney

Serve this sweet, tangy chutney with roasted lamb, pork, chicken or turkey (or on the next day's sandwiches). It's a treat in the morning with eggs and sausage or bacon, too.

9 cups chopped **fresh apricots**

2 cups **granulated sugar**

1¼ cups **cider vinegar**

1 cup chopped **red onion**

1 cup chopped **sweet red pepper**

1 cup **golden raisins**

2 tsp **mustard seeds**

½ tsp **salt**

½ tsp each **cinnamon** and **ground coriander**

¼ tsp **curry powder**

Pinch **cayenne pepper**

In large heavy saucepan, combine apricots, sugar, vinegar, onion, red pepper, raisins, mustard seeds, salt, cinnamon, coriander, curry powder and cayenne pepper; bring to boil.

Reduce heat to medium; simmer, stirring often, until thick enough that 1 tbsp dropped onto chilled plate flows slowly in single stream when plate is tilted, about 50 minutes.

Fill hot 1-cup (250 mL) canning jars, leaving ½-inch (1 cm) headspace. Remove any air bubbles.

Cover with prepared discs. Screw on bands until resistance is met; increase to fingertip tight. Boil in boiling water canner for 15 minutes. (See Canning Basics, page 10.)

Turn off heat. Uncover and let jars stand in canner for 5 minutes. Lift up rack. With canning tongs, transfer jars to cooling rack; let cool for 24 hours.

MAKES ABOUT 7 CUPS. PER ½ CUP: about 222 cal, 3 g pro, 1 g total fat (0 g sat. fat), 56 g carb, 4 g fibre, 0 mg chol, 86 mg sodium. % RDI: 3% calcium, 9% iron, 31% vit A, 47% vit C, 5% folate.

Gooseberry Chutney

Gooseberries are so named because they were commonly used as a sauce for roast goose. This classic tart, seedy relish is also wonderful with roast pork or tourtière.

4½ cups packed **brown sugar**

1 cup **cider vinegar**

½ tsp **salt**

2 **whole allspice**

2-inch (5 cm) piece **cinnamon stick,** broken

8 **whole cloves**

10 cups **fresh gooseberries,** topped and tailed

¼ tsp grated **nutmeg**

In large Dutch oven, stir together brown sugar, vinegar, ½ cup water and salt. Tie allspice, cinnamon and cloves in damp square of double-thickness cheesecloth to form bag; hit a few times with rolling pin to crush cinnamon and release flavour. Add to pot.

Cover and bring to boil over high heat; reduce heat to low and simmer, uncovered, for 5 minutes. Add gooseberries and nutmeg; return to boil.

Reduce heat and simmer, stirring often and adjusting heat so sauce bubbles gently, until thickened and berries are tender, about 45 minutes. Remove spice bag; squeeze liquid from bag into pan. Discard bag.

Fill hot 1-cup (250 mL) canning jars, leaving ½-inch (1 cm) headspace. Remove any air bubbles.

Cover with prepared discs. Screw on bands until resistance is met; increase to fingertip tight. Boil in boiling water canner for 15 minutes. (See Canning Basics, page 10.)

Turn off heat. Uncover and let jars stand in canner for 5 minutes. Lift up rack. With canning tongs, transfer jars to cooling rack; let cool for 24 hours.

MAKES ABOUT 8 CUPS. PER 1 TBSP: about 34 cal, trace pro, 0 g total fat (0 g sat. fat), 9 g carb, 1 g fibre, 0 mg chol, 12 mg sodium. % RDI: 1% calcium, 1% iron, 3% vit C.

Chutneys, Salsas & Conserves

Ruby Beet Chutney

Beets are a refreshing change from the usual apples, pears and tomatoes that go into chutneys. Their natural sweetness is a delight in this jewel-toned condiment.

8 **large beets**

1 **lemon**

3 cups chopped peeled **apples**

2 cups chopped **onions**

2 cups **granulated sugar**

2 cups **cider vinegar**

½ cup **raisins**

¼ cup diced **crystallized ginger**

1 tsp **mustard seeds**

½ tsp **salt**

½ tsp **pepper**

Trim beets, leaving root ends and about 1 inch (2.5 cm) of stems intact. In large pot of boiling water, cook beets until tender, about 30 minutes. Drain and let cool; slip off skins. Dice beets to make 4½ cups.

Meanwhile, using zester, remove zest from lemon. (Or pare off thin outer rind and cut into thin strips.) Squeeze and strain juice into large heavy nonaluminum saucepan or Dutch oven.

Stir in lemon zest, apples, onions, sugar, vinegar, raisins, ginger, mustard seeds, salt and pepper; bring to boil. Reduce heat to low; simmer, stirring occasionally, until apples are tender, about 30 minutes.

Stir in beets. Cook until thickened, 10 to 15 minutes.

Fill hot 1-cup (250 mL) canning jars, leaving ½-inch (1 cm) headspace. Remove any air bubbles.

Cover with prepared discs. Screw on bands until resistance is met; increase to fingertip tight. Boil in boiling water canner for 20 minutes. (See Canning Basics, page 10.)

Turn off heat. Uncover and let jars stand in canner for 5 minutes. Lift up rack. With canning tongs, transfer jars to cooling rack; let cool for 24 hours.

MAKES ABOUT 6 CUPS. PER 1 TBSP: about 30 cal, trace pro, trace total fat (0 g sat. fat), 8 g carb, trace fibre, 0 mg chol, 22 mg sodium, 71 mg potassium. % RDI: 2% iron, 2% vit C, 5% folate.

Golden Conserve

This chunky mix of oranges, lemon, apricots and plums bursts with flavour.

2 **large oranges**

1 **large lemon**

4 cups quartered **fresh apricots**

4 cups quartered **fresh golden plums**

⅓ cup freshly squeezed **orange juice**

7 cups **granulated sugar**

Scrub oranges and lemon; cut out stem and blossom ends and any blemishes. Cut in half lengthwise; slice thinly to make about 4 cups.

In large Dutch oven, combine oranges, lemon and 1 cup water; cover and bring to boil. Reduce heat to low and simmer, stirring often, until peel is almost mushy, about 1 hour.

Add apricots, plums and orange juice; bring to boil over medium heat. Reduce heat and simmer, uncovered, until apricots and plums begin to soften, about 15 minutes. Measure 7 cups fruit mixture, adding water to top up or boiling further to reduce to correct amount if necessary.

Add sugar; bring to boil over high heat, stirring constantly. Boil hard, stirring constantly, until firmly set, about 10 minutes. (See Testing for Setting Point, page 17.)

Remove from heat. Stir and skim off foam for 5 minutes.

Fill hot 1-cup (250 mL) canning jars, leaving ¼-inch (5 mm) headspace. Cover with prepared discs. Screw on bands until resistance is met; increase to fingertip tight. Boil in boiling water canner for 10 minutes. (See Canning Basics, page 10.)

Turn off heat. Uncover and let jars stand in canner for 5 minutes. Lift up rack. With canning tongs, transfer jars to cooling rack; let cool undisturbed for 24 hours.

MAKES 8 CUPS. PER 1 TBSP: about 98 cal, trace pro, trace total fat (0 g sat. fat), 25 g carb, 1 g fibre, 0 mg chol, 1 mg sodium. % RDI: 1% calcium, 1% iron, 2% vit A, 12% vit C, 1% folate.

Peach Orange Conserve

A conserve differs from jam, not in the luscious effect it has when spooned on toast, bagels or scones, but in its ingredients. There is always citrus to complement the main fruit, and sometimes dried fruits or nuts.

2 **oranges**

1 tbsp coarsely grated **lemon zest**

8 cups coarsely chopped peeled **fresh peaches**

6 cups **granulated sugar**

¼ cup freshly squeezed **lemon juice**

1 **cinnamon stick** (optional)

¾ cup **slivered blanched almonds** (optional)

Scrub oranges; cut out stem and blossom ends and any blemishes. Slice very thinly; chop coarsely, discarding any seeds. In saucepan, bring oranges, lemon zest and ¾ cup water to boil; reduce heat, cover and simmer until zest is almost mushy, about 15 minutes.

In Dutch oven, bring orange mixture, peaches, sugar, lemon juice, and cinnamon (if using) to boil over high heat. Reduce heat to medium-low and simmer, uncovered and stirring often, for 55 minutes.

Stir in almonds (if using); cook until firmly set, about 5 minutes. (See Testing for Setting Point, page 17.) Discard cinnamon. Remove from heat. Skim off any foam.

Fill hot 1-cup (250 mL) canning jars, leaving ¼-inch (5 mm) headspace. Cover with prepared discs. Screw on bands until resistance is met; increase to fingertip tight. Boil in boiling water canner for 10 minutes. (See Canning Basics, page 10.)

Turn off heat. Uncover and let jars stand in canner for 5 minutes. Lift up rack. With canning tongs, transfer jars to cooling rack; let cool undisturbed for 24 hours.

MAKES ABOUT 12 CUPS. PER 1 TBSP: about 32 cal, trace pro, trace total fat (trace sat. fat), 8 g carb, trace fibre, 0 mg chol, 0 mg sodium. % RDI: 1% vit A, 3% vit C.

Variation
Mixed Cherry Conserve:
Substitute 1 lemon for the oranges, and 4 cups each pitted fresh Bing cherries and tart cherries for the peaches. Precook cherries with ½ cup water until softened, about 10 minutes. Reduce sugar to 4 cups. Omit cinnamon. Reduce almonds to ½ cup. Reduce simmering time to 40 minutes or until thickened.

MAKES ABOUT 6 CUPS.

Rhubarb Orange Conserve

If you're a fan of rhubarb, wait until you taste what a hit of orange and lemon can do to this springtime favourite.

1 **orange,** scrubbed and thinly sliced

4 thin slices **lemon**

5½ cups chopped **fresh rhubarb** (½-inch/1 cm pieces)

3½ cups **granulated sugar**

1 cup **golden raisins**

In small saucepan, combine orange, lemon and 1 cup water; cover and cook over low heat until peel is tender and translucent, 20 to 30 minutes.

In large Dutch oven, stir together orange mixture, rhubarb, sugar and raisins; bring to full rolling boil, stirring constantly. Boil, stirring constantly, until firmly set, about 15 minutes. (See Testing for Setting Point, page 17.)

Remove from heat. Stir and skim off foam for 5 minutes.

Fill hot 1-cup (250 mL) canning jars, leaving ¼-inch (5 mm) headspace. Cover with prepared discs. Screw on bands until resistance is met; increase to fingertip tight. Boil in boiling water canner for 10 minutes. (See Canning Basics, page 10.)

Turn off heat. Uncover and let jars stand in canner for 5 minutes. Lift up rack. With canning tongs, transfer jars to cooling rack; let cool undisturbed for 24 hours.

MAKES 4 CUPS. PER 1 TBSP: about 53 cal, trace pro, 0 g total fat (0 g sat. fat), 14 g carb, trace fibre, 0 mg chol, 1 mg sodium, 50 mg potassium. % RDI: 1% calcium, 1% iron, 5% vit C.

Plum Raisin Conserve

Thick, sweet-tart and utterly satisfying, this old-fashioned conserve is delicious on bread or alongside roasts.

2 **small navel oranges,** scrubbed and cut in chunks

8 cups sliced pitted **plums**

5 cups **granulated sugar**

¾ cup **raisins**

2 tbsp freshly squeezed **lemon juice**

In food processor or grinder and using coarse blade, chop or grind oranges until in medium-fine pieces.

In large shallow heavy saucepan, bring oranges and 1 cup water to boil; cover, reduce heat and simmer gently until softened, about 15 minutes.

Add plums, stirring to coat well; return to simmer, stirring often. Reduce heat to low, cover and simmer until plums are softened and start to release juices, about 10 minutes.

Stir in sugar, raisins and lemon juice; bring to full rolling boil, stirring constantly. Boil hard, stirring constantly, until softly set, about 15 minutes. (See Testing for Setting Point, page 17.)

Remove from heat. Stir and skim off foam for 5 minutes.

Fill hot 1-cup (250 mL) canning jars, leaving ¼-inch (5 mm) headspace. Cover with prepared discs. Screw on bands until resistance is met; increase to fingertip tight. Boil in boiling water canner for 10 minutes. (See Canning Basics, page 10.)

Turn off heat. Uncover and let jars stand in canner for 5 minutes. Lift up rack. With canning tongs, transfer jars to cooling rack; let cool undisturbed for 24 hours.

MAKES ABOUT 7 CUPS. PER 1 TBSP: about 46 cal, trace pro, trace total fat (0 g sat. fat), 12 g carb, trace fibre, 0 mg chol, 0 mg sodium, 32 mg potassium. % RDI: 1% iron, 3% vit C.

Apricot Almond Conserve

With its fresh apricot and lemon aroma, and nutty almond crunch, this softly set conserve is delightful on Buttermilk Scones (page 35), ice cream or cheesecake.

2½ cups packed **dried apricots,** chopped (1 lb/450 g)

2 **large lemons**

2½ cups **granulated sugar**

½ cup toasted **almonds,** chopped

In large Dutch oven, combine apricots with 6 cups water. Cover and bring to boil over high heat. Remove from heat; let stand until apricots are plump, about 1 hour.

Meanwhile, scrub 1 of the lemons; cut out stem and blossom ends and any blemishes. Using vegetable peeler, peel off zest in strips, avoiding white pith. Cut zest crosswise into thin strips. Squeeze enough juice from lemons to make ½ cup total.

Drain apricots, reserving soaking liquid. Measure 4½ cups liquid, adding water if necessary.

In clean Dutch oven, combine apricots, soaking liquid, lemon zest and lemon juice; bring to boil over medium heat, stirring often. Uncover and reduce heat; simmer, stirring often and crushing apricots lightly, until apricots begin to break down, about 15 minutes.

Gradually stir in sugar; bring to boil over high heat, stirring. Boil hard, stirring constantly, until softly set, 30 minutes. (See Testing for Setting Point, page 17.)

Remove from heat. Stir in almonds. Stir and skim off foam for 5 minutes.

Fill hot 1-cup (250 mL) canning jars, leaving ¼-inch (5 mm) headspace. Cover with prepared discs. Screw on bands until resistance is met; increase to fingertip tight. Boil in boiling water canner for 10 minutes. (See Canning Basics, page 10.)

Turn off heat. Uncover and let jars stand in canner for 5 minutes. Lift up rack. With canning tongs, transfer jars to cooling rack; let cool undisturbed for 24 hours.

MAKES ABOUT 6 CUPS. PER 1 TBSP: about 36 cal, trace pro, trace total fat (0 g sat. fat), 8 g carb, trace fibre, 0 mg chol, 1 mg sodium, 62 mg potassium. % RDI: 1% iron, 2% vit A, 2% vit C.

tip
Toasted almonds have a richer flavour. To toast, spread whole unblanched almonds on baking sheet; bake in 375°F (190°C) oven until fragrant, eight to 10 minutes. Let cool, then chop.

Chutneys, Salsas & Conserves

Fig and Wine Conserve

When you need a rich conserve fast, this non-citrus refrigerator version comes together in no time. It's glossy, well spiced and particularly good with creamy blue cheese or old Cheddar – or even ice cream!

1 lb (450 g) **dried light-coloured figs** (such as Calimyrna)

1½ cups **white wine**

1 cup **granulated sugar**

2 **cinnamon sticks,** broken in pieces

4 **cardamom pods,** crushed

2 **whole cloves**

Trim tough tips off figs and discard; quarter figs.

In saucepan, bring wine and sugar to boil. Tie cinnamon, cardamom and cloves in cheesecloth square to form bag; add to pan along with figs.

Reduce heat and simmer until figs are tender and liquid is thick and syrupy, about 25 minutes.

Let cool to room temperature. Refrigerate in airtight container for up to 2 weeks.

MAKES 3 CUPS. PER 1 TBSP: about 47 cal, trace pro, trace total fat (0 g sat. fat), 10 g carb, 1 g fibre, 0 mg chol, 1 mg sodium. % RDI: 1% calcium, 1% iron, 2% vit C.

tip
If you prefer a darker conserve, dried dark purple Mission figs work well.

Peach and Pear Conserve With Lemon

Here's an easy conserve that will release the heavenly scent of freshly picked pears when you open the jar.

1½ **lemons**

6 **fresh peaches**

3 **fresh pears**

3½ cups **granulated sugar**

¼ cup **golden raisins**

⅓ cup halved **maraschino cherries**

Squeeze juice from half lemon; reserve juice and discard peel. Scrub remaining lemon; cut out stem and blossom ends and any blemishes. Cut lemon into chunks. In food processor or grinder fitted with medium blade, process until finely chopped.

In saucepan, combine reserved lemon juice, chopped lemon and juices, and ¼ cup water; cover and simmer over low heat until peel is translucent and very tender, about 45 minutes. Add more water to keep mixture moist, if necessary.

Meanwhile, peel peaches and pears; cut into ½-inch (1 cm) chunks. In heavy saucepan, combine peaches, pears and ¼ cup water; cover and simmer, stirring often, until slightly softened, about 10 minutes.

Add lemon mixture to peach mixture. Stir in sugar and raisins. Bring to full rolling boil, stirring often; boil hard, stirring constantly, until firmly set, 10 to 15 minutes. (See Testing for Setting Point, page 17.) Remove from heat. Stir in cherries.

Fill hot 1-cup (250 mL) canning jars, leaving ¼-inch (5 mm) headspace. Cover with prepared discs. Screw on bands until resistance is met; increase to fingertip tight. Boil in boiling water canner for 10 minutes. (See Canning Basics, page 10.)

Turn off heat. Uncover and let jars stand in canner for 5 minutes. Lift up rack. With canning tongs, transfer jars to cooling rack; let cool undisturbed for 24 hours.

MAKES ABOUT 4 CUPS. PER 1 TBSP: about 53 cal, trace pro, 0 g total fat (0 g sat. fat), 14 g carb, 1 g fibre, 0 mg chol, 0 mg sodium, 31 mg potassium. % RDI: 1% iron, 3% vit C.

Plum Orange Conserve

Thick with chunks of fruit, this is a pleasing spread for scones or English muffins at a leisurely breakfast.

1 **orange**

8 cups coarsely chopped **fresh plums**

4 cups **granulated sugar**

1 **cinnamon stick**

Scrub orange. Slice very thinly; chop, discarding any seeds. In small saucepan, combine orange with 1 cup water; cover and simmer over medium heat until peel is tender, about 40 minutes.

In large Dutch oven, combine orange mixture, plums, sugar and cinnamon stick; bring to full rolling boil over high heat, stirring often. Boil hard, stirring almost constantly, until firmly set, 10 to 12 minutes. (See Testing for Setting Point, page 17.)

Remove from heat; discard cinnamon stick. Stir and skim off foam for 5 minutes.

Fill hot 1-cup (250 mL) canning jars, leaving ¼-inch (5 mm) headspace. Cover with prepared discs. Screw on bands until resistance is met; increase to fingertip tight. Boil in boiling water canner for 10 minutes. (See Canning Basics, page 10.)

Turn off heat. Uncover and let jars stand in canner for 5 minutes. Lift up rack. With canning tongs, transfer jars to cooling rack; let cool undisturbed for 24 hours.

MAKES ABOUT 7 CUPS. PER 1 TBSP: about 34 cal, 0 g pro, 0 g total fat (0 g sat. fat), 9 g carb, 0 g fibre, 0 mg chol, 0 mg sodium. % RDI: 3% vit C.

Chutneys, Salsas & Conserves

Bourbon Vanilla Preserved Apricots

Bourbon-laced apricots make an elegant dessert, either on their own or on pound cake or angel food cake. Firm, barely ripe apricots will keep their shape during cooking.

1 cup **granulated sugar**

8 cups halved **firm fresh apricots**

1 **vanilla bean,** split lengthwise

⅔ cup **bourbon,** amber rum or brandy

In large shallow Dutch oven, bring sugar and 1 cup water to boil. Add apricots and vanilla bean; reduce heat to medium. Cover with circle of parchment paper and lid; simmer, stirring occasionally, until apricots are slightly tender, about 5 minutes.

Reserving liquid, drain apricots. Pack apricots into hot 1-cup (250 mL) canning jars. Divide bourbon among jars.

Meanwhile, return reserved liquid to boil over high heat; boil until reduced to about 1¼ cups, 4 minutes. Divide among jars to cover apricots, leaving ½-inch (1 cm) headspace. Remove any air bubbles.

Cover with prepared discs. Screw on bands until resistance is met; increase to fingertip tight. Boil in boiling water canner for 20 minutes. (See Canning Basics, page 10.)

Turn off heat. Uncover and let jars stand in canner for 5 minutes. Lift up rack. With canning tongs, transfer jars to cooling rack; let cool for 24 hours.

MAKES ABOUT 7 CUPS. PER ½ CUP: about 105 cal, 1 g pro, trace total fat (0 g sat. fat), 24 g carb, 2 g fibre, 0 mg chol, 2 mg sodium. % RDI: 1% calcium, 4% iron, 17% vit A, 10% vit C, 2% folate.

tip
Don't have a vanilla bean? Add 2 tsp vanilla to the boiled syrup.

Chutneys, Salsas & Conserves

Spiced Peaches

Enjoy peach season long after summer is over. Choose ripe, firm blush-red peaches for vibrant-looking syrup. The lemon mixture prevents the peaches from discolouring.

½ cup freshly squeezed **lemon juice**

8 large or 12 small **fresh peaches** (3½ lb/1.5 kg)

3¼ cups **granulated sugar**

6 **dried red hot peppers**

4 **whole cloves**

2 **cinnamon sticks,** broken in pieces

2 **whole star anise**

4 strips **orange zest**

4 slices **fresh ginger**

In large bowl, mix 6 cups water with ¼ cup of the lemon juice to make acidulated water.

With sharp knife, score X into bottom of each peach. In saucepan of boiling water, blanch each peach for 30 seconds. Transfer to cold water; peel off skin. Transfer peach to acidulated water.

In large Dutch oven, bring remaining lemon juice, 5 cups water and sugar to boil. Add hot peppers, cloves, cinnamon, star anise, orange zest and ginger; boil for 4 minutes.

Quarter large peaches or halve small peaches. Add to pan; cook over medium heat, in 2 batches, until tender-firm, about 3 minutes.

Remove peaches with slotted spoon; tightly pack into 6 hot 2-cup (500 mL) canning jars to within ¾ inch (2 cm) of rim.

Strain syrup; divide spices among jars. Divide syrup among jars, leaving ½-inch (1 cm) headspace. Cover with prepared discs. Screw on bands until resistance is met; increase to fingertip tight. Boil in boiling water canner for 10 minutes. (See Canning Basics, page 10.)

Turn off heat. Uncover; let stand in canner for 5 minutes. Lift up rack. With canning tongs, transfer jars to cooling rack; let cool for 24 hours.

MAKES SIX 2-CUP (500 mL) JARS.
PER QUARTER PEACH: about 45 cal, trace pro, 0 g total fat (0 g sat. fat), 11 g carb, 1 g fibre, 0 mg chol, 1 mg sodium. % RDI: 1% iron, 1% vit A, 3% vit C.

Variation
Spiced Pears: Replace peaches with 5 lb (2.25 kg) small pears, such as Anjou or Bartlett. Peel, core and quarter before cooking in sugar syrup for 5 minutes.

MAKES FIVE 2-CUP (500 mL) JARS.

Spirited Peaches

Sweet peaches with a hint of rum make a scrumptious adults-only dessert over ice cream or waffles. For a twist, add a cinnamon stick to the syrup.

¾ cup **granulated sugar**

8 cups sliced peeled **fresh peaches**

⅔ cup **amber rum** or dark rum

In large saucepan, bring 1½ cups water and sugar to boil. Add peaches; boil gently for 5 minutes.

Pack peaches into hot 1-cup (250 mL) canning jars to within ¾ inch (2 cm) of rim. Divide rum among jars.

Return syrup to boil; divide among jars to cover peaches, leaving ¼-inch (5 mm) headspace. Remove any air bubbles.

Cover with prepared discs. Screw on bands until resistance is met; increase to fingertip tight. Boil in boiling water canner for 20 minutes. (See Canning Basics, page 10.)

Turn off heat. Uncover and let jars stand in canner for 5 minutes. Lift up rack. With canning tongs, transfer jars to cooling rack; let cool for 24 hours.

MAKES ABOUT 7 CUPS. PER ¼ CUP: about 52 cal, trace pro, 0 g total fat (0 g sat. fat), 11 g carb, 1 g fibre, 0 mg chol, 0 mg sodium. % RDI: 1% iron, 2% vit A, 3% vit C.

Variation

Grape Peaches: Substitute white grape juice for the amber rum.

Preserved Lemons

Preserved lemons usually take a month to soften to tangy perfection. This quicker method yields similar results in just five days. Use thin-skinned lemons, preferably organic or Meyer, for the best texture and floral flavour.

4 **lemons**

¼ cup **coarse sea salt**

With brush, scrub lemons in warm soapy water; rinse well and pat dry.

With paring knife, make eight 2-inch (5 cm) long cuts lengthwise around each lemon, cutting just to but not through membrane.

In saucepan, bring 4 cups water, lemons and salt to boil, covered; reduce heat and simmer until peels soften, about 15 minutes. Remove from heat and let cool to room temperature.

Pack lemons into sterilized 4-cup (1 L) canning jar; pour in cooking liquid. Seal tightly; shake gently. Let stand for 5 days at room temperature.

Rinse before using. After opening, refrigerate lemons for up to 1 week.

MAKES 4 LEMONS. PER QUARTER LEMON: about 5 cal, trace pro, trace total fat (0 g sat. fat), 3 g carb, 1 g fibre, 0 mg chol, 494 mg sodium, 39 mg potassium. % RDI: 2% calcium, 1% iron, 33% vit C.

tip

Sterilizing the jar ensures that it is free of bacteria and mould. This allows you to store the lemons at room temperature without processing them in a boiling water canner. To sterilize, submerge the jar in boiling water in a large canning pot and boil for 10 minutes. Leave it in the water and dry just before you're ready to fill it.

Chutneys, Salsas & Conserves

Spiced Pears

Deliciously scented with warm spices, these sweet pickled pears are as beautiful as they are tasty. Try the variation, vinegar-free Riesling Pears (below), as a simple dessert with a dollop of crème fraîche or whipped cream.

2 **cinnamon sticks,** broken in thirds

1 tbsp **whole cloves**

3 thick slices **fresh ginger**

2⅔ cups **granulated sugar**

1⅓ cups **white vinegar**

½ cup freshly squeezed **lemon juice**

16 **small firm ripe fresh pears** (about 4 lb/1.8 kg)

Tie cinnamon, cloves and ginger in square of double-thickness cheesecloth to form bag. In Dutch oven, bring spice bag, sugar, 2 cups water and vinegar to boil. Boil for 5 minutes. Set aside.

In large bowl, stir lemon juice with 6 cups water to make acidulated water. Peel and halve pears; with melon baller or teaspoon, scoop out cores, adding each pear to acidulated water as you work.

Drain pears; add to pan. Bring to boil; cover with round of parchment paper. Reduce heat and simmer until pears are slightly translucent and barely tender, 5 minutes. Discard spice bag.

Pack pears into 5 hot 2-cup (500 mL) canning jars; divide syrup among jars, leaving ½-inch (1 cm) headspace. Remove any air bubbles.

Cover with prepared discs. Screw on bands until

resistance is met; increase to fingertip tight. Boil in boiling water canner for 20 minutes. (See Canning Basics, page 10.)

Turn off heat. Uncover and let jars stand in canner for 5 minutes. Lift up rack. With canning tongs, transfer jars to cooling rack; let cool for 24 hours.

MAKES FIVE 2-CUP (500 mL) JARS.
PER PEAR: about 104 cal, trace pro, trace total fat (0 g sat. fat), 27 g carb, 2 g fibre, 0 mg chol, 1 mg sodium. % RDI: 1% calcium, 1% iron, 5% vit C, 2% folate.

Variation

Riesling Pears: Omit spice bag and vinegar; reduce sugar to 1½ cups. Bring 3 cups Riesling wine, sugar, 1½ cups water, 1 strip each lemon and orange zest, and 1 cinnamon stick to boil. Boil for 5 minutes before adding pears. Discard zest and cinnamon. If desired, add 1 tbsp brandy to each jar before filling with pears.

Chutneys, Salsas & Conserves

Brandied Sweet Cherries

These gourmet delights are delicious on ice cream, pudding or cake. You can sip the leftover brandy as a cordial or use it as a flavouring in baking.

7 cups **fresh sweet cherries**

1 cup **granulated sugar**

1 bottle (750 mL) **brandy**

Snip off top half of each cherry stem; with toothpick, prick each cherry 2 or 3 times.

In each of 7 sterilized 1-cup (250 mL) canning jars, place 1 cup cherries and rounded 2 tbsp sugar; pour in brandy to cover cherries.

Seal jars tightly. Shake gently to dissolve sugar; let stand for 24 hours, shaking occasionally.

Store jars in cool dark place, turning periodically, for 2 months before opening.

MAKES 7 CUPS. PER ¼ CUP: about 107 cal, trace pro, trace total fat (trace sat. fat), 12 g carb, trace fibre, 0 mg chol, 0 mg sodium. % RDI: 1% iron, 1% vit A, 3% vit C.

tip

Jars that will be boiled in a boiling water canner for 10 minutes or more don't need to be sterilized. But because these cherries aren't processed (and are stored at room temperature), it's a good idea to sterilize the jars before filling them to be sure they're free of bacteria. Simply submerge the jars in boiling water in a large canning pot and boil for 10 minutes. Leave them in the water and dry them just before you're ready to fill them.

Chutneys, Salsas & Conserves

Preserved Tart Cherries in Syrup

The season for tart cherries is short, so use easier-to-find frozen cherries and preserve them to enjoy throughout the winter. Use these in your favourite pie or tart filling, or on a Black Forest cake. Or thicken them into a sundae sauce.

3½ cups **granulated sugar**

7 lb (3.15 kg) **unsweetened individually quick frozen (IQF) pitted tart cherries,** thawed

In saucepan, stir sugar with 5½ cups water. Bring to boil over medium heat, stirring until sugar is dissolved. Reduce heat to low; cover and keep syrup hot.

Pour ½ cup of the syrup into each of 7 hot 2-cup (500 mL) canning jars. Pack about 1⅔ cups cherries into each jar to within 1 inch (2.5 cm) of rim, shaking gently to help cherries settle.

Divide remaining syrup among jars to cover cherries, leaving ½-inch (1 cm) headspace. Remove any air bubbles.

Cover with prepared discs. Screw on bands until resistance is met; increase to fingertip tight. Boil in boiling water canner for 25 minutes. (See Canning Basics, page 10.)

Turn off heat. Uncover and let jars stand in canner for 5 minutes. Lift up rack. With canning tongs, transfer jars to cooling rack; let cool for 24 hours.

MAKES SEVEN 2-CUP (500 mL) JARS.
PER ¼ CUP: about 77 cal, 1 g pro, trace total fat (0 g sat. fat), 19 g carb, 1 g fibre, 0 mg chol, 2 mg sodium, 98 mg potassium. % RDI: 1% calcium, 1% iron, 5% vit A, 7% vit C, 1% folate.

tips

• Let the cherries thaw in a colander set over a bowl to capture juice. You can use up to 2½ cups of this juice in place of an equal amount of the water called for to make the syrup. Add the thawed cherries to the syrup and return to boil, stirring, before filling the jars.

• Fresh cherries have a much larger volume than thawed frozen ones. If you want to use fresh for this recipe, either cut the initial amount of cherries or make a double batch of syrup. The final yield will vary.

Classic Mincemeat

You can make this freezable, old-fashioned fruit mixture with suet or butter, as you prefer. It makes the most delicious holiday pies and tarts (see opposite).

6 **Golden Delicious apples,** peeled and grated (about 5 cups)

2 cups **raisins**

2 cups **seeded lexia raisins**

2 cups **dried currants**

1¾ cups packed **brown sugar**

1½ cups shredded **suet** (or ½ cup butter, softened)

1 cup **candied mixed peel**

¼ cup grated **lemon zest**

¾ cup freshly squeezed **lemon juice**

¾ cup **apple cider** or apple juice

2 tsp each **cinnamon** and **nutmeg**

1 tsp each **ground cloves, ground allspice** and **salt**

½ cup **rum** or brandy

In Dutch oven, combine apples, raisins, lexia raisins, currants, brown sugar, suet, mixed peel, lemon zest, lemon juice, cider, cinnamon, nutmeg, cloves, allspice and salt; bring to boil.

Reduce heat and simmer until thickened and syrupy, about 45 minutes. Stir in rum; let cool.

Fill airtight containers; seal with lids. Refrigerate for up to 3 weeks or freeze for up to 3 months.

MAKES ABOUT 12 CUPS. PER ¼ CUP: about 141 cal, 1 g pro, 4 g total fat (2 g sat. fat), 29 g carb, 2 g fibre, 2 mg chol, 58 mg sodium. % RDI: 2% calcium, 6% iron, 7% vit C, 1% folate.

Chutneys, Salsas & Conserves

Mincemeat Pie

There's no better way to serve mincemeat than in a flaky, hot-from-the-oven pie. The tart variation provides the ideal opportunity to bake special treats for gifts.

3 cups **all-purpose flour**

1 tsp **salt**

½ cup cold **butter,** cubed

½ cup cold **shortening,** cubed

1 **egg**

2 tsp **white vinegar** or lemon juice

Ice water

1 **egg yolk**

2 tsp **granulated sugar**

FILLING:

1 **apple,** peeled and grated

3½ cups **Classic Mincemeat** (opposite)

In bowl, mix flour with salt. Using pastry blender or 2 knives, cut in butter and shortening until mixture is in fine crumbs with a few larger pieces.

In liquid measure, whisk egg with vinegar; whisk in enough ice water to make ⅔ cup. Drizzle over flour mixture, stirring briskly with fork until pastry holds together. Press into 2 discs. Wrap in plastic wrap and refrigerate for 30 minutes. *(Make-ahead: Refrigerate for up to 3 days or freeze for up to 3 months. Let thawed pastry stand at room temperature for 15 minutes before rolling out.)*

On lightly floured surface, roll out 1 disc pastry to fit 9-inch (23 cm) pie plate; fit into plate.

FILLING: Stir apple into mincemeat; scrape into pie shell. Roll out remaining pastry and fit over top; trim and flute edge.

Whisk egg yolk with 1 tbsp water; brush over pastry. Sprinkle with sugar. Cut steam vents in top. Bake in bottom third of 400°F (200°C) oven until golden, 50 to 60 minutes.

MAKES 8 TO 10 SERVINGS. PER EACH OF 10 SERVINGS: about 525 cal, 6 g pro, 25 g total fat (11 g sat. fat), 70 g carb, 4 g fibre, 65 mg chol, 418 mg sodium. % RDI: 4% calcium, 19% iron, 10% vit A, 10% vit C, 22% folate.

Variation

Mincemeat Tarts: Roll out each half of pastry to ⅛-inch (3 mm) thickness. Using 3½-inch (9 cm) round cutter, cut out 30 circles. Using smaller decorative cutters (such as stars), cut out 30 shapes from remaining pastry, rerolling scraps. Fit circles into 2¼-inch (5.5 cm) tart cups; fill each with 1 tbsp filling. Top with cutouts and glaze as above. Refrigerate for 30 minutes. Reduce baking time to 20 minutes.

MAKES 30 TARTS.

Chutneys, Salsas & Conserves

chapter six

Sauces, Syrups & Vinegars

Freezer Tomato Sauce

The acidity level of tomatoes is at the edge of what's safe to process at home in a boiling water canner. This sauce has excellent tomato flavour and waits patiently in the freezer. Use it as is, or as the base of a more complex sauce.

10 lb (4.5 kg) **plum tomatoes** (about 80)

2½ cups chopped **onions**

3 cloves **garlic,** chopped

2 **bay leaves**

1 tbsp **granulated sugar**

1 tbsp **dried basil**

1 tbsp **dried marjoram**

2 tsp **salt**

1 tsp **pepper**

½ tsp **hot pepper flakes**

Core and coarsely chop tomatoes to make about 28 cups. In very large heavy Dutch oven, combine tomatoes, onions, garlic, bay leaves, sugar, basil, marjoram, salt, pepper and hot pepper flakes; bring to boil, stirring often to prevent scorching.

Reduce heat and simmer, stirring occasionally, until thick enough to stand wooden spoon in sauce, about 2 hours. Discard bay leaves. Press through fine disc of food mill or large fine-mesh sieve to remove seeds and skins.

Let tomato mixture cool; fill airtight containers, leaving ½-inch (1 cm) headspace. Seal with lids; freeze for up to 6 months.

MAKES ABOUT 15 CUPS. PER ¼ CUP: about 18 cal, 1 g pro, trace total fat (trace sat. fat), 4 g carb, 1 g fibre, 0 mg chol, 83 mg sodium. % RDI: 1% calcium, 3% iron, 8% vit A, 18% vit C, 3% folate.

Tomato Pizza Sauce

This simple, easy-to-freeze sauce is always ready for an impromptu pizza night. It's stored in small portions because you won't be able to refreeze any leftover defrosted sauce.

1 can (28 oz/796 mL)
  plum tomatoes

2 tbsp **extra-virgin olive oil**

½ cup finely chopped **onion**

2 cloves **garlic,** minced

½ tsp **dried oregano**

½ tsp **red wine vinegar**

¼ tsp each **salt** and **pepper**

Pinch **granulated sugar**

Reserving juice, drain, seed and chop tomatoes. Set aside.

In saucepan, heat oil over medium heat; cook onion, garlic and oregano, stirring occasionally, until onion is translucent, about 4 minutes.

Add tomatoes and reserved juice, vinegar, salt, pepper and sugar; simmer until thickened, 15 to 20 minutes.

Let cool slightly. Transfer to food processor; blend until smooth. Fill ½-cup (125 mL) airtight containers, leaving ½-inch (1 cm) headspace. Seal with lids; freeze for up to 2 months.

MAKES 2 CUPS. PER 1 TBSP: about 13 cal, trace pro, 1 g total fat (trace sat. fat), 1 g carb, trace fibre, 0 mg chol, 49 mg sodium, 50 mg potassium. % RDI: 1% calcium, 2% iron, 5% vit C, 1% folate.

Pizza Dough

The dough for this crisp, airy crust is a dream to work, especially after 24 hours, because the gluten is relaxed, making it easy to roll.

3 cups **all-purpose flour** (approx)

2 tsp **quick-rising** (instant) **dry yeast**

1 tsp **salt**

1¼ cups hot **water** (120°F/50°C)

1 tbsp **extra-virgin olive oil**

In bowl, combine 2¾ cups of the flour, yeast and salt. With wooden spoon, gradually stir in water and oil, using hands if necessary, until ragged dough forms.

Turn dough out onto lightly floured surface; knead until smooth and elastic, about 8 minutes, adding up to ¼ cup more flour, 1 tbsp at a time, if necessary.

Place in greased bowl, turning to grease all over. Cover and let rise in warm draft-free place until doubled in bulk, about 1 hour. (*Make-ahead: Refrigerate unrisen dough and let rise for 24 hours. Or freeze in plastic bag for up to 1 month; let thaw and rise in refrigerator overnight.*)

MAKES ABOUT 1½ LB (675 G) DOUGH, ENOUGH FOR ONE 14-INCH (35 CM) PIZZA BASE.

Variation
Bread Machine Pizza Dough:
Into pan of 2-lb (900 g) machine, place (in order) water, oil, salt, flour and yeast. (Do not let yeast touch liquid.) Choose dough setting.

Basil Pesto

This sauce is the best reason to plant basil in your garden. For convenience, freeze pesto in an ice-cube tray; transfer cubes to a freezer bag and defrost a few when you want to top a pizza or toss together a simple weeknight pasta.

¼ cup **pine nuts**

2 cups packed **fresh basil leaves**

¼ tsp each **salt** and **pepper**

⅓ cup **extra-virgin olive oil**

½ cup grated **Parmesan cheese**

1 clove **garlic,** minced

In dry small skillet, toast pine nuts over medium heat, shaking pan often, until light golden, 3 to 5 minutes. Transfer to food processor; let cool.

Add basil, salt and pepper; finely chop together. With motor running, add oil in thin steady stream until puréed. Pulse in Parmesan cheese and garlic.

Fill airtight container, leaving ½-inch (1 cm) headspace. Seal with lid; refrigerate for up to 3 days or freeze for up to 6 months.

MAKES ABOUT 1 CUP. PER 1 TBSP: about 69 cal, 2 g pro, 7 g total fat (1 g sat. fat), 1 g carb, trace fibre, 3 mg chol, 84 mg sodium, 42 mg potassium. % RDI: 4% calcium, 3% iron, 3% vit A, 2% vit C, 2% folate.

tip

Pine nuts can be pricey and harder to find than other nuts. Walnuts are an excellent substitute, so use them if you prefer. Buy California walnut halves and chop enough to make the ¼ cup called for in this recipe.

Sauces, Syrups & Vinegars

Pumpkin Seed Pesto

High in fibre and rich in flavour, pumpkin seeds make an excellent pesto. Pumpkin seed oil is an Austrian specialty item available at gourmet food shops. It's expensive, but used sparingly, it imparts an intense toasted flavour.

⅓ cup shelled **raw pumpkin seeds** (pepitas)

1 cup lightly packed **fresh cilantro**

½ cup lightly packed **fresh parsley**

2 tbsp **pumpkin seed oil** or extra-virgin olive oil

2 tbsp freshly squeezed **lime juice**

1 clove **garlic,** minced

1 **small red hot pepper** or green hot pepper (optional), coarsely chopped

¼ tsp **salt**

In dry skillet over medium heat, toast pumpkin seeds, shaking pan often, until popping starts to subside and seeds are golden, about 5 minutes.

Transfer to food processor; add cilantro, parsley, ¼ cup water, oil, lime juice, garlic, hot pepper (if using) and salt. Purée until smooth, adding up to 2 tbsp more water, if necessary, to make thick sauce.

Fill airtight container, leaving ½-inch (1 cm) headspace. Seal with lid; refrigerate for up to 3 days or freeze for up to 6 months.

MAKES ⅔ CUP. PER 1 TBSP: about 48 cal, 1 g pro, 5 g total fat (1 g sat. fat), 1 g carb, trace fibre, 0 mg chol, 57 mg sodium, 63 mg potassium. % RDI: 1% calcium, 6% iron, 4% vit A, 8% vit C, 4% folate.

tip

This pesto is particularly delicious on grilled or broiled fish (opposite) but it also makes a tasty vegan sauce for whole wheat pasta.

Broiled Fish With Pumpkin Seed Pesto

Any firm-fleshed fish, such as halibut, salmon or tilapia, tastes terrific with this nutty, seed-based pesto.

1½ lb (675 g) **firm-fleshed fish fillets**

1 tbsp **pumpkin seed oil** or extra-virgin olive oil

¼ tsp **salt**

Pumpkin Seed Pesto (opposite)

1 tbsp shelled **raw pumpkin seeds** (pepitas)

Lime wedges

Arrange fish on baking sheet. Brush with pumpkin seed oil; sprinkle with salt.

Broil, turning once, until fish flakes easily when tested, 6 to 8 minutes.

Stir pesto; drizzle over fish. Sprinkle with pumpkin seeds. Serve with lime wedges.

MAKES 4 SERVINGS. PER SERVING: about 395 cal, 43 g pro, 23 g total fat (3 g sat. fat), 5 g carb, 3 g fibre, 54 mg chol, 389 mg sodium. % RDI: 10% calcium, 37% iron, 14% vit A, 23% vit C, 20% folate.

Sun-Dried Tomato Pesto

Sun-dried tomatoes give this pesto a rich, savoury-sweet taste. Try it on sandwiches, pizzas and burgers.

¼ cup **pine nuts**

½ cup **dry-packed sun-dried tomatoes**

3 tbsp **tomato paste**

¼ tsp **pepper**

Pinch **salt**

⅓ cup **extra-virgin olive oil**

¼ cup grated **Parmesan cheese**

1 clove **garlic,** minced

In dry small skillet, toast pine nuts over medium heat, shaking pan often, until light golden, 3 to 5 minutes. Transfer to food processor; let cool.

In heatproof bowl, cover sun-dried tomatoes with ½ cup boiling water; soak until softened, about 10 minutes. Reserving 2 tbsp soaking liquid, drain.

Add tomatoes, reserved soaking liquid, tomato paste, pepper and salt to food processor; finely chop.

With motor running, add oil in thin steady stream until puréed. Pulse in Parmesan cheese and garlic.

Fill airtight container, leaving ½-inch (1 cm) headspace. Seal with lid; refrigerate for up to 5 days or freeze for up to 6 months.

MAKES ABOUT 1 CUP. PER 1 TBSP: about 69 cal, 1 g pro, 7 g total fat (1 g sat. fat), 2 g carb, 1 g fibre, 1 mg chol, 69 mg sodium, 115 mg potassium. % RDI: 2% calcium, 3% iron, 1% vit A, 2% vit C, 1% folate.

Taco Sauce

Commercial taco sauce can be extremely high in sodium. This homemade canned version is just as tasty without as much salt. Keep it on hand for fun family taco nights.

16 cups coarsely chopped **tomatoes**

1 cup chopped **onions**

1 cup **cider vinegar**

2 cloves **garlic,** minced

½ cup **granulated sugar**

2 tbsp **chili powder**

1 tsp **salt**

1 tsp **ground cumin**

½ tsp **cayenne pepper**

In large saucepan, combine tomatoes, onions, vinegar and garlic; bring to boil. Reduce heat, cover and simmer until very tender, about 1 hour.

Press through fine disc of food mill or fine-mesh sieve into clean saucepan. Stir in sugar, chili powder, salt, cumin and cayenne pepper; bring to boil. Reduce heat and simmer, stirring often, until thick enough to coat spoon, about 25 minutes.

Fill hot 2-cup (500 mL) canning jars, leaving ½-inch (1 cm) headspace. Cover with prepared discs. Screw on bands until resistance is met; increase to fingertip tight. Boil in boiling water canner for 30 minutes. (See Canning Basics, page 10.)

Turn off heat. Uncover and let jars stand in canner for 5 minutes. Lift up rack. With canning tongs, transfer jars to cooling rack; let cool for 24 hours.

MAKES ABOUT 8 CUPS. PER 1 TBSP: about 8 cal, trace pro, trace total fat (0 g sat. fat), 2 g carb, trace fibre, 0 mg chol, 20 mg sodium, 60 mg potassium. % RDI: 1% iron, 2% vit A, 5% vit C, 1% folate.

Smoky Barbecue Sauce

This simple barbecue sauce makes a tasty glaze, not only on ribs, but also on chicken, steak, pork chops and burgers. It keeps for two weeks in the fridge, so make a double batch during barbecue season.

1 tbsp **vegetable oil**

1 **small onion,** finely chopped

2 cloves **garlic,** minced

1 tbsp **smoked paprika**

1 tsp **dry mustard**

¼ tsp **salt**

1 cup **ketchup** or chili sauce

2 tbsp packed **brown sugar**

2 tbsp **cider vinegar**

In saucepan, heat oil over medium heat; fry onion, garlic, paprika, mustard and salt, stirring occasionally, until onion is softened, about 3 minutes.

Stir in ketchup, ½ cup water, sugar and vinegar; bring to boil. Reduce heat and simmer until sauce is consistency of thick ketchup, about 20 minutes.

In food processor or blender, purée sauce until smooth. Fill airtight container, leaving ½-inch (1 cm) headspace. Seal with lid; refrigerate for up to 2 weeks.

MAKES ABOUT 1¼ CUPS. PER 1 TBSP: about 24 cal, trace pro, 1 g total fat (0 g sat. fat), 5 g carb, trace fibre, 0 mg chol, 159 mg sodium. % RDI: 1% iron, 3% vit A, 3% vit C, 1% folate.

Variation

Smoky Red Wine Barbecue Sauce: Substitute ½ cup red wine for the water.

Rhubarbecue Sauce

Tart rhubarb adds its tantalizing tang to this sweet barbecue sauce. And, with frozen rhubarb, you can make this sauce any time of year and freeze it for later.

2 cups chopped **rhubarb**

1 cup **ketchup**

1 **onion,** chopped

2 cloves **garlic,** minced

¼ cup packed **brown sugar**

2 tbsp **Dijon mustard**

1 tbsp **cider vinegar**

2 tsp **Worcestershire sauce**

¼ tsp **salt**

¼ tsp **hot pepper sauce**

In large saucepan, bring rhubarb, ketchup, ½ cup water, onion, garlic, brown sugar, mustard, vinegar, Worcestershire sauce, salt and hot pepper sauce to boil. Reduce heat and simmer, stirring often, until rhubarb is tender, about 20 minutes.

Transfer to blender or food processor; purée until smooth. Let cool.

Fill airtight container, leaving ½-inch (1 cm) headspace. Seal with lid; refrigerate for up to 1 week or freeze for up to 1 month.

MAKES 2½ CUPS. PER 1 TBSP: about 16 cal, trace pro, 0 g total fat (0 g sat. fat), 4 g carb, trace fibre, 0 mg chol, 109 mg sodium. % RDI: 1% calcium, 1% iron, 1% vit A, 2% vit C.

Sweet-and-Sour Barbecue Sauce

This classic barbecue sauce is so flavourful you won't even notice that it has no added salt. It's great on pork, chicken or beef.

2 tbsp **vegetable oil**

1 **onion,** diced

2 cloves **garlic,** minced

1 can (28 oz/796 mL) **diced tomatoes**

1 can (8 oz/227 mL) **pineapple tidbits,** drained

⅓ cup **cider vinegar**

¼ cup **cooking molasses**

3 tbsp packed **brown sugar**

3 tbsp **tomato paste**

1 tbsp **Dijon mustard**

2 tsp **sweet paprika**

1 tsp **dried oregano**

½ tsp **chipotle chili powder** or chili powder

½ tsp **pepper**

In large saucepan, heat oil over medium heat; fry onion, stirring, until golden, about 10 minutes.

Add garlic; cook, stirring, until fragrant, about 1 minute.

Add tomatoes, pineapple, vinegar, molasses, brown sugar, tomato paste, mustard, paprika, oregano, chili powder and pepper; bring to boil. Reduce heat and simmer, stirring occasionally, until sauce is thickened, about 2 hours. Let cool slightly.

In blender, purée sauce, in batches, until smooth. Let cool.

Fill airtight containers, leaving ½-inch (1 cm) headspace. Seal with lids; refrigerate for up to 1 week or freeze for up to 2 months.

MAKES ABOUT 3 CUPS. PER 1 TBSP: about 21 cal, trace pro, 1 g total fat (trace sat. fat), 4 g carb, trace fibre, 0 mg chol, 28 mg sodium. % RDI: 1% calcium, 3% iron, 1% vit A, 5% vit C, 1% folate.

Sauces, Syrups & Vinegars

Grainy Mustard

This rustic-looking blend of partially ground beer-infused mustard seeds is delicious on sandwiches, sausages and just about everything in between.

¼ cup each **yellow mustard seeds** and **brown mustard seeds**

¾ cup **beer** or water

1 tbsp **dry mustard**

¼ tsp **turmeric**

½ cup **cider vinegar**

1 tsp **granulated sugar**

1 tsp **salt**

In glass bowl, combine yellow and brown mustard seeds and beer; let seeds soak overnight.

Stir in dry mustard and turmeric; let stand for 20 minutes. Scrape into food processor along with vinegar, sugar and salt; process until smooth with some seeds remaining.

Fill 2-cup (500 mL) canning jar. Seal with lid; refrigerate for 4 days before opening.

Refrigerate for up to 2 weeks.

MAKES 2 CUPS. PER 1 TBSP: about 10 cal, trace pro, trace total fat (0 g sat. fat), 1 g carb, trace fibre, 0 mg chol, 72 mg sodium. % RDI: 1% calcium, 1% iron.

Sweet and Hot Maple Mustard

Give this to the sandwich lover in your life. For a gift, include it in a basket with other tasty sandwich fixings: pickles, hot peppers and assorted breads and cheeses.

1 cup **dry mustard**

½ cup packed **brown sugar**

½ cup **maple syrup**

⅓ cup **vegetable oil**

3 tbsp **cider vinegar**

½ tsp **salt**

2 tbsp boiling **water**

In food processor or blender, blend together mustard, sugar, maple syrup, oil, vinegar and salt until smooth. With motor running, add water, scraping down side of bowl as necessary.

Scrape into sterilized decorative jars. (See Tip, page 268.) Seal with lids. Use immediately for hot mustard or store at room temperature for 2 weeks before using for mild mustard.

Store at room temperature for up to 6 months.

MAKES 1½ CUPS. PER 1 TBSP: about 78 cal, 1 g pro, 4 g total fat (trace sat. fat), 9 g carb, 0 g fibre, 0 mg chol, 50 mg sodium. % RDI: 2% calcium, 3% iron, 2% vit C.

Sauces, Syrups & Vinegars

Hot Honey Mustard

This spicy mustard mellows as it ages, so use it right away if you like it hot. For a milder result, let the jars stand in the fridge for a couple of weeks before opening.

1 cup **dry mustard**

¼ cup cold **water**

½ cup **granulated sugar**

½ cup **liquid honey**

¼ cup **cider vinegar**

3 tbsp **canola oil**

½ tsp **kosher salt**

½ tsp freshly squeezed **lemon juice**

In food processor, whirl mustard with water, scraping down side and bottom of bowl once, until thick smooth paste forms.

Add sugar, honey, vinegar, oil, salt and lemon juice. Whirl, scraping down side and bottom of bowl once, until smooth, about 1 minute.

Scrape into hot sterilized ½-cup (125 mL) canning jars. (See Tip, below.) Seal with lids; let cool.

Store in refrigerator for up to 6 months.

MAKES 2 CUPS. PER 1 TSP: about 18 cal, trace pro, 1 g total fat (0 g sat. fat), 3 g carb, 0 g fibre, 0 mg chol, 8 mg sodium, 7 mg potassium. % RDI: 1% iron.

tip

Sterilizing the jars ensures that they are free of bacteria and mould. This allows you to store the mustard for a long time in the fridge without processing the jars in a boiling water canner. To sterilize, simply submerge the jars in boiling water in a large canning pot and boil for 10 minutes. Leave them in the water and dry them just before you're ready to fill them.

Sauces, Syrups & Vinegars

Korean Marinade

This salty-sweet marinade is the flavour base for many Korean-style meat dishes. It's particularly tasty on beef, such as Korean Beef Short Ribs (opposite).

1 **small apple,** sliced

1 **small onion,** thinly sliced

2 cups **soy sauce**

1 cup **granulated sugar**

½ cup **sake** or dry sherry

½ cup **mirin** (Japanese sweet rice wine)

1 piece (1 inch/2.5 cm) **fresh ginger,** thinly sliced

5 cloves **garlic,** thinly sliced

15 **black peppercorns**

In saucepan, bring apple, onion, soy sauce, sugar, sake, mirin, ginger, garlic and peppercorns to boil. Reduce heat and simmer until reduced by half, about 40 minutes.

Cover and refrigerate for 12 hours. Strain through fine sieve into airtight container. Seal with lid; refrigerate for up to 2 weeks.

MAKES 2 CUPS. PER ¼ CUP: about 162 cal, 4 g pro, trace total fat (0 g sat. fat), 35 g carb, 0 g fibre, 0 mg chol, 4,126 mg sodium. % RDI: 2% calcium, 12% iron, 3% vit C, 6% folate.

tip

If you don't have mirin, you can increase the sake to ¾ cup and add ¼ cup corn syrup.

Korean Beef Short Ribs

Beef short ribs are a tough but intensely flavourful cut of meat favoured by many Korean cooks. You only need half a batch of the marinade, so try the rest on pork or lamb ribs or chops, or use it to baste beef or lamb kabobs.

3 lb (1.35 kg) **lean beef simmering short ribs,** trimmed

1 cup **Korean Marinade** (opposite)

Place beef ribs in large shallow glass baking dish; pour marinade over top, turning to coat.

Cover and marinate in refrigerator for 4 hours, turning occasionally. *(Make-ahead: Marinate for up to 48 hours, turning occasionally.)*

Bake, covered, in 350°F (180°C) oven, turning once, until tender, about 1 hour.

MAKES 4 SERVINGS. PER SERVING: about 655 cal, 39 g pro, 38 g total fat (16 g sat. fat), 36 g carb, 1 g fibre, 105 mg chol, 4,213 mg sodium. % RDI: 5% calcium, 33% iron, 3% vit C, 10% folate.

Thai Sauce

Here is a gingery, spicy sauce for marinating and basting meat or poultry, or for stir-frying. It keeps well in the fridge, so make lots.

⅔ cup **corn syrup**

½ cup **unseasoned rice vinegar** or cider vinegar

¼ cup grated **fresh ginger**

4 cloves **garlic,** sliced

½ tsp **hot pepper sauce**

1 tbsp **cornstarch**

¼ cup **soy sauce**

2 tbsp **sesame oil**

In saucepan, bring corn syrup, vinegar, ⅓ cup water, ginger, garlic and hot pepper sauce to boil. Reduce heat and simmer, stirring, for 1 minute.

Dissolve cornstarch in 1 tbsp water; stir into pan. Bring to boil; boil until thickened, about 1 minute.

Remove from heat. Stir in soy sauce and sesame oil; let cool.

Strain into 2-cup (500 mL) canning jar. Seal with lid; refrigerate for up to 2 weeks.

MAKES 1¼ CUPS. PER 1 TBSP: about 50 cal, trace pro, 1 g total fat (trace sat. fat), 9 g carb, 0 g fibre, 0 mg chol, 174 mg sodium. % RDI: 1% calcium, 4% iron.

Hot Pepper Sauce

Fresh red hot peppers make a wonderful homemade hot sauce. The sauce can separate as it stands, so shake it before using. Transfer a small amount to a shaker bottle to keep on hand for sprinkling over pizza, wings and more.

1¾ cups stemmed **Thai bird's-eye peppers**

1½ cups chopped **sweet red peppers**

2 tbsp **pickling salt,** kosher salt or noniodized sea salt

1 tbsp **mustard seeds**

1½ tsp **coriander seeds**

1 tsp crumbled **mace blades**

½ tsp **cumin seeds**

1¾ cups **white vinegar**

2 tbsp **fish sauce** (optional)

1 tsp **granulated sugar**

2 tbsp **all-purpose flour**

In food processor, purée together Thai bird's-eye peppers, sweet red peppers and salt until paste forms. Stir in 1 cup water.

In saucepan over low heat, toast mustard seeds, coriander seeds, mace and cumin seeds until fragrant, about 4 minutes. Stir in hot pepper mixture, vinegar, fish sauce (if using), and sugar; bring to boil. Reduce heat, cover and simmer for 40 minutes.

Strain through fine sieve into clean saucepan; discard solids. Whisk flour with 2 tbsp water. Whisk into hot pepper mixture; bring to boil. Boil until slightly thickened, about 2 minutes. Strain.

Fill hot ½-cup (125 mL) canning jars, leaving ½-inch (1 cm) headspace. Cover with prepared discs. Screw on bands until resistance is met; increase to fingertip tight. Boil in boiling water canner for 10 minutes. (See Canning Basics, page 10.)

Turn off heat. Uncover and let jars stand in canner for 5 minutes. Lift up rack. With canning tongs, transfer jars to cooling rack; let cool for 24 hours.

MAKES ABOUT 2 CUPS. PER 1 TBSP: about 11 cal, trace pro, trace total fat (0 g sat. fat), 2 g carb, trace fibre, 0 mg chol, 292 mg sodium, 45 mg potassium. % RDI: 1% iron, 3% vit A, 37% vit C, 2% folate.

tips

• For a fiery Caribbean-style sauce, substitute coarsely chopped red Scotch bonnet or habanero peppers for the Thai bird's-eye peppers. For a tamer sauce, try red finger hot peppers.

• If you can't find mace blades, you can substitute one-quarter whole nutmeg, smashed into small pieces with side of knife.

Sauces, Syrups & Vinegars

Chili Garlic Sauce

This Asian-inspired sauce is delicious on noodles and in Vietnamese-style soups – or even on pizza and burgers.

3 lb (1.35 kg) **red hot peppers**

4 heads **garlic**

1⅓ cups **unseasoned rice vinegar**

¼ cup **granulated sugar**

2 tbsp + 2 tsp **pickling salt**

Cut hot peppers lengthwise; remove seeds. Chop peppers coarsely. Separate garlic into cloves and peel; cut off tough, woody base of each clove. Smash garlic.

In batches in food processor, pulse hot peppers with garlic until minced (do not purée).

Scrape into saucepan; stir in vinegar, sugar and salt. Bring to boil; reduce heat to medium and simmer, uncovered, until mixture tastes cooked and is slightly thickened, about 15 minutes.

Fill hot 1-cup (250 mL) canning jars, leaving ¼-inch (5 mm) headspace. Remove any air bubbles.

Cover with prepared discs. Screw on bands until resistance is met; increase to fingertip tight. Boil in boiling water canner for 15 minutes. (See Canning Basics, page 10.)

Turn off heat. Uncover and let jars stand in canner for 5 minutes. Lift up rack. With canning tongs, transfer jars to cooling rack; let cool for 24 hours.

MAKES 7¾ CUPS. PER 1 TBSP: about 7 cal, trace pro, 0 g total fat (0 g sat. fat), 2 g carb, trace fibre, 0 mg chol, 101 mg sodium, 31 mg potassium. % RDI: 1% iron, 1% vit A, 17% vit C, 1% folate.

tips

• This sauce is wonderful made with crimson hot or shepherd peppers. If you want to boost the heat, add six to 10 red Scotch bonnet or habanero peppers, or 20 to 30 Thai bird's-eye peppers. If you use cayenne or red finger hot peppers, they should be hot enough on their own.

• If you have any sauce left over when filling the jars, let it cool, then refrigerate and use within one month.

Banana Pepper Hot Sauce

Banana peppers taste only moderately hot, but this fruity sauce becomes quite spicy when the peppers are cooked with their seeds and membranes. For a milder sauce, seed the peppers first.

3 lb (1.35 kg) **hot banana peppers,** sliced

2 **large white onions,** chopped

2 cups sliced quartered **apples** (unpeeled and uncored)

2 cups **cider vinegar**

⅓ cup **mustard seeds**

3 tbsp minced **garlic**

2 tbsp **salt**

1 tbsp **mace blades**

¾ tsp **turmeric**

In large saucepan, bring banana peppers, onions, apples, vinegar, mustard seeds, garlic, salt, mace and turmeric to boil; reduce heat, cover and simmer over medium-low heat, stirring occasionally, about 1 hour.

Press through fine disc of food mill or, in batches, through fine-mesh sieve.

Fill 7 hot 2-cup (500 mL) canning jars, leaving ½-inch (1 cm) headspace. Cover with prepared discs. Screw on bands until resistance is met; increase to fingertip tight. Boil in boiling water canner for 15 minutes. (See Canning Basics, page 10.)

Turn off heat. Uncover and let jars stand in canner for 5 minutes. Lift up rack. With canning tongs, transfer jars to cooling rack; let cool for 24 hours.

Let jars stand for 3 days before opening.

MAKES SEVEN 2-CUP (500 mL) JARS.
PER 1 TBSP: about 4 cal, trace pro, trace total fat (0 g sat. fat), 1 g carb, trace fibre, 0 mg chol, 54 mg sodium, 21 mg potassium. % RDI: 1% iron, 5% vit C, 1% folate.

tips

• A food mill makes short work of straining this sauce; it is much tougher to press it through a sieve.

• If you can't find mace blades, you can substitute three-quarters whole nutmeg, smashed into small pieces with side of knife.

Pawpaw Hot Sauce

Papaya, a.k.a. pawpaw, is the base of this hot sauce, which is used like ketchup in the Caribbean. Decrease the peppers to two for a mild sauce; increase to six if you like it superhot. Careful, though: The heat intensifies with age.

2 **carrots,** chopped

Half **English cucumber,** peeled and seeded

4 **Scotch bonnet (habanero) peppers,** halved and seeded

2 cups chopped **papaya**

½ cup **white vinegar**

2 tsp packed **brown sugar**

½ tsp **salt**

In food processor, pulse carrots with cucumber. Add peppers and papaya; pulse until finely chopped. Scrape into saucepan.

Stir in vinegar, ¼ cup water, brown sugar and salt; bring to boil. Reduce heat and simmer for 30 minutes.

Fill airtight container, leaving ½-inch (1 cm) headspace. Seal with lid; refrigerate for up to 3 weeks.

MAKES 2 CUPS. PER 1 TBSP: about 8 cal, trace pro, 0 g total fat (0 g sat. fat), 2 g carb, trace fibre, 0 mg chol, 39 mg sodium. % RDI: 1% iron, 11% vit A, 12% vit C.

Peach Melba Fruit Sauce

Enjoy the fresh flavours of raspberries and peaches all year long in this sweet dessert sauce. Drizzle it generously over ice cream or cake.

4 cups **fresh raspberries**

2 cups **granulated sugar**

¼ cup **corn syrup**

½ tsp grated **lemon zest**

¼ cup freshly squeezed **lemon juice**

6 cups chopped peeled **fresh peaches** (about 6)

¼ cup **raspberry liqueur** or framboise

In food processor, purée raspberries; press through fine-mesh sieve set over large saucepan. Discard seeds.

Add sugar, 1¼ cups water, corn syrup, lemon zest and lemon juice. Bring to boil over medium-high heat; boil, stirring, for 2 minutes.

Add peaches; return to boil. Reduce heat to medium and cook, stirring often, until thickened, about 15 minutes. Stir in raspberry liqueur.

Fill hot 1-cup (250 mL) canning jars, leaving ¼-inch (5 mm) headspace. Remove any air bubbles.

Cover with prepared discs. Screw on bands until resistance is met; increase to fingertip tight. Boil in boiling water canner for 10 minutes. (See Canning Basics, page 10.)

Turn off heat. Uncover and let jars stand in canner for 5 minutes. Lift up rack. With canning tongs, transfer jars to cooling rack; let cool for 24 hours.

MAKES ABOUT 8 CUPS. PER 1 TBSP: about 18 cal, 0 g pro, 0 g total fat (0 g sat. fat), 4 g carb, 0 g fibre, 0 mg chol, 1 mg sodium. % RDI: 2% vit C

Sauces, Syrups & Vinegars

Cranberry Port Sauce

Preserving is one of the easiest ways to make holiday gifts. Each batch of this Port-laced sauce makes enough for four households to enjoy with a holiday turkey dinner.

2 pkg (each 12 oz/340 g) **fresh cranberries** or frozen cranberries

1¾ cups **granulated sugar**

¾ cup **Port**

In large saucepan, bring cranberries, sugar and 1¾ cups water to boil; boil until berries pop and form sauce, about 7 minutes.

Stir in Port; return to boil. Boil until thickened and sauce darkens and clears, about 2 minutes.

Fill hot 1-cup (250 mL) canning jars, leaving ¼-inch (5 mm) headspace. Remove any air bubbles.

Cover with prepared discs. Screw on bands until resistance is met; increase to fingertip tight. Boil in boiling water canner for 10 minutes. (See Canning Basics, page 10.)

Turn off heat. Uncover and let jars stand in canner for 5 minutes. Lift up rack. With canning tongs, transfer jars to cooling rack; let cool undisturbed for 24 hours.

MAKES ABOUT 4 CUPS. PER 2 TBSP: about 59 cal, trace pro, trace total fat (0 g sat. fat), 14 g carb, 1 g fibre, 0 mg chol, 1 mg sodium. % RDI: 1% iron, 3% vit C.

Sauces, Syrups & Vinegars

Peach Dipping Sauce

This peachy sweet-and-sour take on plum sauce depends on ripe fruit for the best flavour. It's nice with roasted pork, duck or goose; with spring rolls, pakoras or other fried savouries; or alongside pâtés and cheeses.

10 cups chopped peeled **fresh peaches**

1¾ cups **granulated sugar**

1 cup stemmed **fresh red currants** (or ¼ cup freshly squeezed lemon juice)

⅔ cup **cider vinegar**

¾ tsp finely grated **lemon zest**

½ cup freshly squeezed **lemon juice**

20 **black peppercorns**

10 **green cardamom pods,** crushed

3-inch (8 cm) piece **cinnamon stick**

1 tsp **ground ginger**

¾ tsp **salt**

½ tsp **cayenne pepper**

In saucepan, bring peaches, sugar, currants, ¾ cup water, vinegar, lemon zest, lemon juice, peppercorns, cardamom, cinnamon, ginger, salt and cayenne to boil, stirring often. Reduce heat to medium; simmer, uncovered and stirring every 10 minutes, until peaches break down and mixture is consistency of applesauce, about 1¼ hours.

In batches in food processor, purée until smooth. Press through fine disc of food mill or fine-mesh sieve into clean saucepan, pushing through as much of the solids as possible. Return to boil.

Fill hot 1-cup (250 mL) canning jars, leaving ½-inch (1 cm) headspace. Remove any air bubbles.

Cover with prepared discs. Screw on bands until resistance is met; increase to fingertip tight. Boil in boiling water canner for 15 minutes. (See Canning Basics, page 10.)

Turn off heat. Uncover and let jars stand in canner for 5 minutes. Lift up rack. With canning tongs, transfer jars to cooling rack; let cool for 24 hours.

MAKES ABOUT 9 CUPS. PER 1 TBSP: about 14 cal, trace pro, 0 g total fat (0 g sat. fat), 4 g carb, trace fibre, 0 mg chol, 12 mg sodium, 22 mg potassium. % RDI: 2% vit C.

Spiced Whole Cranberry Sauce

This perennial accompaniment to roast turkey has a spiced edge that's also tasty with roast or grilled pork, or roast goose or duck. The star anise gives it a prominent licorice taste, but you can omit it if you prefer.

1 **large orange**

1 **cinnamon stick**

1½-inch (4 cm) piece **fresh ginger,** thinly sliced

8 **whole cloves**

3 **whole star anise** (optional)

5 cups **apple juice**

3½ cups **granulated sugar**

Pinch **salt**

10 cups **fresh cranberries** or frozen cranberries

Using vegetable peeler, peel zest off orange in strips, scraping off pith. Tie zest, cinnamon, ginger, cloves, and star anise (if using) in cheesecloth square to form bag.

In saucepan, combine apple juice, sugar, salt and spice bag. Bring to full rolling boil over high heat, stirring often; boil hard, stirring constantly, for 6 minutes.

Add cranberries; return to boil. Reduce heat to medium; boil until berries are soft and split and juices are lightly jelled, 30 to 45 minutes.

To test, chill small plate in freezer; place 1 tsp cooking liquid on plate and return to freezer for 1 minute. Tilt plate; mixture shouldn't run and should be consistency of soft jelly. If not set, continue cooking, repeating test every 2 minutes.

Fill hot 2-cup (500 mL) canning jars, leaving ¼-inch (5 mm) headspace. Remove any air bubbles.

Cover with prepared discs. Screw on bands until resistance is met; increase to fingertip tight. Boil in boiling water canner for 15 minutes. (See Canning Basics, page 10.)

Turn off heat. Uncover and let jars stand in canner for 5 minutes. Lift up rack. With canning tongs, transfer jars to cooling rack; let cool undisturbed for 24 hours.

MAKES ABOUT 8 CUPS. PER ¼ CUP: about 117 cal, trace pro, trace total fat (0 g sat. fat), 30 g carb, 1 g fibre, 0 mg chol, 2 mg sodium, 72 mg potassium. % RDI: 1% iron, 23% vit C.

tip

The liquid for this sauce shouldn't be as thick as for jelly, but it should be nicely thickened and lightly set, so the testing method is slightly different than for jellies or jams.

Cranberry Croissant Bread Pudding

Cranberries and croissants combine deliciously in this pudding, which is beautiful on a buffet table.

6 **eggs,** lightly beaten

2 cups **milk**

2 cups **10% cream**

¾ cup **granulated sugar**

2 tsp grated **orange zest**

1 tsp **vanilla**

6 large (5- x 3-inch/ 12 x 8 cm) **croissants**

1 cup **whole berry cranberry sauce,** such as Spiced Whole Cranberry Sauce (page 283)

In large bowl, stir together eggs, milk, cream, sugar, orange zest and vanilla.

Cut croissants into 1¼-inch (3 cm) cubes; evenly scatter half in greased 13- x 9-inch (3 L) baking dish. Spoon cranberry sauce evenly over cubes; scatter remaining croissant cubes over top.

Drizzle with milk mixture; let stand for 15 minutes, pressing occasionally. *(Make-ahead: Cover and refrigerate for up to 12 hours.)*

Bake in 350°F (180°C) oven until puffy and knife inserted in centre comes out clean, about 50 minutes.

MAKES 8 TO 10 SERVINGS. PER EACH OF 10 SERVINGS: about 365 cal, 10 g pro, 16 g total fat (9 g sat. fat), 46 g carb, 1 g fibre, 173 mg chol, 345 mg sodium. % RDI: 13% calcium, 9% iron, 17% vit A, 3% vit C, 10% folate.

Clementine Cranberry Sauce

Clementines and orange liqueur give a fresh, citrusy tang to this traditional homemade cranberry sauce.

6 **clementines** or mandarins

2 pkg (each 12 oz/340 g) **fresh cranberries** or frozen cranberries

2 cups **granulated sugar**

¼ cup **orange liqueur** (optional)

Scrub clementines; pat dry. Cut out stem and blossom ends and any blemishes. Cut in half crosswise; squeeze out juice, discarding seeds. Cut peels into fine slivers. Set juice aside.

In Dutch oven or large heavy saucepan, combine peels with 2 cups water; bring to simmer over medium heat.

Reduce heat to low; cover and simmer very gently, adding a little more water if necessary to prevent burning, until peel turns to mush when pressed between fingers, about 30 minutes.

Add clementine juice; return to boil over medium heat. Stir in cranberries and sugar; bring to boil. Boil hard, stirring often, until berries pop and sauce is thickened, about 5 minutes. Stir in liqueur (if using).

Fill hot 1-cup (250 mL) canning jars, leaving ½-inch (1 cm) headspace. Remove any air bubbles.

Cover with prepared discs. Screw on bands until resistance is met; increase to fingertip tight. Boil in boiling water canner for 10 minutes. (See Canning Basics, page 10.)

Turn off heat. Uncover and let jars stand in canner for 5 minutes. Lift up rack. With canning tongs, transfer jars to cooling rack; let cool undisturbed for 24 hours.

MAKES ABOUT 8 CUPS. PER ¼ CUP: about 68 cal, trace pro, trace total fat (trace sat. fat), 17 g carb, 1 g fibre, 0 mg chol, 1 mg sodium. % RDI: 1% calcium, 1% iron, 2% vit A, 17% vit C, 1% folate.

tip

If you're sure you'll serve the sauce within three weeks, you can skip the canning step and just pour the cooked cranberry mixture into sterilized jars, then seal and refrigerate. For longer storage, process as directed.

Wild Blueberry Topping

This dark, shiny topping captures the deep, ripe flavour of wild blueberries. Enjoy it on waffles, pancakes, yogurt or ice cream, or warm it up and use it as a syrup.

1 **lemon**

6 cups **fresh wild blueberries** or thawed frozen wild blueberries (1½ lb/675 g)

3 cups **granulated sugar**

Using vegetable peeler, peel strips of zest from lemon, avoiding pith. Cut lemon in half crosswise; squeeze out juice, discarding seeds. Measure ¼ cup juice. Set zest and juice aside.

In large saucepan, bring blueberries and 1½ cups water to boil over medium-high heat; reduce heat, cover and simmer, stirring often, until softened, about 10 minutes. Let cool slightly.

In batches, transfer blueberry mixture to blender or food processor; coarsely chop. Press through fine-mesh sieve to make about 3½ cups.

In saucepan, bring 3 cups water, sugar and reserved lemon zest to boil over high heat, stirring constantly until sugar is dissolved. Boil, without stirring, until reduced to about 2 cups and candy thermometer registers 240°F (116°C), or soft-ball stage, 15 to 20 minutes.

Remove from heat; discard zest. Whisk in blueberry purée. Return to boil; boil, stirring, until reduced to 4 cups, about 10 minutes. Skim off any foam. Stir in reserved lemon juice.

Fill hot 1-cup (250 mL) canning jars, leaving ½-inch (1 cm) headspace. Remove any air bubbles.

Cover with prepared discs. Screw on bands until resistance is met; increase to fingertip tight. Boil in boiling water canner for 20 minutes. (See Canning Basics, page 10.)

Turn off heat. Uncover and let jars stand in canner for 5 minutes. Lift up rack. With canning tongs, transfer jars to cooling rack; let cool for 24 hours.

MAKES ABOUT 4 CUPS. PER 1 TBSP: about 41 cal, 0 g pro, 0 g total fat (0 g sat. fat), 11 g carb, 0 g fibre, 0 mg chol, 1 mg sodium. % RDI: 2% vit C.

Sauces, Syrups & Vinegars

Strawberry Sundae Topping

This tasty, not-too-sweet sauce is particularly delectable over vanilla or chocolate ice cream.

8 cups halved hulled **fresh strawberries**

1 tbsp coarsely grated **orange zest**

1 cup **granulated sugar**

½ cup **corn syrup**

½ cup freshly squeezed **orange juice**

In large heavy saucepan, combine strawberries, ¼ cup water and orange zest; bring to boil over medium heat. Reduce heat to medium-low, cover and simmer for 10 minutes.

Stir in sugar, corn syrup and orange juice; return to boil. Boil, uncovered and stirring often, for 10 minutes.

Fill hot 1-cup (250 mL) canning jars, leaving ¼-inch (5 mm) headspace. Remove any air bubbles.

Cover with prepared discs. Screw on bands until resistance is met; increase to fingertip tight. Boil in boiling water canner for 10 minutes. (See Canning Basics, page 10.)

Turn off heat. Uncover and let jars stand in canner for 5 minutes. Lift up rack. With canning tongs, transfer jars to cooling rack; let cool for 24 hours.

MAKES 6 CUPS. PER 1 TBSP: about 18 cal, trace pro, 0 g total fat (0 g sat. fat), 5 g carb, trace fibre, 0 mg chol, 2 mg sodium, 23 mg potassium. % RDI: 1% iron, 10% vit C, 1% folate.

Sauces, Syrups & Vinegars

Pineapple Sundae Topping

Once you try this vanilla-scented dessert sauce packed with pineapple, you'll never go back to store-bought sauce. It's perfect for homemade banana splits, but try it on spice cake, over fresh fruit and in blender cocktails too.

5 cups finely chopped
   fresh pineapple

4 cups **granulated sugar**

1 cup **corn syrup**

1 pkg (85 mL) **liquid fruit pectin**

1 tbsp **vanilla**

In large Dutch oven, combine pineapple with ½ cup water. Cover and bring to boil over high heat, stirring often. Boil, uncovered and stirring often, until pineapple starts to soften, about 3 minutes.

Stir in sugar and corn syrup. Return to full rolling boil over high heat, stirring often. Boil hard, stirring constantly, for 1 minute.

Remove from heat; stir in pectin and vanilla. Stir and skim off any foam for 8 minutes.

Fill hot 1-cup (250 mL) canning jars, leaving ¼-inch (5 mm) headspace. Remove any air bubbles.

Cover with prepared discs. Screw on bands until resistance is met; increase to fingertip tight. Boil in boiling water canner for 10 minutes. (See Canning Basics, page 10.)

Turn off heat. Uncover and let jars stand in canner for 5 minutes. Lift up rack. With canning tongs, transfer jars to cooling rack; let cool for 24 hours.

MAKES ABOUT SIX 1-CUP (250 mL) JARS. PER 1 TBSP: about 46 cal, 0 g pro, 0 g total fat (0 g sat. fat), 12 g carb, trace fibre, 0 mg chol, 5 mg sodium, 10 mg potassium. % RDI: 3% vit C.

tip

Stirring after removing the sauce from the heat helps keep the pineapple from floating to the top of the jar. If it does float, gently tilt the jars from side to side after the 24-hour cooling period to distribute the pineapple throughout the sauce. Or just give the topping a stir before serving.

Sauces, Syrups & Vinegars

Spiced Brandied Fruit Sauce

It takes about five minutes to put together this sensational, old-fashioned sauce. In four days, it mellows into a great little hostess gift.

1 cup chopped **candied mixed peel**

1 cup **red candied cherries,** quartered

1 cup **dark seedless raisins**

¼ cup diced **preserved ginger in syrup**

3 **whole allspice**

3 **whole cloves**

1 **cinnamon stick,** broken in pieces

1½ cups **brandy** or rum (approx)

In hot sterilized 4-cup (1 L) canning jar, stir together candied peel, cherries, raisins and ginger until well mixed. (See Tip, page 268.)

Tie allspice, cloves and cinnamon in cheesecloth square to form bag; bury in fruit mixture. Pour in brandy, adding more if necessary to cover fruit. Seal with lid; store in cool, dark, dry place for 4 days.

Remove and discard spice bag. Spoon sauce into sterilized decorative jars; seal with lids. Store in cool, dark, dry place for up to 3 months.

MAKES ABOUT 3 CUPS. PER 2 TBSP: about 107 cal, trace pro, trace total fat (0 g sat. fat), 19 g carb, 1 g fibre, 0 mg chol, 13 mg sodium, 109 mg potassium. % RDI: 1% calcium, 4% iron, 3% vit C.

Butterscotch Sauce

Sundaes will never be the same once you start crowning them with this rich, decadent sauce. And try a drizzle on almost any pie or cake to transform it into a fabulous dessert.

1½ cups packed **brown sugar**

1 cup **whipping cream**

¾ cup **corn syrup**

½ cup **butter,** cubed

1 tbsp **vanilla**

In heavy-bottomed saucepan, stir together sugar, cream, corn syrup and butter; bring to boil over medium heat, stirring until sugar is dissolved. Boil, stirring often, until sauce is thick enough to coat back of wooden spoon, about 5 minutes (mixture will thicken further as it cools).

Remove from heat; stir in vanilla.

Fill hot sterilized 1-cup (250 mL) canning jars. (See Tip, page 268.) Seal with lids; let cool.

Refrigerate for up to 3 weeks.

MAKES 2⅔ CUPS. PER 1 TBSP: about 83 cal, trace pro, 4 g total fat (3 g sat. fat), 12 g carb, 0 g fibre, 13 mg chol, 27 mg sodium, 32 mg potassium. % RDI: 1% calcium, 1% iron, 4% vit A.

tips

• The butter and whipping cream in this sauce make it unsuitable for home canning and room temperature storage, but the sauce does keep well in the refrigerator. Storing in sterilized canning jars isn't strictly necessary, but it can extend the shelf life.

• If the sauce gets too thick after refrigerating, simply warm it gently in the microwave or set the jar in a dish of hot water.

Sauces, Syrups & Vinegars

Apple Spread

Delicate and fresh, this spread is a lighter cousin of dark brown apple butter. It's delicious on toast or with grilled cheese sandwiches made with extra-old Cheddar.

2 lb (900 g) **red apples** (unpeeled and uncored), chopped

1½ cups **granulated sugar**

½ tsp **cinnamon**

Pinch **ground cloves**

In heavy saucepan, bring apples and 1½ cups water to boil; reduce heat, cover and simmer, stirring often, until very soft, about 30 minutes. Press through fine disc of food mill or fine-mesh sieve into clean saucepan.

Add sugar, cinnamon and cloves; simmer, stirring often, until wooden spoon scraped across bottom of pan leaves trail that take 3 seconds to fill in, about 35 minutes.

Fill hot 1-cup (250 mL) canning jars, leaving ¼-inch (5 mm) headspace. Seal with lids; refrigerate for up to 1 month.

MAKES ABOUT 3 CUPS. PER 1 TBSP: about 31 cal, 0 g pro, 0 g total fat (0 g sat. fat), 8 g carb, trace fibre, 0 mg chol, 0 mg sodium, 14 mg potassium.

Chocolate Fudge Sauce

To make a classic Tin Roof Sundae, drizzle this gooey sauce over a scoop of vanilla ice cream and sprinkle with chopped peanuts. For the full effect, garnish with whipped cream and a maraschino cherry.

⅓ cup **cocoa powder,** sifted

⅓ cup **corn syrup**

4 oz (115 g) **bittersweet chocolate,** chopped

1 tsp **vanilla**

In small saucepan over medium heat, bring ½ cup water, cocoa and corn syrup to boil, whisking constantly; boil for 2 minutes.

Reduce heat to low. Add chocolate; cook, stirring, until melted. Remove from heat; stir in vanilla.

Fill airtight container; serve warm or seal with lid and refrigerate until chilled.

Refrigerate for up to 2 weeks. Reheat in saucepan over low heat or in microwave at low (10%) until pourable.

MAKES 1 CUP. PER 2 TBSP: about 125 cal, 2 g pro, 7 g total fat (4 g sat. fat), 19 g carb, 2 g fibre, 0 mg chol, 38 mg sodium. % RDI: 2% calcium, 12% iron, 1% folate.

Peanut Butter Caramel Sundae Sauce

There's something about the combination of sweet and salty in this sauce that makes it utterly divine.

¼ cup **unsalted butter**

½ cup packed **brown sugar**

¼ cup **granulated sugar**

¼ cup **corn syrup**

¼ tsp **salt**

⅓ cup **whipping cream**

½ cup **smooth peanut butter**

In saucepan, melt butter over medium-low heat; stir in brown and granulated sugars, corn syrup, 2 tbsp water and salt. Cook, stirring, until thickened, about 5 minutes.

Stir in whipping cream; cook for 30 seconds. Remove from heat.

Stir in peanut butter; let cool slightly. Serve warm or at room temperature.

Fill airtight container; seal with lid and refrigerate for up to 1 week. Reheat in saucepan over low heat or in microwave at low (10%) until pourable.

MAKES ABOUT 1⅔ CUPS. PER 2 TBSP: about 170 cal, 3 g pro, 10 g total fat (5 g sat. fat), 19 g carb, 1 g fibre, 17 mg chol, 101 mg sodium, 98 mg potassium. % RDI: 1% calcium, 2% iron, 5% vit A, 4% folate.

Oatmeal Buttermilk Pancakes

Oats and whole wheat flour add fibre and nutty flavour to these pancakes. They're delicious with Spiced Maple-Apple Pancake Sauce (opposite) or straight-up maple syrup.

2¼ cups **buttermilk**

1½ cups **quick-cooking** (not instant) **rolled oats**

½ cup **all-purpose flour**

½ cup **whole wheat flour**

1 tbsp packed **brown sugar**

1 tsp **baking powder**

1 tsp **baking soda**

¼ tsp **salt**

2 **eggs**

3 tbsp **vegetable oil**

In bowl, pour buttermilk over oats; let stand for 5 minutes.

In separate bowl, whisk together all-purpose and whole wheat flours, sugar, baking powder, baking soda and salt. Whisk eggs with 2 tbsp of the oil; pour over dry ingredients. Pour buttermilk mixture over top; stir just until combined.

Heat large nonstick skillet over medium heat; brush with some of the remaining oil. Pour about ¼ cup of the batter into skillet for each pancake, brushing skillet with remaining oil as necessary.

Cook until underside is golden and bubbles break on top but do not fill in, 1½ to 2 minutes. Turn and cook until underside is golden, 30 to 60 seconds.

MAKES ABOUT 15 PANCAKES. PER PANCAKE: about 123 cal, 5 g pro, 5 g total fat (1 g sat. fat), 15 g carb, 1 g fibre, 28 mg chol, 184 mg sodium. % RDI: 6% calcium, 6% iron, 2% vit A, 8% folate.

Sauces, Syrups & Vinegars

Spiced Maple-Apple Pancake Sauce

Serve this sweet maple-apple combo warm or at room temperature over Oatmeal Buttermilk Pancakes (opposite). It's equally delicious over ice cream.

2 tbsp **butter**

1 **Golden Delicious apple,** peeled and diced

1 cup **apple cider**

1 cup **maple syrup**

¼ tsp **cinnamon**

¼ tsp **nutmeg**

¼ tsp **ground ginger**

In saucepan, melt butter over medium heat; cook apple, stirring occasionally, until golden, 8 minutes.

Add cider, maple syrup, cinnamon, nutmeg and ginger; bring to boil. Reduce heat to medium and simmer until syrupy, about 12 minutes. Let cool.

Pour sauce into decorative bottle or jar; seal with lid. Refrigerate for up to 1 month. Rewarm to serve.

MAKES 1½ CUPS. PER 1 TBSP: about 51 cal, 0 g pro, 1 g total fat (1 g sat. fat), 11 g carb, trace fibre, 3 mg chol, 8 mg sodium. % RDI: 1% calcium, 1% iron, 1% vit A.

Sauces, Syrups & Vinegars

Dulce de Leche

This South American caramel sauce is so simple to make that you'll want to keep it on hand all the time. It's delicious on cake or ice cream – or even straight out of the jar!

2 cans (each 385 mL)
    2% evaporated milk

1¼ cups **milk**

1 tbsp **cornstarch**

½ tsp **baking soda**

1 cup **granulated sugar**

In large heavy saucepan, bring evaporated milk and ¾ cup of the milk to boil. Whisk together remaining milk, cornstarch and baking soda; pour into boiling milk mixture. Reduce heat to low; simmer, stirring occasionally.

Meanwhile, in large stockpot, stir sugar with ¾ cup water over medium heat until dissolved, brushing down side of pan with brush dipped in cold water. Bring to boil; boil, without stirring but brushing down side of pan often, until light golden, about 15 minutes. Remove caramel from heat.

Averting face, slowly pour milk mixture through sieve into caramel; whisk vigorously until well blended. Return to heat; simmer, stirring occasionally, until dark golden and thick enough to coat back of wooden spoon, 1 to 1½ hours.

Strain through fine sieve into decorative jar or airtight container; seal with lid. Let cool. Refrigerate for up to 1 month. Rewarm to liquefy.

MAKES ABOUT 2 CUPS. PER 2 TBSP: about 107 cal, 4 g pro, 1 g total fat (1 g sat. fat), 19 g carb, 0 g fibre, 5 mg chol, 104 mg sodium. % RDI: 15% calcium, 1% iron, 4% vit A, 7% vit C, 2% folate.

Pear Butter

Brown butter gives this spread both caramel and nut nuances, which pair exceptionally well with the bright, fresh pear flavour. Make batches of the butter during pear season, when the fruit is at its most fragrant.

2 lb (900 g) **fresh Bartlett pears** (about 5), peeled and thinly sliced

½ cup **apple cider**

2 strips **orange zest**

1 tsp grated **fresh ginger**

¼ cup **unsalted butter**

2 tbsp **wildflower honey** or other liquid honey

Pinch **salt**

In large saucepan, bring pears, apple cider, orange zest and ginger to boil over medium heat. Reduce heat and simmer, stirring often, until thickened, pears are broken down and almost no liquid remains, 45 to 60 minutes. Discard orange zest. Let cool.

In small saucepan, melt butter over medium-low heat; reduce heat and simmer until foaming and browned, 8 to 10 minutes. Let cool slightly. Strain through fine sieve into bowl to make 3 tbsp. Let cool.

In food processor, purée pear mixture until smooth. Add browned butter, honey and salt; pulse to combine. Transfer to airtight container; refrigerate for up to 2 weeks.

MAKES ABOUT 1 CUP. PER 1 TBSP: about 59 cal, trace pro, 2 g total fat (1 g sat. fat), 10 g carb, 1 g fibre, 6 mg chol, 1 mg sodium. % RDI: 1% iron, 2% vit A, 3% vit C, 1% folate.

Sauces, Syrups & Vinegars

Peach Butter

Homemade fruit butters aren't quite as thick as commercially made ones, but their flavour is just as wonderful. This is a terrific way to capture perfectly ripe summer peaches in a jar to enjoy throughout the year.

4½ lb (2.025 kg) **fresh peaches** (about 16)

¼ cup freshly squeezed **lemon juice**

3 cups **granulated sugar**

¾ cup packed **brown sugar**

½ tsp **cinnamon** (optional)

tips

• The peaches are unpeeled because the skins give the butter a nice colour. Once they're puréed, you can't taste them.

• If your food mill doesn't make the peach mixture smooth enough, use an immersion blender after the sugar is added to purée the mixture to a smoother consistency.

• As the mixture thickens, keep a close eye on the pot to prevent burning. Maintain a gentle boil by gradually decreasing the heat and stirring more frequently.

Scrub peaches to remove excess fuzz. Cut into quarters, or sixths if large. In large Dutch oven, combine peaches, ½ cup water and lemon juice. Using potato masher, crush peaches. Partially cover and bring to boil over medium-high heat.

Reduce heat to medium-low and simmer, partially covered and stirring, until peaches are very soft and can be mashed easily with spoon, about 25 minutes.

Chill 2 plates in freezer. Press peach mixture through fine disc of food mill or purée in food processor until smooth. In clean Dutch oven, combine peach mixture, granulated and brown sugars, and cinnamon (if using). Bring to boil over medium heat, stirring until sugar is dissolved. Reduce heat and simmer, stirring often, until thick enough to mound softly on spoon, 1 hour.

To test for correct consistency, place 1 tsp hot peach butter on 1 chilled plate. Butter should stay in place without flattening or seeping at edges. If not, continue cooking, repeating test every 2 minutes, until correct consistency, always using coldest clean plate.

Fill hot 1-cup (250 mL) canning jars, leaving ¼-inch (5 mm) headspace. Cover with prepared discs. Screw on bands until resistance is met; increase to fingertip tight. Boil jars in boiling water canner for 20 minutes. (See Canning Basics, page 10.)

Turn off heat. Uncover and let jars stand in canner for 5 minutes. Lift up rack. With canning tongs, transfer jars to cooling rack; let cool for 24 hours.

MAKES ABOUT 7 CUPS. PER 1 TBSP: about 33 cal, trace pro, 0 g total fat (0 g sat. fat), 9 g carb, trace fibre, 0 mg chol, 1 mg sodium, 39 mg potassium. % RDI: 1% iron, 2% vit C.

Vanilla Syrup

With infused syrups, you can turn coffee, tea, steamed milk or sparkling water into your favourite coffee-house treats. Or try the flavourful infusions in creative cocktails.

1½ cups **granulated sugar**

1 **vanilla bean**

In saucepan, combine sugar with 1½ cups water. Cut vanilla bean in half lengthwise; scrape seeds into pan. Add pod.

Bring to boil over medium heat, stirring often until sugar is dissolved. Boil for 1 minute. Remove from heat; cover and let stand for 1 hour or for up to 8 hours.

Strain through fine-mesh sieve into liquid measure or pitcher; discard solids.

Fill glass bottles or canning jars; seal with lids. Refrigerate for up to 1 month.

MAKES ABOUT 2 CUPS. PER 1 TBSP: about 37 cal, 0 g pro, 0 g total fat (0 g sat. fat), 9 g carb, 0 g fibre, 0 mg chol, 0 mg sodium, 1 mg potassium.

Variations

Honey Ginger Syrup: Omit vanilla. Reduce sugar to 1¼ cups. Add ¼ cup each chopped fresh ginger and liquid honey to pan. Heat, strain and store as directed.

Orange Syrup: Omit vanilla. Using vegetable peeler, peel strips of zest from 1 orange, avoiding pith. Add zest after syrup has been boiled and removed from heat. Let stand for 3 hours. Strain and store as directed.

Sauces, Syrups & Vinegars

Tarragon Vinegar

Fresh herb vinegars like this one are excellent bases for vinaigrettes to drizzle over salads and grilled vegetables.

½ cup **fresh tarragon leaves**

1 strip **lemon zest**

1½ cups **white wine vinegar**

Lightly crush tarragon leaves to bruise and release oil. Place in heatproof jar along with lemon zest.

In saucepan, heat vinegar just until boiling; pour over tarragon mixture. Let cool to room temperature; discard lemon zest. Seal with lid and refrigerate for 1 week.

Strain through cheesecloth-lined sieve into decorative jar(s); seal with lid(s). Refrigerate for up to 1 month.

MAKES 1½ CUPS. PER 1 TBSP: about 3 cal, 0 g pro, 0 g total fat (0 g sat. fat), trace carb, 0 g fibre, 0 mg chol, 1 mg sodium, 9 mg potassium. % RDI: 1% iron, 2% vit C.

Variations

Chive Vinegar: Substitute ½ cup fresh chive pieces (1 inch/2.5 cm) and 1 tsp black peppercorns for tarragon and lemon zest. Do not discard before refrigerating for 1 week.

Dill Orange Vinegar: Omit tarragon and lemon zest. Increase vinegar to 2 cups. Using vegetable peeler, peel zest from 1 orange, avoiding pith. Place zest in canning jar; add 1 cup packed fresh dill. In saucepan, toast 1 tbsp mustard seeds over medium heat until popping, about 2 minutes. Add vinegar; bring just to boil. Pour over dill mixture. Let cool; cover and let stand for 24 hours. Strain through cheesecloth-lined sieve into airtight jar; seal with lid. Store in cool, dark, dry place for up to 6 months.

MAKES 2 CUPS.

Cranberry Vinegar

Fruit vinegars make welcome presents, so use this recipe to get you started on your holiday gifts. Fresh or thawed frozen cranberries work equally well.

6 cups **cranberries**
4 cups **white vinegar**
½ cup **granulated sugar**
2 strips **orange zest**

In large saucepan, bring cranberries, vinegar, sugar and orange zest to boil. Reduce heat, cover and simmer for 5 minutes. Let cool for 30 minutes, stirring once.

Scoop into dampened jelly bag suspended over large glass measure or bowl. Let drip, without squeezing bag, for 2 hours.

In saucepan, bring vinegar mixture to boil.

Fill hot 1-cup (250 mL) canning jars, leaving ¼-inch (5 mm) headspace. Cover with prepared discs. Screw on bands until resistance is met; increase to fingertip tight. Boil in boiling water canner for 10 minutes. (See Canning Basics, page 10.)

Turn off heat. Uncover and let jars stand in canner for 5 minutes. Lift up rack. With canning tongs, transfer jars to cooling rack; let cool for 24 hours.

MAKES ABOUT 3⅓ CUPS. PER 1 TBSP: about 10 cal, 0 g pro, 0 g total fat (0 g sat. fat), 3 g carb, 0 g fibre, 0 mg chol, 0 mg sodium.

tip
If you don't have a jelly bag and frame, you can make a simple substitute. Scoop cooked fruit mixture into colander lined with damp square of triple-thickness fine cheesecloth. Bring up sides; tie with kitchen string to form bag. Tie bag to cupboard handle over large glass measure or bowl. Let drip as directed.

Sauces, Syrups & Vinegars

Raspberry Vinegar

Whether it's used to add zip to salad dressings, to brighten a bowl of berries or to splash into the pan while making a quick sauce after browning chicken, this fruity vinegar is worth every single step it takes to make it.

6 cups **frozen raspberries** (about two 300 pkg)

3 cups **white wine vinegar** or unseasoned rice vinegar

2 tsp **granulated sugar**

GARNISH:
Fresh or thawed frozen **raspberries**

In food processor, chop together frozen raspberries, vinegar and sugar. Transfer to large microwaveable bowl; cover and microwave at medium-high (70%) for 7 minutes (or heat in saucepan over medium heat until steaming, about 10 minutes). Let cool.

Refrigerate for 12 hours, stirring occasionally. Strain mixture through fine-mesh sieve into bowl, pressing solids to extract liquid. Discard solids.

Line funnel with coffee filter or damp square of double-thickness fine cheesecloth; strain raspberry mixture into sterilized decorative bottles. (See Tip, below.) Let stand until completely filtered, topping up funnel and changing to new bottles as necessary, about 8 hours.

GARNISH: Add about 3 raspberries to each bottle; seal with cork. Store in cool, dark, dry place for up to 6 months.

MAKES ABOUT 5 CUPS. PER 1 TBSP: about 5 cal, trace pro, 0 g total fat (0 g sat. fat), 1 g carb, 0 g fibre, 0 mg chol, 1 mg sodium, 16 mg potassium. % RDI: 1% iron, 2% vit C.

tip

Sterilizing the bottles and jars ensures that they are free of bacteria and mould. This allows you to store the vinegar at room temperature without processing the bottles in a boiling water canner. To sterilize, simply submerge the bottles and jars in boiling water in a large canning pot and boil for 10 minutes. Leave them in the water and dry them just before you're ready to fill them.

From left: Thai
Lemongrass Vinegar
(page 308) and
Tarragon and Pink
Peppercorn Vinegar
(opposite)

Tarragon and Pink Peppercorn Vinegar

Tarragon's citrus and licorice notes are complemented by the delicate taste of pink peppercorns. To make a simple vinaigrette, whisk one part vinegar with four parts extra-virgin olive oil.

1½ cups packed **fresh tarragon sprigs**

2 tbsp **pink peppercorns**

6 cups **white wine vinegar**

GARNISH:
Pink peppercorns
Tarragon sprigs

Place tarragon and peppercorns in sterilized wide-mouth 6-cup (1.5 L) canning jar. (See Tip, page 305.)

In saucepan, bring vinegar to boil; pour over tarragon mixture. Let cool to room temperature. Seal jar; let stand in sunny location at room temperature for 10 days, shaking occasionally. Strain through cheesecloth-lined sieve. Discard solids.

GARNISH: Place a few pink peppercorns and 1 sprig tarragon in each of several sterilized decorative bottles.

Pour in vinegar mixture. Seal; store in cool, dark, dry place for up to 6 months.

MAKES ABOUT 6 CUPS. PER 1 TBSP: about 2 cal, 0 g pro, 0 g total fat (0 g sat. fat), 1 g carb, 0 g fibre, 0 mg chol, 0 mg sodium. % RDI: 1% iron.

tip
The colour of the tarragon naturally fades over time, so bottle the vinegar just before giving as a gift.

Sauces, Syrups & Vinegars

Thai Lemongrass Vinegar

Use this lemon-scented vinegar in vinaigrettes to drizzle over simple cucumber or vegetable salads.

2 stalks **fresh lemongrass**

1 **Thai bird's-eye pepper**

2 tbsp **coriander seeds**

6 cups **unseasoned rice vinegar**

GARNISH:
Lemongrass stalks
Thai bird's-eye peppers
Coriander seeds

Coarsely chop lemongrass. Halve pepper lengthwise. Using bottom of heavy pan, crack coriander seeds. Place lemongrass, pepper and coriander seeds in sterilized wide-mouth 6-cup (1.5 L) canning jar. (See Tip, page 305.)

In saucepan, bring vinegar to boil; pour over lemongrass mixture. Let cool to room temperature. Seal jar; let stand in sunny location at room temperature for 10 days, shaking occasionally. Strain through cheesecloth-lined sieve. Discard solids.

GARNISH: Cut lemongrass into pieces; place piece in each of several sterilized decorative bottles. Add 1 pepper and a few coriander seeds to each; pour in vinegar mixture. Seal; store in cool, dark, dry place for up to 6 months.

MAKES ABOUT 6 CUPS. PER 1 TBSP: about 2 cal, 0 g pro, 0 g total fat (0 g sat. fat), 1 g carb, 0 g fibre, 0 mg chol, 0 mg sodium.

Mint Vinegar

Nothing is more pleasant than the fresh flavour of herbed vinegars on crisp greens. Whisk this vinegar with olive oil and honey to make a smashing, summery vinaigrette.

1 cup packed **fresh mint sprigs**

4 cups **cider vinegar**

GARNISH:

Fresh mint sprigs

Wash and thoroughly dry mint sprigs. Place in 4-cup (1 L) sterilized canning jar; pour in vinegar, submerging mint completely. Seal with lid; let stand in cool, dark, dry place for 2 weeks.

GARNISH: Place mint sprig in each of several sterilized decorative bottles. (See Tip, page 305.)

Line funnel with coffee filter or damp square of double-thickness fine cheesecloth; discarding mint, strain vinegar into bottles.

Seal; store in cool, dark, dry place for up to 1 year.

MAKES 4 CUPS. PER 1 TBSP: about 2 cal, 0 g pro, 0 g total fat (0 g sat. fat), 1 g carb, 0 g fibre, 0 mg chol, 0 mg sodium, 15 mg potassium. % RDI: 1% iron.

chapter seven

Liqueurs
& Seasonings

Peach Liqueur

Peach pits and skins give this sweet liqueur a delicate, peachy, almond-like flavour. Make it when you're putting up other peach preserves that use only the flesh, such as Peach Dipping Sauce (page 280) or Peach Jam (page 58).

2 baskets (each 3 L) **fresh peaches** (7 to 8 lb/ 3.15 to 3.6 kg)

1½ cups **granulated sugar**

1 **dried tangerine peel** (see Tips, below)

2½ cups **vodka**

1½ cups **brandy**

With sharp knife, score X into bottom of each peach. In saucepan of boiling water, blanch each peach for 30 seconds. Transfer to cold water. Reserving skin and pit, peel skin and remove pit (save flesh for another use).

In small saucepan, bring sugar and ½ cup water to boil; reduce heat and simmer, swirling pan, until sugar is dissolved. Let cool.

Pour syrup into hot sterilized 8-cup (2 L) canning jar or divide between 2 hot sterilized 4-cup (1 L) canning jars. (See Tip, page 314.) Add tangerine peel. Add reserved peach skins and pits; pour in vodka and brandy. Stir; seal jar(s) with lid(s).

Let stand in cool, dark, dry place for 6 weeks. Strain through fine-mesh sieve lined with double-thickness cheesecloth; discard solids. Pour into sterilized decorative bottle(s).

MAKES ABOUT 4½ CUPS. PER ½ OZ (1 TBSP): about 46 cal, 0 g pro, 0 g total fat (0 g sat. fat), 5 g carb, trace fibre, 0 mg chol, 0 mg sodium, 8 mg potassium.

tips

• You can buy dried tangerine peel in Chinese grocery stores, but it's easy to make at home. Just peel tangerine; let peel dry on rack until brittle, about one week. Make sure peel is completely dry before using to avoid any bitterness.

• Clingstone peaches give this liqueur a slightly peachier flavour, as some of the flesh sticks to the pits.

Liqueurs & Seasonings

Black Currant Liqueur

French crème de cassis is the inspiration for this sweet and fruity liqueur. For a refreshing cocktail, pour 1 oz (2 tbsp) liqueur into a tall glass; top with 4 oz (½ cup) chilled white wine, sparkling white wine or soda water.

¾ cup **granulated sugar**

3 cups **fresh black currants** or frozen black currants, stemmed

1 bottle (750 mL) **vodka**

¼ cup **brandy** (optional)

In saucepan over medium heat, whisk sugar with ¼ cup water until clear; remove from heat. Stir in currants; let stand for 5 minutes. Stir in vodka, and brandy (if using).

In batches, transfer black currant mixture to blender and purée. Divide between 2 hot sterilized wide-mouth 4-cup (1 L) canning jars. (See Tip, below.)

Seal with lids; let stand in cool, dark, dry place, shaking occasionally, for 5 days or for up to 3 months.

Strain through fine-mesh sieve lined with double-thickness cheesecloth, gently pressing black currants to release liquid; discard solids. Pour into sterilized decorative bottle(s).

MAKES 4½ CUPS. PER ½ OZ (1 TBSP): about 10 cal, 0 g pro, 0 g total fat (0 g sat. fat), 3 g carb, 0 g fibre, 0 mg chol, 0 mg sodium. % RDI: 1% iron, 12% vit C.

tip

Sterilizing jars and bottles ensures that they are free of bacteria and mould. This allows you to store them at room temperature without processing them in a boiling water canner. To sterilize, submerge the jars or bottles in boiling water in a large canning pot and boil for 10 minutes. Leave them in the water and dry just before you're ready to fill them.

Apple Schnapps

During long, dark winter evenings, what could be more welcome than a whiff of apples fresh from the orchard? This schnapps preserves their heady aroma and flavour.

4 **apples**
½ cup **granulated sugar**
1 bottle (750 mL) **vodka**

Remove stems from apples. Scrub apples in warm soapy water; rinse well and let dry. Quarter and seed apples; slice thinly, without peeling or coring.

In hot sterilized wide-mouth 6-cup (1.5 L) canning jar (see Tip, opposite), mix apples with sugar; seal with lid. Let stand in cool, dark, dry place for 3 days.

Add vodka; seal with lid. Let stand in cool, dark, dry place for 3 weeks or for up to 2 months.

Strain through fine-mesh sieve lined with double-thickness cheesecloth, pressing apples to release liquid; discard solids.

Line funnel with coffee filter; strain liqueur through filter into sterilized decorative bottle(s). Store at room temperature for up to 6 months.

MAKES 3 CUPS. PER 1 OZ (2 TBSP): about 96 cal, 0 g pro, 0 g total fat (0 g sat. fat), 7 g carb, trace fibre, 0 mg chol, 0 mg sodium. % RDI: 2% vit C.

Variations
Ginger Apple Schnapps:
Add 10 thin slices fresh ginger along with sliced apples.

Spiced Apple Schnapps:
Add 2 whole star anise and half cinnamon stick along with vodka.

tip
Serve this schnapps chilled in small shot glasses alongside hors d'oeuvres. Or enjoy it at room temperature as a digestif with dessert or after dinner.

Liqueurs & Seasonings

Apple Cider Schnapps

Dried apples, cinnamon and cloves give this liqueur an apple cider flavour and a spicy fragrance. Sip it straight up or use it in cocktails.

1 cup **dried apples,** chopped

2 tbsp packed **brown sugar**

6 **whole cloves**

1 **cinnamon stick**

1 bottle (750 mL) **vodka**

In saucepan over medium-low heat, bring apples, sugar, cloves, cinnamon stick and ½ cup water to boil. Boil, stirring, until sugar is dissolved and no liquid remains, 5 minutes. Let cool to room temperature.

Stir in vodka. Pour into hot sterilized wide-mouth 4-cup (1 L) canning jar. (See Tip, page 314.) Seal with lid. Let stand in cool, dark, dry place, shaking occasionally, for 1 to 2 weeks.

Strain through fine-mesh sieve lined with double-thickness cheesecloth, gently pressing apple mixture to release liquid; discard solids. Pour into sterilized decorative bottle(s). Store in cool, dark, dry place for up to 3 months.

MAKES 3 CUPS. PER 1 OZ (2 TBSP): about 80 cal, 0 g pro, 0 g total fat (0 g sat. fat), 3 g carb, 0 g fibre, 0 mg chol, 4 mg sodium. % RDI: 1% iron.

Liqueurs & Seasonings

Cran-Raspberry Cordial

With its festive colour and fabulous flavour, this infused vodka is ideal for gift-giving during the holiday season.

2 cups **frozen cranberries**

2 cups **frozen raspberries**

2 cups **granulated sugar**

1 bottle (750 mL) **vodka**

In food processor, coarsely chop together cranberries, raspberries and sugar; transfer to hot sterilized wide-mouth 8-cup (2 L) canning jar. (See Tip, page 314.)

Pour in vodka; seal with lid. Shake to combine. Refrigerate for 2 weeks, shaking often.

Strain through fine-mesh sieve lined with double-thickness cheesecloth, pressing berry mixture firmly to release liquid; discard solids. Pour into sterilized decorative bottle(s).

MAKES ABOUT 6 CUPS. PER 1 OZ (2 TBSP): about 70 cal, 0 g pro, 0 g total fat (0 g sat. fat), 9 g carb, 0 g fibre, 0 mg chol, 0 mg sodium. % RDI: 3% vit C.

Blueberry Vodka

Deep purple-black and brimming with wild blueberry flavour, this vodka makes a mean mixed drink. Try it in a Blueberry Martini (page 320).

3 cups **fresh wild blueberries** or thawed frozen wild blueberries

3 strips (each 4- x 1-inch/ 10 x 2.5 cm) **lemon zest** (pith removed)

Half **vanilla bean,** split lengthwise

1 bottle (750 mL) **vodka**

In large glass bowl and using potato masher, lightly crush blueberries. Add lemon zest and vanilla bean; stir in vodka. Cover with plastic wrap; let stand in cool, dark, dry place, stirring occasionally, for 3 days.

Strain through fine-mesh sieve lined with double-thickness cheesecloth, gently pressing blueberries to release liquid; discard solids. Pour into sterilized decorative bottle(s). (See Tip, page 314.) Refrigerate for up to 1 month.

MAKES 3½ CUPS. PER 1 OZ (2 TBSP): about 66 cal, trace pro, trace total fat (0 g sat. fat), 2 g carb, 0 g fibre, 0 mg chol, 0 mg sodium, 12 mg potassium. % RDI: 3% vit C.

Blueberry Martini
(page 320)

Blueberry Martini

This cocktail is like a melted Freezie – adult-style. Infuse the Blueberry Vodka at least three days ahead for the best flavour. Top with a skewer of blueberries and lemon zest.

Ice cubes

4 oz (½ cup) **Blueberry Vodka** (page 318)

1 tbsp **Simple Syrup** (right)

2 tsp **lemon juice**

GARNISH:
Lemon wedge

Granulated sugar

GARNISH: Rub lemon over rims of 2 martini glasses; press into sugar to coat.

Half-fill cocktail shaker with ice. Add vodka, simple syrup and lemon juice; shake. Strain into prepared glasses.

MAKES 2 MARTINIS. PER MARTINI: about 150 cal, trace pro, trace total fat (0 g sat. fat), 8 g carb, 0 g fibre, 0 mg chol, 1 mg sodium, 31 mg potassium. % RDI: 1% iron, 8% vit C, 1% folate.

Simple Syrup:

In small saucepan over medium-high heat, bring ½ cup each granulated sugar and water to boil. Boil, stirring occasionally, until sugar is dissolved and mixture turns clear, about 2 minutes. Let cool. Refrigerate in airtight jar for up to 1 week.

Lychee Martini

This tropical-style, easy-to-drink martini is delicious garnished with a canned lychee – or two. Keep in mind that the longer the homemade Lychee Vodka steeps, the better the flavour.

Ice cubes

1½ oz (3 tbsp) strained **Lychee Vodka** (opposite)

¼ oz (1½ tsp) **white vermouth**

1 strip **lime zest**

Splash **club soda**

1 drained canned **whole lychee** (optional)

Half-fill cocktail shaker with ice. Add vodka, vermouth and lime zest; shake. Strain into martini glass; add soda. Garnish with lychee (if using).

MAKES 1 MARTINI. PER MARTINI: about 68 cal, 0 g pro, 0 g total fat (0 g sat. fat), 3 g carb, 0 g fibre, 0 mg chol, 1 mg sodium. % RDI: 1% iron, 2% vit C.

Lychee Vodka

Lychees have an exotic, perfumy scent that's enticing. Try some of this small-batch, fragrant infused vodka in a Lychee Martini (opposite).

1 can (20 oz/530 mL)
  whole lychees in syrup

1½ cups **vodka**

Reserving ⅔ cup of the syrup, drain lychees. In bowl and using potato masher, coarsely crush lychees; transfer to sterilized wide-mouth 4-cup (1 L) canning jar. (See Tip, page 314.)

Pour in reserved syrup and vodka; seal with lid. Let stand in cool, dark, dry place for 24 hours before opening. Store in cool, dark, dry place for up to 1 month.

MAKES 3 CUPS. PER 1 OZ (2 TBSP): about 38 cal, 0 g pro, 0 g total fat (0 g sat. fat), 1 g carb, trace fibre, 0 mg chol, 0 mg sodium, 6 mg potassium. % RDI: 1% iron, 2% vit C.

Limoncello

Limone, which means "lemon" in Italian, is the refreshing base for this sweet liqueur. It couldn't be simpler to make.

8 **lemons**
1 bottle (750 mL) **vodka**
2 cups **granulated sugar**

Scrub lemons in hot soapy water; rinse well and pat dry. Using vegetable peeler or zester, peel off zest, avoiding pith (save flesh for another use). Place zest in hot sterilized wide-mouth 4-cup (1 L) canning jar. (See Tip, page 314.) Pour in vodka. Seal with lid. Let stand in cool, dark, dry place for 5 days.

In small saucepan, bring 2½ cups water and sugar to boil; reduce heat and simmer for 15 minutes. Let cool to room temperature. Stir into vodka mixture.

Line funnel with coffee filter or double thickness cheesecloth; strain liqueur through filter into sterilized decorative bottle(s), discarding zest.

MAKES 6 CUPS. PER 1 OZ (2 TBSP): about 66 cal, 0 g pro, 0 g total fat (0 g sat. fat), 8 g carb, 0 g fibre, 0 mg chol, 1 mg sodium.

Pineapple Lime Schnapps

This fruity liqueur is a delicious base for a pineapple mimosa. Pour 1½ oz (3 tbsp) schnapps into a champagne flute; top with 5 oz (½ cup + 2 tbsp) chilled sparkling wine.

1 **pineapple**
Juice of 1 **lime**
1 tbsp **granulated sugar**
1 bottle (750 mL) **vodka**

Peel, core and cut pineapple into 1-inch (2.5 cm) cubes. In hot sterilized wide-mouth 4-cup (1 L) canning jar. (See Tip, page 314.) Combine pineapple, lime juice and sugar; seal with lid. Refrigerate for 2 hours.

Stir in vodka; seal with lid. Let stand in cool, dark, dry place, shaking occasionally, for 2 weeks.

Strain through fine-mesh sieve lined with double-thickness cheesecloth, gently pressing pineapple mixture to release liquid; discard solids. Pour into sterilized decorative bottle(s). Refrigerate for up to 3 months.

MAKES 3 CUPS. PER 1 OZ (2 TBSP): about 79 cal, trace pro, 0 g total fat (0 g sat. fat), 3 g carb, 0 g fibre, 0 mg chol, 1 mg sodium. % RDI: 1% iron, 13% vit C, 1% folate.

Liqueurs & Seasonings

Cranberry Almond Schnapps

Cranberries turn this vodka a gorgeous deep red, while almonds add a hint of toasted nutty flavour. Fresh or frozen cranberries work equally well.

¼ cup **blanched almonds**

1 pkg (12 oz/340 g) **fresh cranberries** or frozen cranberries

⅓ cup **granulated sugar**

¼ cup chopped **crystallized ginger**

4 thin strips **orange zest** (pith removed)

1 bottle (750 mL) **vodka**

Spread almonds on baking sheet; toast in 350°F (180°C) oven until fragrant, 7 to 8 minutes.

In saucepan over medium-low heat, bring cranberries, sugar, almonds, ginger, ¼ cup water and orange zest to boil. Boil, stirring, until sugar is dissolved and cranberries pop, about 5 minutes. Let cool to room temperature.

Stir in vodka. Pour into hot sterilized wide-mouth 4-cup (1 L) canning jar. (See Tip, page 314.) Seal with lid. Let stand in cool, dark, dry place, shaking occasionally, for 2 weeks.

Strain through fine-mesh sieve lined with double-thickness cheesecloth, gently pressing cranberry mixture to release liquid; discard solids. Pour into sterilized decorative bottle(s). Refrigerate for up to 3 months.

MAKES 3 CUPS. PER 1 OZ (2 TBSP): about 83 cal, 0 g pro, 0 g total fat (0 g sat. fat), 4 g carb, 0 g fibre, 0 mg chol, 1 mg sodium. % RDI: 2% vit C.

Liqueurs & Seasonings

From left: Pineapple Lime
Schnapps (page 323)
and Cranberry Almond
Schnapps (opposite)

Peppermint Patty Liqueur

You can whisk together this minty liqueur in a flash for the ultimate after-dinner treat. Since it contains dairy, it will only keep for two weeks in the fridge, so enjoy it right away.

1 cup **vodka**

¾ cup **whipping cream**

1 can (300 mL) **sweetened condensed milk**

½ cup **chocolate syrup**

1 tsp **vanilla**

Dash **peppermint extract**

In large bowl, whisk together vodka, cream, condensed milk, chocolate syrup, vanilla and peppermint extract.

Pour into decorative bottle(s). Refrigerate for up to 2 weeks.

MAKES 4 CUPS. PER 1 OZ (2 TBSP): about 89 cal, 1 g pro, 4 g total fat (2 g sat. fat), 9 g carb, trace fibre, 11 mg chol, 22 mg sodium. % RDI: 4% calcium, 1% iron, 3% vit A, 1% folate.

Marroni al Liquore

This Italian-inspired concoction, which translates to "chestnuts in spirits," is two treats in one. Spoon the chestnuts over ice cream, and enjoy the liqueur in coffee or as a digestif.

1½ cups **granulated sugar**

4 **whole allspice**

2 **whole cloves**

2 **bay leaves**

Half **vanilla bean,** split lengthwise (or ½ tsp vanilla)

2½ cups **prepared chestnuts** (see Tip, below)

1 bottle (750 mL) **brandy**

In wide saucepan, bring sugar, 1 cup water, allspice, cloves, bay leaves and vanilla bean to boil over medium-high heat; boil, stirring occasionally, until sugar is dissolved. Stir in chestnuts; reduce heat, cover and simmer for 30 minutes.

Stir in brandy; bring to boil. Reduce heat and simmer for 2 minutes. Skim off any foam. Discard allspice, cloves, bay leaves and vanilla bean.

Divide chestnuts among 6 hot sterilized 1-cup (250 mL) canning jars. (See Tip, page 314.) Divide liqueur among jars to cover chestnuts; seal with lids.

Let stand in cool, dark, dry place for 2 weeks before opening. Store for up to 2 months.

MAKES 6 CUPS. PER SERVING OF 5 CHESTNUTS: about 88 cal, 1 g pro, trace total fat (trace sat. fat), 14 g carb, 2 g fibre, 0 mg chol, 7 mg sodium. % RDI: 1% calcium, 3% iron, 10% vit C, 4% folate.

PER 1 OZ (2 TBSP) LIQUEUR: about 64 cal, trace pro, trace total fat (0 g sat. fat), 9 g carb, 0 g fibre, 0 mg chol, 2 mg sodium. % RDI: 1% iron, 2% vit C, 1% folate.

tip

To prepare fresh chestnuts for cooking: Cut X on flat side of each. In saucepan of boiling water, cook chestnuts, four at a time, until points of cut curl, about two minutes; drain. With knife, pull off skins. In saucepan, cover peeled chestnuts with water and bring to boil; cook over medium heat until tender, about five minutes.

Coffee Liqueur

Freshly ground coffee beans are the key to the deep coffee flavour of this homemade liqueur. It's delicious in drinks or in your favourite baking recipes.

¼ cup **dark-roast coffee beans**

1½ cups **vodka**

1½ cups **granulated sugar**

1 tbsp **vanilla**

In coffee grinder, coarsely grind coffee beans. Place in hot sterilized wide-mouth 4-cup (1 L) canning jar. (See Tip, page 314.) Pour in vodka; seal with lid. Let stand in cool, dark, dry place for 5 days.

In saucepan, bring 2½ cups water and sugar to boil; reduce heat and simmer for 15 minutes. Let cool to room temperature.

In large glass measure, stir together vodka mixture, sugar mixture and vanilla. Strain through fine-mesh sieve lined with double-thickness cheesecloth; discard coffee grounds.

Line funnel with coffee filter; strain liqueur through filter into sterilized decorative bottle(s). Store in cool, dark, dry place for up to 6 months.

MAKES 4 CUPS. PER 1 OZ (2 TBSP): about 62 cal, 0 g pro, 0 g total fat (0 g sat. fat), 9 g carb, 0 g fibre, 0 mg chol, 1 mg sodium.

Liqueurs & Seasonings

Espresso Liqueur

This rum-based liqueur has an intense flavour that coffee lovers will savour. Sip it on the rocks or in a mixed drink, such as a classic White Russian.

1 cup **granulated sugar**

1 cup **brewed espresso**

1½ cups **white rum**

½ tsp **vanilla**

In saucepan, bring sugar and espresso to boil, stirring until sugar is dissolved; boil for 1 minute. Remove from heat; let stand for 10 minutes.

Stir in rum and vanilla; pour into hot sterilized bottles. (See Tip, page 314.) Store in cool, dark, dry place for up to 6 months.

MAKES 3 CUPS. PER 1 OZ (2 TBSP): about 65 cal, 0 g pro, 0 g total fat (0 g sat. fat), 8 g carb, 0 g fibre, 0 mg chol, 2 mg sodium.

tip

One cup brewed espresso is equivalent to eight 1-oz (2 tbsp) shots. If you don't have an espresso machine, brew triple-strength espresso in a drip coffee maker.

Liqueurs & Seasonings

Chili Vodka

Fiery hot peppers give this vodka a delicious burn that's excellent in mixed drinks, such as Caesars. It's also a delicious base for Oyster Shooters (below).

1 bottle (750 mL) **vodka**
1 **red finger hot pepper**
1 **green finger hot pepper**
6 grains **coarse sea salt**

Remove 1 oz (2 tbsp) vodka from bottle. Cut slits lengthwise down sides of red and green hot peppers; insert into vodka bottle along with salt. Seal with lid.

Let stand for 3 days. Strain, discarding hot peppers; return to bottle and store in freezer for up to 1 year.

MAKES 1 BOTTLE. PER ½ OZ (1 TBSP): about 32 cal, 0 g pro, 0 g total fat (0 g sat. fat), 0 g carb, 0 g fibre, 0 mg chol, 3 mg sodium, 1 mg potassium.

Oyster Shooters: Mince 3 tbsp finely chopped sweet onion with 2 tbsp finely chopped fresh cilantro until almost paste. Mix together paste, 2 cups tomato juice, ⅓ cup lime juice, 2 tsp Worcestershire sauce and ½ tsp celery salt. Refrigerate until chilled, 1 hour. Shuck 24 fresh oysters; slide each, with juices, into large shot glass. Pour about 1½ tbsp tomato juice mixture into each; top with ½ oz (1 tbsp) chilled Chili Vodka.

MAKES 24 SHOOTERS.

Liqueurs & Seasonings

Oyster Shooters
(opposite)

Irish Cream Liqueur

This liqueur has a luxurious taste and texture that makes it delicious on its own, over ice, or in coffee or hot chocolate.

½ tsp **instant coffee granules**

2 tsp **vanilla**

1 cup **Irish whiskey**

1 cup **whipping cream**

1 can (300 mL) **sweetened condensed milk**

⅓ cup **chocolate syrup**

In large bowl, dissolve coffee granules in vanilla; whisk in whiskey, cream, condensed milk and chocolate syrup.

Pour into decorative bottles. Refrigerate for up to 2 weeks.

MAKES 4 CUPS. PER 1 OZ (2 TBSP): about 91 cal, 1 g pro, 4 g total fat (3 g sat. fat), 9 g carb, 0 g fibre, 14 mg chol, 21 mg sodium. % RDI: 4% calcium, 1% iron, 4% vit A, 1% folate.

tip

If you have crème de cacao, add 2 tbsp and reduce chocolate syrup to 2 tbsp.

Liqueurs & Seasonings

Rhubarb Nectar

OK, this is not a liqueur, but it is a refreshing, sweet-tart base for a beverage. If you don't feel like processing the jars, the nectar will keep in the fridge for one week. To serve, mix equal parts nectar and sparkling water.

10 cups chopped **rhubarb** (about 3 lb/1.35 kg)

1 strip each **orange zest** and **lemon zest**

2 cups **granulated sugar**

In large saucepan, combine rhubarb, 3 cups water, orange zest and lemon zest; bring to boil over high heat. Reduce heat to medium-low, cover and simmer until rhubarb is broken up, about 10 minutes.

Strain through fine-mesh sieve lined with cheesecloth into clean saucepan. Stir in sugar and bring to boil.

Fill hot 1-cup (250 mL) canning jars, leaving ¼-inch (5 mm) headspace. Cover with prepared discs. Screw on bands until resistance is met; increase to fingertip tight. Boil in boiling water canner for 10 minutes. (See Canning Basics, page 10.)

Turn off heat. Uncover and let jars stand in canner for 5 minutes. Lift up rack. With canning tongs, transfer jars to cooling rack; let cool for 24 hours.

Shake or stir before using.

MAKES 6 CUPS. PER ½ CUP: about 146 cal, 1 g pro, trace total fat (0 g sat. fat), 36 g carb, 0 g fibre, 0 mg chol, 5 mg sodium, 264 mg potassium. % RDI: 8% calcium, 1% iron, 1% vit A, 13% vit C, 3% folate.

tip
Fresh or frozen rhubarb works equally well in this drink.

Porcini Salt

Flavoured sea salts are trendy in specialty food shops, but they're so easy to make at home. Sprinkle this woodsy-flavoured salt over roasts and steaks to take them to new heights of deliciousness.

1 pkg (14 g) **dried porcini mushrooms**

¼ cup **sea salt**

Pinch grated **nutmeg**

In clean spice or coffee grinder, pulse together mushrooms, salt and nutmeg, in 2 batches, until powdery with a few larger mushroom pieces.

Store in airtight container in cool, dark, dry place for up to 1 month.

MAKES ABOUT ½ CUP. PER PINCH: about 0 cal, 0 g pro, 0 g total fat (0 g sat. fat), 0 g carb, 0 g fibre, 0 mg chol, 48 mg sodium.

Liqueurs & Seasonings

Clockwise from top:
Porcini Salt (opposite),
Baked Lemon Rosemary
Salt (page 336) and
Saffron Salt (page 337)

Lemon Salt

Use this salt in fish dishes and salads, or as a finishing salt to add a pinch of zesty lemon aroma and flavour. Meyer lemons have particularly fragrant rinds. Orange, lime or mixed citrus zests are other delicious alternatives.

¾ cup **pickling salt,** kosher salt or noniodized sea salt

¼ cup grated **lemon zest**

Mix salt with lemon zest. Pack into 1-cup (250 mL) canning jar or divide between two ½-cup (125 mL) canning jars. Store in cool, dark, dry place for up to 1 month.

MAKES ABOUT 1 CUP. PER PINCH: about 0 cal, 0 g pro, 0 g total fat (0 g sat. fat), 0 g carb, 0 g fibre, 0 mg chol, 108 mg sodium, 0 mg potassium.

Variation
Baked Lemon Rosemary Salt: Increase lemon zest to 6 tbsp. Coarsely chop ¼ cup fresh rosemary leaves. In clean spice or coffee grinder, pulse together salt, rosemary and lemon zest, in 2 batches, until combined. Spread on parchment paper–lined rimmed baking sheet; bake in 225°F (110°C) oven until dry, about 10 minutes. Let cool. Break up dried salt. Store in airtight container in cool, dark, dry place for up to 1 month.

MAKES ABOUT 1⅓ CUPS.

tip
Organic lemons are preferable in this recipe because their peels don't contain pesticide residues. In any case, when zesting citrus fruits, always scrub them in hot soapy water, rinse well and pat dry.

Liqueurs & Seasonings

Saffron Salt

This aromatic, golden salt adds Middle Eastern flair to grilled chicken, fish or vegetables.

⅓ cup **sea salt**

2 tsp **saffron threads**

In clean spice or coffee grinder, pulse together salt, saffron and ½ tsp water until vibrant yellow with a few saffron threads still intact.

Store in airtight container in cool, dark, dry place for up to 1 month.

MAKES ABOUT ½ CUP. PER PINCH: about 0 cal, 0 g pro, 0 g total fat (0 g sat. fat), 0 g carb, 0 g fibre, 0 mg chol, 65 mg sodium.

Liqueurs & Seasonings

Spiced Rosemary Salt for Roasts

Make this salt when you have a bumper crop of fresh rosemary in your garden. Use it to season roast meats, especially lamb, pork, chicken and turkey.

½ cup minced **fresh rosemary**

½ cup **pickling salt,** kosher salt or noniodized sea salt

4 tsp **fennel seeds,** crushed

1 tbsp coarsely ground **pepper**

1 tbsp **sweet paprika**

2 tsp **ground dried hot peppers** (or 1 tsp cayenne pepper)

1½ tsp **smoked paprika**

Mix together rosemary, salt, fennel seeds, pepper, sweet paprika, ground hot peppers and smoked paprika.

Pack into 1-cup (250 mL) canning jar or divide between two ½-cup (125 mL) canning jars.

Store in cool, dark, dry place for up to 1 month.

MAKES ABOUT ¾ CUP. PER PINCH: about 0 cal, 0 g pro, 0 g total fat (0 g sat. fat), 0 g carb, 0 g fibre, 0 mg chol, 96 mg sodium, 1 mg potassium.

tip
Dried rosemary is a poor substitute for fresh, and the needle-like leaves can be quite unpleasant to eat. Don't substitute it in this recipe, where the rosemary flavour is the main event.

Herb Salt for Poultry

This herb-and-salt mixture is especially good for roasted, stewed or braised poultry. It can also be used to excellent effect in egg and liver dishes.

¾ cup finely chopped
fresh savory

½ cup finely chopped
fresh sage

½ cup finely chopped
fresh parsley

½ cup **pickling salt,** kosher salt
or noniodized sea salt

⅓ cup **fresh thyme leaves**

Mix together savory, sage, parsley, salt and thyme.

Pack into 1-cup (250 mL) canning jar or divide between two ½-cup (125 mL) canning jars.

Store in cool, dark, dry place for up to 1 month.

MAKES ABOUT 2 CUPS. PER ½ TSP: about 0 cal, 0 g pro, 0 g total fat (0 g sat. fat), trace carb, 0 g fibre, 0 mg chol, 144 mg sodium, 1 mg potassium.

Liqueurs & Seasonings

Vanilla Sugar

Flavoured sugars add a special touch to baked goods. They're also delicious as drink rimmers or stirred into your favourite coffee or tea. Try this simple vanilla version or a herb or citrus variation.

1 **vanilla bean**

2 cups **granulated sugar**

Cut vanilla bean in half crosswise. Cut 1 half in half lengthwise; scrape seeds into food processor. Set scraped pods aside.

Add 1 cup of the sugar and remaining vanilla bean half to food processor; pulse until vanilla is finely chopped. In bowl, stir vanilla mixture with remaining sugar.

Fill 2-cup (500 mL) canning jar. Add reserved vanilla pods to jar; seal with lid. Store in cool, dark, dry place for 2 days before opening. Store for up to 6 months.

To use, sift sugar mixture through fine-mesh sieve to remove any large pieces of vanilla bean.

MAKES ABOUT 2 CUPS. PER 1 TSP: about 16 cal, 0 g pro, 0 g total fat (0 g sat. fat), 4 g carb, 0 g fibre, 0 mg chol, 0 mg sodium, 0 mg potassium.

Variations

Lavender Sugar: Omit vanilla bean. Stir 1½ tsp dried culinary lavender into sugar. (Do not chop in food processor.) Seal in jar and store as directed.

Lime and Mint Sugar: Omit vanilla bean. Spread sugar on parchment paper–lined rimmed baking sheet. Using zester, peel strips of zest from 1 lime evenly over sugar. Cut 4 fresh mint leaves into thin strips; sprinkle over sugar. Stir to combine; spread in thin layer over baking sheet. Let dry in cool, dark, dry place until zest and mint are dry and brittle, 18 to 24 hours. Seal in jar and store as directed.

From left: Lavender Sugar, Lime and
Mint Sugar, and Vanilla Sugar

CREATING A BOOK LIKE THIS is like preserving the fruits of the harvest. First, you select the best ingredients, then you carefully prepare them and finally, you seal them up in a beautiful package to be enjoyed for a long time to come. And what a tasty result this is!

To start, I want to offer my heartfelt thanks to the members of The Canadian Living Test Kitchen. Their knowledge and good taste make them a delight to be around. I was also pleased to work with former staff members Andrew Chase and Jennifer MacKenzie, who created a number of new recipes for this book.

A helping of gratitude goes to Test Kitchen manager Adell Shneer for heading up the retesting of these recipes. Another generous helping goes to our fearless food director, Annabelle Waugh. From choosing recipes from our 37-year archive to making the final tweaks on proofs, she was there for every step of this project, with good humour and sharp insights.

Dreaming up the beautiful interior design of this book was our talented art director, Chris Bond, while our creative director, Michael Erb, designed the sharp-looking cover. It has been exciting watching their vision for this book unfold.

I owe a deep debt of gratitude to photographer Edward Pond, food stylist Nicole Young and prop stylist Madeleine Johari, who shot a number of new photos for this book. They made a sea of jams, jellies and pickles look fresh and inviting, shot after shot after shot. For a list of the other photographers and stylists who contributed their talents to this book, turn to page 351.

For her eagle eye, I want to thank copy editor Jill Buchner, who pored over miles of preserving methods with a smile. Thanks also to Gillian Watts for the handy index and to Sharyn Joliat at Info Access for the nutrient analysis on each recipe.

It goes without saying that I am grateful to the folks at the top. Thanks to Transcontinental Books publisher Jean Paré, *Canadian Living* publisher Lynn Chambers and *Canadian Living* editor-in-chief Susan Antonacci for the chance to do this thoroughly enjoyable job every day.

Finally, thanks to the team at Random House Canada for distributing and promoting this book across the continent.

– *Christina Anson Mine,*
project editor

Index

Recipes

All recipes developed by The Canadian Living Test Kitchen, except the following:

Andrew Chase: pages 81, 132, 152, 208, 214, 220, 273, 274, 280, 283, 312, 336, 338 and 339.

Kate Gammal: page 244.

Heather Howe: page 49.

Jennifer MacKenzie: pages 22, 38, 54, 66, 70, 90, 99, 108, 112, 116, 235, 247, 289, 291, 300, 302 and 340.

Photography

Mark Burstyn: pages 121, 134, 139, 143, 146 and 158.

Christopher Campbell: page 245.

Yvonne Duivenvoorden: pages 77, 97, 101, 107, 171, 176, 182, 227, 287 and 325.

Geoff George: pages 5, 14, 15 and 47.

Kevin Hewitt: page 114.

Edward Pond: hardcover; endpapers; pages 4, 6, 8, 12, 16, 20, 23, 28, 39, 53, 59, 64, 67, 71, 72, 78, 85, 86, 91, 98, 113, 117, 118, 133, 153, 194, 197, 209, 215, 221, 233, 241, 250, 253, 257, 262, 275, 281, 282, 293, 301, 306, 310, 313, 319, 335 and 341.

Jodi Pudge: pages 11, 127, 163, 203 and 269.

David Scott: page 190.

Felix Wedgwood: page 331.

Food Styling

Julie Aldis: pages 97 and 227.

Donna Bartolini: pages 77 and 176.

Andrew Chase: pages 127 and 163.

Lucie Richard: pages 53, 101, 182, 190 and 287.

Claire Stancer: pages 306 and 335.

Claire Stubbs: pages 11, 12, 16, 59, 64, 72, 107, 171, 203, 241, 269, 319, 325 and 331.

Rosemarie Superville: pages 121, 134, 139, 143, 146 and 158.

Sandra Watson: page 197.

Nicole Young: hardcover; endpapers; pages 4, 6, 8, 20, 23, 28, 39, 67, 71, 78, 85, 86, 91, 98, 113, 117, 118, 133, 153, 194, 209, 215, 221, 233, 250, 253, 257, 262, 275, 281, 282, 293, 301, 310, 313 and 341.

Prop Styling

Martine Blackhurst: page 331.

Laura Branson: page 53.

Catherine Doherty: pages 121, 127, 134, 139, 143, 146, 158, 163 and 319.

Mandy Gyulay: pages 11, 203 and 269.

Madeleine Johari: hardcover; endpapers; pages 4, 6, 8, 20, 23, 28, 39, 67, 71, 78, 85, 86, 91, 98, 113, 117, 118, 133, 153, 194, 209, 215, 221, 233, 250, 253, 257, 262, 275, 281, 282, 293, 301, 310, 313 and 341.

Maggi Jones: page 197.

Oksana Slavutych: pages 12, 16, 59, 64, 72, 77, 97, 101, 107, 114, 171, 176, 182, 190, 227, 241, 287, 306, 325 and 335.

Illustrations

Monica Hellström: pages 7, 9, 21, 87, 119, 195, 251 and 311.

TRANSCONTINENTAL BOOKS
1100 René-Lévesque Boulevard West
24th Floor
Montreal, Que. H3B 4X9
Tel: 514-340-3587
Toll-free: 1-866-800-2500
canadianliving.com

Bibliothèque et Archives nationales du Québec
and Library and Archives Canada cataloguing
in publication

Main entry under title :
The complete preserving book
"Canadian living".
Includes index.
ISBN 978-0-9877474-1-9
1. Canning and preserving. I. Canadian Living Test
Kitchen. II. Title: Canadian living.
TX603.C65 2012   641.4'2   C2011-942832-6

Project editor: Christina Anson Mine
Copy editor: Jill Buchner
Indexer: Gillian Watts
Art direction and design: Chris Bond
Front cover design: Michael Erb

Printed in Canada
© Transcontinental Books, 2012
Legal deposit – 2nd quarter 2012
National Library of Quebec
National Library of Canada
ISBN 978-0-9877474-1-9

We acknowledge the financial support of our
publishing activity by the Government of Canada
through the Canada Book Fund.

For information on special rates for corporate
libraries and wholesale purchases, please call
1-866-800-2500.